PLAYERS ALL

DRAMA AND PERFORMANCE STUDIES

TIMOTHY WILES, GENERAL EDITOR

PLAYERS ALL

PERFORMANCES

IN

CONTEMPORARY

SPORT

Robert E. Rinehart

INDIANA UNIVERSITY PRESS   BLOOMINGTON & INDIANAPOLIS

The paper used in this publication meets
the minimum requirements of American National
Standard for Information Sciences—Permanence
of Paper for Printed Library Materials,
ANSI Z39. 48-1984.

Manufactured in the United States of America

Library of Congress Cataloging-in-Publication Data

Rinehart, Robert E., date
Players all : performances in contemporary sport / Robert E.
Rinehart
p.   cm. — (Drama and performance studies)
Includes bibliographical references and index.
ISBN 0-253-33426-8 (alk. paper). — ISBN 0-253-21223-5 (pbk. :
alk. paper)
1. Sports—Sociological aspects. 2. Performance art.   I. Title.
II. Series.
GV706.5.R56   1998
796—dc21   98-19008
1 2 3 4 5 03 02 01 00 99 98

For my mother,

Mavis Lorraine (Burns) Rinehart

(1909–1996),

who gave me life

C O N T E N T S

FOREWORD

"Peter Ueberroth as commissioner in the 1980s," says
Giants general manager Bob Quinn . . . , "liked to say,
'The field is your stage. Always make it look good.'"

—Tom Verducci, 1996

In late-twentieth-century North America, institutions seem to overwhelm individuals. The agency of people is questioned; multinational corporations urge
us to "Just Do It," but few of us know exactly what "It" might be. The erasure of
the distinction between individuality (or the ideology of individuality) and
group membership is complete, and we find ourselves joining self-help groups,
after-work recreational softball leagues, Bible study sessions, or electronic mail
services simply to belong to something. We often mistrust the motives of
others, bringing to this ontological dilemma the suspicion that altruistic behavior has never, when you really get down to it, been a motivating factor in
human relations.

And in the sports arena, we no longer enjoy sports the simple, childlike way
we might have before (or the way we might have been told we did). We are
slammed by insecurities: when we begin to admire an athlete, a little further
digging unearths facts that make our admiration seem sullied and shallow. The
purity that we once ascribed to sport has eroded, so that the hero structure we
learned as children elides into sad listings: "Dennis Rodman kicks a camera
man. Jeff George rages in the face of his coach after he is benched. . . . Roberto
Alomar, incensed, spits at an umpire."[1] We seek an idealized, nostalgic past—
and are frustrated by our inability to find it. We yearn for a simpler, more easily
defined characterization of complex issues, and so are easily duped into slogan
admiration (or, in much the same way we suspend disbelief when we enter
into a fictional world, allow ourselves to be duped): Nike's "Just Do It" campaign seamlessly elides into Nancy Reagan's "Just Say No" [to drugs] and Magic
Johnson's "Just Say No" [to sex]. Even our politics have taken on the simplicity
of recurring sound and visual bites.

We seek answers, yearning for sense-making, for (often) fundamental solutions, which seem to mirror what we have been told was a better, simpler,

purer time. We use and overuse metaphors, as if their very repetition would make the world we see—the world of disjointed, fragmented, non-sensical open texts—magically evolve into a world of order and sense. And sport has become one of the final refuges of this semblance of order and sense.

Thus we are told, for example, that by the early 1800s, "cricket had become theater: two teams and two umpires were not enough, and spectators became a *necessary* part of the activity."[2] It was seemingly logical that spectators would become a part of modern sport, and that theater would become the abiding metaphor for sport.[3] Theater is part of the known, and the known is an integral part of theater: every statement and every movement in theater is scripted, ordered, practiced, and sensical.

But sport, though it has become highly rationalized, often scripted, does not always demonstrate such predictability. Sport, in short, is no longer strictly modernist in its orientation. Yet we constantly strive to pull it back, to order it, to rationally make sense of it—and, by doing so, to deny other incarnations of what it is that might be sport.

One of the central themes of this book, then, is that spectator sport has become more than a simple observed game between two contestants or two teams: it is defined and enjoyed, sampled and gobbled up, casually and causally participated in, by, as Bakhtin puts it of the novel, a "revealed and actualized . . . dialogic nature of heteroglossia."[4] There are a myriad of folks out there who have, in one way or another, become players of sport. And their participation ranges from blatant to subtle, active to passive, deliberate to coerced, authentic to contrived, and local to global. In the following chapters, I hope to reveal some of the players, their motivations and hopes and dreams, and how sport has become what it is in these few years preceding the dawn of the third millennium.

Coupled with a yearning for a nostalgic and simplified past in our world is an ever-increasing information glut. We now have the capacity to receive more information (some of it actually useful) than we have the capacity to comprehend. No wonder that modern (wo)man seeks shelter in health clubs, resort time-sharing, leisure activities, and the pursuit of sport tourism. Highly influenced by sport, western contemporary life has become, for many, a quest for self-pleasure, a sort of body-as-subject/body-as-object hedonism. But with this self-pleasure came a mistrust of things institutional.

A part of the recent mistrust toward established sport institutions may be the nagging suspicion that there exists no real "amateurism" anymore. When, in the 1890s, Baron Pierre de Coubertin urged his fellow Anglophiles to regenerate the Olympic movement, to create an international fellowship of premier athletes exhibiting their skills, he likely never dreamed that his accent on upper-class talent would be viewed with increasing skepticism. He likely never envisioned that the very precepts upon which he based his "egalitarianism" would be questioned, that his lofty ideals of amateurism and professionalism would be criticized as thin veils for a "haves versus have nots," privileged upper-class snobbery. The ideology that allowed sports commentator Al Michaels, at the 1980 Winter Olympic Games, to enthuse, "Do you believe in miracles?" after an "amateur" United States hockey team (made up of college athletes, most of whom were on athletic scholarship) defeated the "professional" USSR team—this ideology has, in the 1990s, been quietly dismissed. Now both Western and former Eastern Bloc countries eagerly anticipate and enjoy the United States Dream Teams' games, praising athletic prowess, female or male, paid or not.

Closely linked with this distrust of sports based on an amateur/professional dichotomy are the blatant economic trappings of contemporary mass sport. Before the 1996 Super Bowl, for example, Sports Direct took out a full-page advertisement in USA Today hawking "Super Bowl and NBA All-Star Banners Available for Only $129." Tied in with Coca-Cola sponsorship (and logos), each of these banners "displays the trademarked logo of the event featured, enhancing its authenticity." ("Authenticity" is a key trope: witness the expansion of shops selling sports trading cards and sports memorabilia—and the relative value placed on varying degrees of authenticity for each item. As well, notice the importance and relative stature that the sport tourism industry—indeed, all of tourism—places on "authentic" experience.)[5] In the age of postmodern virtuality, the "authentic" has become an ideal to be approached rather than a clearly defined quality of being.

Furthermore, potential buyers are advised that the banners—the Super Bowl XXIX banner and the NBA All-Star Weekend banner, both from 1995—are "more than just a beautiful piece of home decor, these valuable collectibles will be treasured keepsakes for generations." The justification for spending "$129 plus $9.95 shipping and handling"?

> America's premier sporting events have become larger than the contests themselves—taking on a flavor renowned throughout the world. Much of this unique flavor is trimmed around the host city and respective venues.[6]

But not only are "professional" sports the hub of cottage industries; the encroachment of money into "amateur" sports has changed the face of such events as the Olympics, college athletics, and even youth sports. Money drives sport—all sport:

> In 1992, the International Olympic Committee executive board urged world sports federations to set qualifying standards before 1994 and weed out

> Olympians who border on impersonation. . . . "There were 'tourists' who fell
> six or seven times in giant slalom," says IOC member Marc Hodler, president
> of skiing's international body. . . . Ironically, Olympic founder Pierre de Cou-
> bertin once wrote: what's key "is not the triumph but the struggle."[7]

Ideologically, to nations of people, the idea of Pierre de Coubertin's "triumph"
still matters, but pragmatically, from sports entrepreneurs, it is difficult to
imagine a more rampant cynicism. And people know it.

Reportedly, the NFL doled out the 75,156 seats in Sun Devil Stadium (where
Super Bowl XXX was played on January 28, 1996) thus:

> About 5,000 seats are reserved for overflow media, box suites for league and
> team officials, NFL mail-in drawing winners and the league's international
> needs.

> For the 70,000 remaining Super Bowl seats, 25.3 percent are kept by the
> league office, 17.5 percent go to each competing team and 10 percent to the
> host team.

> Only about 1.1 percent go to the NFL's 27 other teams.

> The league and most teams give or sell their tickets to large corporate spon-
> sors and prominent supporters.

> Twenty-one companies paid $150,000 each for corporate sponsorship pack-
> ages. A recent NFL survey . . . put the median salary of . . . ticket holders at
> $70,000 with more than a third making more than $100,000.[8]

The "stories" of sports continue, now-familiar stories to most readers of newspapers. "'This year's [1996] Final Four is one of the most expensive tickets
we've ever seen . . . in the $6,000 range,' says Steven Tick, general manager
of Murray's Tickets and Tours."[9] And yet, though the "average" fan is shut
out of live attendance at these "premier" sporting events, interest in professional, college, and Olympic sport is at an all-time high.

Despite the apparent inequities among the masses of people who emotion-
ally and financially support "their" teams (or "their" country—or even, as we
shall see, "their" multinational corporation), however, there is still a sense that
sport can be a pure refuge, safe from the vagaries of everyday life. There is a
sense that we—that is, the players in sport—can recapture a purity of purpose.
That we can somehow rekindle the magic that sport can be. That we can be all
that we can be. That we can lift our games to another level. That joy will reign
in Mudville. And so on.

For example, just two years after the baseball strike, newspapers were
trumpeting the fans' rebirth of spirit toward the game. *USA Today* carried a
short preview story in which two fans exemplified the love-hate relationship
between spectators and other players of the game:

"The feeling is so incredible, I can't explain it," Pressman said. "You feel it in your heart. . . . It's been a long winter, and the thought of the baseball season starting makes me smile."

"I still have some hard feelings about the strike," said Chicago's Dorice Pepin, keeping score at a Cubs exhibition game. "It was too much about money."[10]

The paradox of postmodern sport is that it is too much about money, and it has nothing to do with money.

Spectators, fans, fanatics, hot dog vendors, coaches who direct traffic, parking lot attendants, coaches who choreograph plays, strength and conditioning coaches, makeup artists, groundskeepers, cheerleaders, merchandisers, fitness consultants, sport psychologists and sociologists, front office personnel, owners, sport entrepreneurs, sport agents, ticket sellers, hawkers, face painters, scalpers, sport tourists who go on a Bambino Trail tour,[11] equipment vendors, cleanup crews, college presidents, voyeurs, corporate award winners, sport clothiers and sellers, sellers of sport paraphernalia, trading card shop owners, youth athletes, interscholastic athletes, intercollegiate athletes, semi-pro athletes, Olympic aspirants and contenders, professional athletes, steroid vendors, sport physiologists, sportswriters, sport scholars, television producers and directors, sports editors, Hulkamaniacs, sports beat reporters, team mascots, organ players, band members, halftime entertainers, stadium designers, city officials, anti-fungal cream producers, multinational corporation sponsors, International Olympic Committee members, Hall of Fame boards, athletic directors, street lugers, teachers who coach, coaches who teach, athletic boosters, videocam operators, road crews, talk show hosts, governing boards, intramural participants, recreational enthusiasts, hobbyists, vacationers, watchers, participants: players all.

ACKNOWLEDGMENTS

Portions of this material have previously appeared in either largely or some-what altered form in the following: chapter 2 as "Dropping Hierarchies: To-ward the Study of a Contemporary Sporting Avant-Garde," *Sociology of Sport Journal* 13, no. 2 (1996): 159–175; chapter 3 as "Sport as Kitsch: A Case Study of *The American Gladiators*," *Journal of Popular Culture* 28, no. 2 (1994): 25–35; chapter 6 as "The Emergence of Contemporary Sport Forms: Paintball," in N. K. Denzin, ed., *Cultural Studies: A Research Annual,* vol. 1 (Greenwich, Conn.: JAI Press, 1996), pp. 241–255; and chapter 8 as "Warp Speed in Barcelona: Olympism, Ideology, and Experience," in N. K. Denzin, ed., *Studies in Symbolic Interaction,* vol. 16 (Greenwich, Conn.: JAI Press, 1994), pp. 123–159.

I wish to thank a few people whose personal support has made this book possible. I cherish my interaction with my children, Nicholas and Alyssa, and appreciate their return love and understanding of their daddy's work. I am grateful to my brother, Jim Rinehart, for recording televised sports programs, for saving newspapers, and for his continuing faith in my work; to his family, Karen Forcum and Gabriele Rinehart; to Kim, Wayne, and Jennifer Lang, whose love and friendship have held me up for decades; to Dwight Hunt and Claudine Hunt, who taught me about relationships; to Vicky Paraschak; to Harry and Gloria Rott; to Robert Wichert; to Donna Mae Miller; and to Maurya, Maureen, and Corinne Walker.

Additionally, I owe great debts of gratitude for professional support to my colleagues at the University of Illinois: Jim Denison, Pirrko Markula, David Andrews, Steve Jackson, Toni Bruce, Nancy Spencer, and Amy Hribar; to my colleagues in the Physical Education and Dance Department at Idaho State University: Mike Lester, Dave Bale, Ann Sebren, Sandra Noakes, Marcia Lloyd, John Gorman, Gina Lay, and Timothy P. Winter; to students who have helped me to formulate my ideas more simply, including Rafi Tanay, Carolyn Smith, Eli Mimouni, Avigail Bergman, Gil Goshen, Sari Katz, Steven Hayward, Jenni-fer Daniels, Nitsan Yacov, Gary Delozier, Sheila Garcia, Nurit Ron-Rankin, Steve Nemeth, Gary Clark, Betsy Waughn, April Anderson, and Debbie Hadley, among many others; to Norman K. Denzin and Chuck Springwood, whose commentary has helped the manuscript immeasurably; and to Timothy J. Wiles, from whose commentary the manuscript has profited. Finally, I wish to thank Syndy Sydnor, my Ph.D. advisor, for her feedback, comments, and positive support of this book project.

Though I have gained greatly from all these people, the usual caveat applies: any errors are my own.

PLAYERS ALL

ONE | **Sport as Performance**
Setting the Stage

[In] music . . . there are wonderful clearings in the wilderness.
. . . We used to talk to Bill Walton, the basketball star, about
being on, you know—hitting it just right. There's a great
correlation between professional sports and music.
They're both improvisational.

—Jerry Garcia, of the Grateful Dead

The working title of an earlier version of this book was simply "Been There, Did That." This homage to a collector mentality, extending even to the immediate gratification and nearly as immediate obsolescence inherent in contemporary travel experience, stems directly from an experience I had while traveling to a conference in Halifax, Nova Scotia, in May of 1992. After an arduous couple of days of travel (to keep expenses down), I found myself on the M/S *Scotia Prince*, a casino-ferry cruising from Portland, Maine, to Yarmouth, Nova Scotia. There was a myriad of types on board, including a group of high school seniors returning from Washington, D.C., college students preparing to work the summer in Canada, and many older, apparently retired couples. But, strangely, there were no business types, commuters to the United States or Canada.

Among the retired group, I espied one older snowy-haired man, casually dressed in a bright yellow sweatshirt emblazoned with the ironed-on block-capitalized BEEN THERE, DID THAT. His life, I guessed, had become a series of collections, to the extent that travel experience was now a collection—a sort of commodity, preserved and highly polished, for him to enjoy.[1] This man wore his (tongue-in-cheek) philosophy on his shirt, yet his bemusement at the irony of collecting experience was tangible. His sweatshirt served a purpose similar to that of collections of slides and photographs, souvenirs, and other key memorabilia of (self-defined) important life events. It created, at least for him, a sense of uniqueness and singularity within a highly commoditized and standardized, mass-produced society. His sweatshirt was a protestation that his attitude toward the best the world had to offer was within his control; that, as an individual, he could collect and classify experience, rather than having experience collect and classify him. His markers—I imagine them as tangible markers, photographs, videos, or even stories which locked the experience into place and time and situation for him—individuated him, and turned back against the tourist site strategy of counting "visitors," classifying them demographically, reducing them to easily manipulable blips on an economic screen. In his own mind, by trumpeting to the world that he had BEEN THERE, DID THAT, this tourist carried the sheen of selective control over those people and systems that might control him.

As commoditization has changed the former ethereal (and certainly imperialist)[2] experience for travelers, so too has it changed the formerly "innocent" stage of sport.[3] Sport and commoditization no longer remain separate entities.

Similarly, until fairly recently, much of the critical work in the study of sport has endlessly intertwined with lived experience and autobiography.[4] This distinction—between lived experience in sport and the scholarly, critical work of those who study sport—has become blurred and conflated.

Certainly, writings critical of sport such as Gary Shaw's *Meat on the Hoof: The Hidden World of Texas Football* have served to enlighten (and possibly disenfranchise) a public gradually growing in its knowledge of public personalities. But there is more at work here. There are media that build up sport figures (and civic figures) only to tear them down in the name of truthful reporting—but are they reporting, or creating, the "story"? Sport scholars are yet another remora-like shadow hovering around the shark that is sport. They talk to each other, generally unwilling or unable to deal with sport as the public sees it. It appears that a dialogue between the various sports publics and various sports players might advantage both: listening to and hearing critical—and anecdotal—discussion by sport spectators may serve to enlighten the sport scholar as to what is *really* going on (if we could ever know). But giving voice to the previously voiceless also serves another purpose: it deprivileges the sports scholar—as sole expert—in terms of specific knowledge and understanding, so that sports spectators may, for example, interactively create their own stories. Frightening as this strategy may be, the shared understanding of all might benefit.

As more and more of the sporting public become knowledgeable and sophisticated in their knowledge, sport scholars' position of importance may appear to dwindle. But the sharing of knowledge may lead to deeper understanding, at deeper levels. Thus, the stolid recitation of statistics, for example, may evolve into what those statistics mean politically in a democratic society. This reciprocity—between scholars, public organizational monoliths, and private concerns—can be examined in light of the performances of all the players in sport: scholars, athletes, coaches, the media, and spectators.

▼ ▼ ▼ ▼

In a sense, I am continuing a project begun by Benjamin Lowe in the mid-1970s, which culminated in his book *The Beauty of Sport: A Cross-Disciplinary Inquiry.*[5] Certain aspects of my personal biography might put this statement in some perspective. In high school, I participated in football and swimming, and swimming has been a large part of my life since the age of six. I have worked out, competed, and coached in swimming at many levels. I also play the saxophone, having learned it in fifth grade—and continued ever since. The rhythms of music have somehow combined in my mind with the rhythms of sport, so that when I swim, I hear a march cadence (2/4 time or 4/4 time) or a waltz tempo (3/4 time). This rhythmicity depends upon whether my breathing pattern is, respectively, once for every two arm strokes or once for every three arm strokes. The waltz rhythm for bilateral breathing is like a voice inside my head, calling "One, two, three, *breathe; one*, two, three, *breathe!*" And the waltz tempo not only creates a different, relaxed feel to swimming and breathing, but has a dramatically different utilitarian aspect to it. The march tempo is reserved for sprinting, the waltz tempo for middle- to long-distance crawl events. So the beauty of affective response to music translates to a cadenced, efficient rhythmicity in sport. And vice versa: I could often prepare myself (psych myself up) for a sport event by playing fast music. We see this type of behavior—this connection between music and sport—all the time when athletes tune in to their own private compact discs prior to a meaningful sport event.

Benjamin Lowe's *The Beauty of Sport* draws parallels between sport and art, but it appears that the parallels are within a modernist framework, descriptive of a modern, oppositional world. His is a study of what might be termed "classical" sport. Such chapter headings as "The Natural Beauty of the Athlete," "The Relationship of Sport and Art," and "Symbolic Communication: Non-definitive Parameters" fit within a "fine art"/"high art" sport rubric. The book betrays a modernist bias. While many observers and participants remain ensconced in such a historical moment (and, indeed, cling to its security, method of seeing the world, and reductionism), that moment appears to be on the wane.[6] We see, for example, movies such as *Pulp Fiction,* in which linear time itself is fractured, shattered, and disjointed; in which life is cartoonish and otherwise serious moments are violently broken with comedic relief; in which the general rule is that there is no general rule.

There is no sense of Bakhtinian polyphonous laughter in Lowe's discussion of sport or art, or of the irony implicit within postmodern discussions and performances. While art, architecture, and literature have clearly emerged into postmodernism and all that it implies, much that surrounds the study of sport is still in a transition phase, containing elements of both.

Thus, in a sense, I amplify and extend Lowe's work,[7] attempting to draw parallels between sport and art in the postmodern moment. But where Lowe saw continuities and consistencies, I see disjuncture and chaos. To accomplish such a project, I make a few assumptions.

One assumption is that contemporary sport is a performance, not unlike the performances that artists of any kind use to demonstrate their art, their selves, their souls. It is, moreover, a cultural performance, and may demonstrate more than anyone has ever surmised the cares, wants, and needs of societies. The professional wrestler Hulk Hogan's self-making, much of it derived from Gorgeous George and Muhammad Ali; Olympian Janet Evans's distinctive straight-arm recovery on crawl; Michael Jordan's self-imitative, self-derivative "style" of slam-dunks; or Ice's personality on *The American Gladiators:* however extreme or atypical they seem at first, all can be viewed as performance art, much as Carolee Schneemann's *Interior Scroll,* in which she draws a written scroll from her vagina to read to the audience, can be considered performance art.[8] There is object in all kinds of performance. As Henry M. Sayre has it, there is also object in two senses of the word: object is the hoped-for resultant of performance, and it is the reason for performance.[9] The "object" of sports performance is not unlike the "object" of performance art. Many athletes hope to have as the result of their performance some sense of success, generally measured against some standard or co-actor. But just as surely, many athletes perform to an object, for a purpose, to an end. The process of training may be that end, or the achievement of fame, glory, and tangible reward may be that end. At any rate, athletes are not the only performers in sport; audiences, coaches, media representatives—all have, in both senses of the word, an "object" of performance.

One of the aims of performance art was to reintegrate the audience with the performance: "performance art developed its own audience separate from theatergoers by establishing a different kind of relationship between audience and performer, one that gave everyone a stake in the work."[10] This instillment of audience/reader into artistic (and athletic) performance carries on Norman K. Denzin's "universal singular" in an arena in which artists (or athletes) are "discussing personal realities" with their audiences.[11] Athletes "discuss" in physical ways, and this physical knowledge resonates with most contemporary audiences simply because audiences share a grain of knowledge of the physical. By being alive, with all that that implicates, the audience has shared with sport performers a semblance of their "art." And by participating, at some level, in sporting practices, the audience "knows" better what makes a good performance. Just as a musician can appreciate a well-played passage, so too may a physically educated populace appreciate—and be drawn into—audience practices for sport.

The blurring of genres that is one facet of postmodernism demands an examination of formerly discrete performance niches. For example, there are many intertextually linked performance areas, such as poetry slams and praise poetry, which borrow from theater and are "reputedly inspired by wrestling matches,"[12] where "three teams of judges hold up scorecards after each poem like their Olympic counterparts after judging a dive."[13]

There are also nesting dolls ("matrioshkas"), claimed to be traditionally Russian after Saava Mamontov appropriated the idea from a Japanese children's toy little more than a hundred years ago, which have evoked debate about their authenticity when new craftspersons have depicted "[the] Beatles, Snow White and the Seven Dwarfs or Magic Johnson and the National Basketball Association all-stars" with their nesting dolls.[14] The authenticity of these matrioshkas' "Russian-ness" (the truth about their origin notwithstanding) is contested ground, because they have included popular figures.

The 1992 Fischer-Spassky chess match held in Yugoslavia, referred to, tongue in cheek, as "The Most Significant Moment in Sports History since that Madison Square Garden matchup in which Randy 'Macho Man' Savage wed The Lovely Miss Elizabeth,"[15] is yet another example of intertextual contestation borrowing from sports. These performances are laden with irony, parody, and a sense of pastiche which, surely, "legitimate," serious sport does not assume.

Decidedly staid and proper, the bastions of sport (American football) propriety have recently become mired in questions of what constitutes inappropriate celebration after a touchdown. The product of football, with its well-established historical epoch and its paean to self-importance, is sacred—and any type of untoward, "frivolous" behavior diminishes the product.

But legitimate sport quite often does assume this crazy quilt of pastiche, if only we were to notice. Witness the intrusion of in-character human M & Ms handing out bags of candy at the Barcelona Olympics venues; the hoopla (and resultant spin control when the hoped-for showdown never materialized) surrounding Reebok's "Dave and Dan" advertising campaign;[16] the hypothesized "moving pregame tribute" to paralyzed NFL player Dennis Byrd, the purpose of which, according to the writers, was "to elicit the paralyzed player's endorsement of what happened to him";[17] the 1993 Super Bowl halftime show, featuring Michael Jackson clutching at his groin, surrounded by virile male performers; or the anticipation of Michael Jordan and his "Nike" Bugs Bunny advertisements (wherein the story lead begins, "Two days before kickoff, the

MVP of the Super Bowl already has been anointed. It's Michael Jordan").[18] These appear laden with irony, parody, and pastiche as well. Perhaps they appear this way, more so than poetry slams, a chess match, or the World Wrestling Federation, because of their protestations of legitimacy. Perhaps because these sport forms work so hard at becoming and remaining "legitimate" sport, the dissonance between play and work becomes parodic of itself.[19]

Embroiled in a Cartesian duality, Americans have dourly celebrated the separation of mind/spirit and body. In popular attitudes toward sports, the mutual exclusion of mind and body is manifest. According to Mikhail Bakhtin, the "new concept of realism has a different way of drawing the boundaries between bodies and objects. It cuts the double body in two and separates the objects of grotesque and folklore realism that were merged within the body."[20] This merging of "grotesque and folklore realism" within the body, almost eastern in its orientation, parallels the merging of mind and body. If we are to celebrate the mind/spirit over the body, then, according to Bakhtin, we should have some sort of release for the body. Carnival was the release point for medieval peoples; physical activity may be the closest thing to carnival in our mass contemporary culture. But again, physical activity is performed—by *all* interested parties—as if it is work, not for renewal.

We are a people who have taken on a degree of superficial hedonism, without an underlying revival and renewal.[21] Bakhtin describes earlier peoples as presuming the cyclic nature of things: "In the world culture of the past there is much more irony, a form of reduced laughter, than our ear can catch."[22] The present-day empty hedonism, the continual pursuit of the obsolescent and transitory, translates out into our games culture, and into our sports culture. Globally, the Americanization of sport (that is, the commercialized, vertically structured, and commodified aspects, which are related to an American postmodernism) is in an advanced stage, and so this empty hedonism, merely unattractive at home, becomes an insidious and hopeless—albeit monetarily successful—export.[23]

Yet one of the prime tenets of a postmodern world is just that sense of playfulness, that selfsame ironic bent, which Bakhtin says is missing in contemporary culture (he wrote circa 1930, in the Union of Soviet Socialist Republics).[24] Is it possible that, as a culture, we have gone so far in our quest for the programmable and predictable that we yearn for a dash of uncertainty? Have we, in other words, virtually come full circle, exhibiting a cultural desire for something as primal as laughter? According to Bakhtin, "Laughter . . . overcomes fear, for it knows no inhibitions, no limitations. Its idiom is never used by violence and authority."[25] Thus the power struggle between NFL authorities and NFL players over something as seemingly innocuous as laughter, celebration.

Elements of laughter, irony, the ludic, regeneration, renewal, reversal—even of the grotesque, in some cases—all "play" out, by varying degrees, in contemporary sport forms and the environments in which these forms are presented.

Despite the mixing of sport games and environs, there are still fans who unquestionably enjoy the actual games, as well as the surrounding experience of sport. The experience of attendance at live versus mediated sporting events is an interesting problematic for those who study sport.[26] Yet the games and sports themselves have become inseparable from their atmosphere: the sport experience is not one that easily lends itself to separating out "the sport" from the totality of "the sporting experience."[27] As I see it, this "sporting experience" includes such esoteric moments as collecting (and displaying on one's ski jacket) expensive metal pins from various ski resorts (or any of a number of sport events); eating hot dogs and drinking beer/soda; scoring a baseball game on an official scorecard; clapping to the music and dance of halftime shows; people-watching; having one's face painted with the symbol of one's sport team. Conversely (but in a related way), fans at home have their own ritualistic behavior: witness the "sporting experience" of Super Bowl parties; the comforting ritual of transplanted nationalists who gather around the only satellite dish in town to watch "their" club play English football (soccer); the easy banter and casual ingestion of food and drink at such gatherings. Furthermore, these sporting experiences, as I hope to indicate in this book, have themselves commingled, so that each borrows from and is informed by the other.

For example, while attending a Pennsylvania State University–University of Illinois women's volleyball match, I was intrigued by the introductions of the two teams.[28] The Penn State players were introduced ordinarily, with little fanfare, the public address announcer's voice flat and without affect. Then— gloriously, dramatically—the interior of Huff Gymnasium (in Champaign, Illinois) darkened. Laser-like beams of light careened across the floor, the stands, the walls, as inspirational music blared from the loudspeakers. The University of Illinois team members, to the frenzied shouts of the crowd, were spotlighted individually, then introduced. I immediately thought of a darkened Assembly Hall at the University of Illinois, where I had recently witnessed nearly identical phenomena: the World Wrestling Federation wrestlers emerged from a tunnel into the darkness, followed by a single spotlight, with an accompanying chaos of laser beams ricocheting off the walls and ceiling; the American Gladiators, to the accompaniment of patriotic music, are bathed in a single light as well. Then I thought of the televised Chicago Bulls games I have seen, in which the introductions follow the same pattern, as well as the NHL All-Star Game openings and the Super Bowl pre-game introductions, which lend no home field advantage to either team, but which individualize and personalize each player for the television viewing audience.[29] In all cases, the athletes are spotlighted and individuated, emerging from a tunnel-like enclosure into the sensory frenzy of a game-show-like atmosphere. Of course, the spotlight itself is a theatrical device. The laser lights, the dusky smoke, the intense sound—all are theatrical devices. Each sport form borrows what works to intensify the experience for the paying fan, and what works is not necessarily what purists in the sport studies professions would constitute as sport.

In fact, Fox Network has carried this creation of a fan base to a new extreme: in broadcasting National Hockey League games, Fox has begun to use a computerized puck that displays colored lights, so that television audiences can better see the puck's movement during telecast games. According to Kevin Maney, technology writer for *USA Today,* the reason is to help Fox

> get better TV ratings. . . . Fox and the NHL believe that one barrier to hockey's popularity is that it's hard to see the fast-moving, little black puck on a TV screen. The compu-puck lets computers track the puck and then lay graphics on top of it. Fox will experiment with making the puck into a glowing blue ball and a blue hoop. It will also give the puck a comet tail that changes colors depending on how fast the puck is moving.[30]

Everywhere, it seems, the performance aspects of contemporary sport bombard the sensitive (and, increasingly, culturally literate) viewer. Certainly, sport has always, to some extent, been performance-based. But a real difference in contemporary sport is the performers' awareness of their performance: thus we see athletes parodying their audiences, turning the focus back on the audience. Much as with Madonna's self-making inversion of the camera's eye, sport performers such as Charles Barkley and David Robinson (who used a video camera at the Barcelona Olympics to "document" the NBC camera's documentation of his participation) have inverted the performance, so that the athletes become audience as well as performers. Likewise, the audiences become performers (integral parts of the performance) as well as spectatorial presence.

A second assumption in this book revolves around a criticism regarding the study of sport, and the apprehension and appreciation of sport in society. Sport studies have followed a modernist framework, consistently asking and attempting to answer questions that assume, as C. Wright Mills writes, that "the world is an object to be manipulated."[31] Furthermore, contemporary study and reflection (in this case, of sport) assumes, following Mills, "that increased rationality may. . . be assumed to make for increased freedom."[32] As Mills warns, this assumption is a fallacious one. Thus, contemporary, *post*modern experience has outstripped modernist philosophy—with its technocracy and its adjunct of prediction and control. A self-conscious search for authenticity, a grasping for reality, a nearly quixotic quest for "true-to-life" experience in the late twentieth century appears to control citizens' lives. Rather than merely living our lives, we watch them in framed, snapshot moments; rather than experiencing the sensory aspects of a single life, we seek representations of it; rather than celebrating the subjectivities and affect which may wash over us at any given time, we assume a mantle of objectivity. Even our poetics have experimented with a mathematical precision that exemplifies feeble attempts at feeling. We have become, in short, a collectivity "in a state of distraction,"[33] unaware in the normal course of things of any degree of "concentration," flitting about from interesting event to interesting event, with, paradoxically, less control over extraneous matters than ever before.

C. Wright Mills calls for a sociology that deals with people, not objects (people "who are not dupes," as Edward Bruner puts it); complex, irreducible relationships, not simplistic, reductionistic, independent components; a sociology that examines the conjunctures of personal and public realms. But modernism in sport studies has grudgingly evolved, and has only recently begun the process of evolving into a cautious postmodernism that calls for different questions, seeking varied answers from equally valid voices.[34]

As Geertz has written,

> A challenge is being mounted to some of the central assumptions of mainstream social science. The strict separation of theory and data, the "brute fact" idea; the effort to create a formal vocabulary of analysis purged of all subjective reference, the "ideal language" idea; and the claim to moral neutrality and the Olympian view, the "God's truth" idea—none of these can prosper when explanation comes to be regarded as a matter of connecting action to its sense rather than behavior to its determinants. . . . Social events do have causes and social institutions effects; but it just may be that the road to discovering what we assert in asserting this lies less through postulating forces and measuring them than through noting expressions and inspecting them.[35]

I propose, in the following pages, to "note and inspect" expressions in sporting milieus and, at the least, to open up avenues of inquiry into what we currently term "sport studies." Furthermore, I propose to learn from the practitioners—the players of sport in contemporary society: fans, athletes, media, coaches, sport tourists, collectors.

Implicit in such a project is my supposition that, much as in art studies (that is, music, literature, visual arts), in sport a

> gradual process of canonization elevated some works over others, separated amateurs from professionals, and divided culture into "high" and "low" spheres. . . . This change stemmed less from the internal properties of these forms of art [sport] than from a desire for social order and a political mobilization on its behalf.[36]

Clearly, such a socially constructed "canonization" and privileging has occurred in sport studies, and—even in critical studies of sport—it follows a largely uncritical agenda, dependent upon perspective and point of view.[37] Men's sports are privileged over women's sports. Certain races are celebrated over others, and certain ages of athletes (it varies somewhat by sport) are given more credence than others. Elite athletes are studied and celebrated before average, mass athletes. "Straight" athletes are assumed to be the norm, so that the "Gay Olympics"[38] receives short shrift from the media.[39] "Expressive" sports (much like "amateur" sports in the quadrennial Olympic debate) in some cases are privileged over "spectacle" sports;[40] in most other, massified, cases, the opposite is true. As the current "canon" stands, there is little overt recognition of these naturalized hierarchies. As naturalized categories, they have become recognized as the natural order of things.

The media, however, are not immune to noticing such delineations, and putting their particular spin on them. In a humorous piece documenting Maryland's dilemma over which sport should be designated as the state's "official sport," one group was said to be promoting duckpin bowling over jousting.[41] Another filler, intended to be ironic, pointed out that an October 1991 poll in *Esquire* magazine determined that the respondents "had watched more episodes of 'American Gladiators' than 'Masterpiece Theater' in the past year."[42] An article in the *Chicago Tribune* pointed out the existence of so-called offbeat high school sports such as "rifle, weightlifting, and alpine and nordic skiing . . . archery, curling, equestrian, judo, fencing, canoeing, water polo, rodeo and crew," as well as the Native Youth Olympics in Alaska, whose ideology is "an effort to preserve the native games of their forefathers."[43] It is clear that the writers of these pieces understand a basic, unchallenged ideology present among the American public: that sport is male, that those sports which do not reproduce dominant images of the maleness of sport are ripe for ridicule. Such verbiage reinforces and reproduces the naturalization process. The very fact that these sports warrant such newspaper pieces demonstrates that they are little-known and less valued. The media in this case are looking for different angles, offbeat and unusual stories, so while they reproduce the dominant ideology, the media continue to provide a vehicle for discussion of resistant and emerging sport forms. In this openness, as sports players, the media are far ahead of sport scholars.

What has made football and hockey and basketball the most lucrative sports in the United States? Is it their inherent nature? The natural excitement within the sports themselves? Or have these sports, which celebrate power, strength, and size, somehow been marketed to reproduce the very maleness that they celebrate?

Likewise, most scholarly classifications of contemporary sport forms have been rather pejorative, in the sense that they have arbitrarily limited, rather than broadened, the scope of study. As well, they are socially constructed, and follow the popular culture. For example, George Sage has argued for a clear binary opposition between legitimate and "trash" sports,[44] which effectively creates scholarly taboos and excludes many contemporary sporting practices from the "sport canon," thereby limiting their examination by scholars. This kind of sport privileging has as its antecedent the relatively recent distinction between high and low culture:

> When Shakespeare, opera, art, and music were subject to free exchange, as they had been for much of the nineteenth century, they became the property of many groups, the companion of a wide spectrum of other cultural genres, and thus their power to bestow distinction was diminished, as was their power to please those who insisted on enjoying them in privileged circumstances, free from the interference of other cultural groups and the dilution of other cultural forms.[45]

Examples of this class distinction in sport, and the resultant "monopoly of access"[46]—whereby certain behaviors are expected, and certain prices are to be paid for admittance—might include live attendance at the races at Ascot, the NCAA Final Four basketball tournament, or the World Series. The "conspicuous consumption,"[47] or bestowal of "distinction," at these events also parallels the high end of the spectrum in package tours of and for travelers to these premier events.

Indeed, some contemporary sport attendance (especially the "highbrow" events) may be privileged. Travel to events, event tickets, and the accouterments (lodging, entertainment, food, souvenirs, shopping in the venue's "culture") which demonstrate that one has "been there," to use Geertz's term, can be financially daunting. Organizers assured potential ticket buyers that the Atlanta Games would be accessible.[48] But to whom?

Merely finding lodging for the Atlanta Olympics was difficult and expensive. Depending on the Atlanta Olympic Committee's 1996 Olympic Games Travel Network as a resource, a case family of four was being charged $2,390 for "a six day 'hotel and parking' package" in a town 80 to 140 miles from Atlanta.[49] But attendance at such "highbrow," or "premier," events also entails, as Levine mentions, a certain expected decorum:

> The patrons of culture at the turn of the century . . . were now able to experience the expressive culture they appreciated, performed, and presented in ways they thought proper, [and] everyone had to experience them in these ways as well. They became both the promoters and the arbiters of this corner of the cultural world and gradually appropriated the term "culture" itself, which in the popular parlance came more and more to signify the high arts.[50]

And as the arbiters of taste (or as the gatekeepers of scholarship or popular culture), these "patrons of culture" subtly shift the focus of culture and what culture itself means—so that a cultural hegemony is instilled.

There are examples other than the high-low distinction of this sport-form classification: Benjamin Lowe examined contemporary sport in a modernist, bipolar framework, designing categorizations of sport that included "expressive" and "spectacle" sport: "Expressive elements underpin 'self-expressive' sport, and spectacle elements accompany sport for social or pecuniary reward."[51] This bipolar classification, while perhaps inclusive of many sport forms, is pragmatically meaningless when, for example, sports containing both expressive and spectacle elements are examined. To what degree, then, are these sports really sports? Do we have to decide whether they are mostly expressive, or generally spectacle? I argue in the following pages that sports that are between categories include most contemporary and many incipient, emerging forms of sports. Thus, this canonization process—the definitional certainty of modernist sport scholars—is exclusionary from the start.

The debate on hierarchical canonization, stemming from literary and social science debates on canonization, has only recently emerged in sport studies.[52] Thus it may be useful to briefly review the debate itself. Dorothy Ross, while not totally decrying some useful "aspects of these social science canons,"[53] demonstrates that the use of canons nevertheless "attempts to set up paradigms to govern work in their disciplines; each, therefore, privileges some kinds of work and excludes others."[54]

The inclusion or exclusion of certain work, which affects how people on the street and scholars alike study and discuss sport and how the construction of such dialogue occurs, elides into a discussion of the politicization of sport. Whether, for example, ballroom dancing is a sport determines whether ballroom dancing is sanctioned by the International Olympic Committee, and whether sponsorship dollars then subsidize its promotion. It would be naive to imagine that decisions which involve funding, power, and status within the academy or outside, on the street—or in nearly any institution—are built upon purely academic or meritocratic concerns.

Likewise, by looking at other areas of study in other disciplines (primarily art, for the art-sport connection seems quite viable), I feel that I can more easily unravel some of the complexities of the sport-player connection, such as the commotidization of sport, the active-passive connection, and the system of international sports tourism. For example, Barrett Watten, speaking of experimental and non-narrative art forms from the Soviet Union and how they tie in with the historicization of the Brezhnev era, looks at non-linear representations, at counterhegemonic artistic attempts, as resistant methods of the Soviet artist.[55] Standard dramaturgical studies (with a linear structure: beginning, middle, end) are not the only way to study art or sport; nor should they be the only objects of study. Henry Sayre, Marjorie Perloff, and others examining art have expanded currently held ideas of the traditional canon of art theory, history, and forms. Their work produces a canonical reflexivity in many traditional disciplines, and it should be included in the study—and resultant discussion—of sport. In sport studies, reflexivity toward this naturalized, socially constructed canonization process has barely begun.[56]

The already cited work by Benjamin Lowe has achieved the status of canon. It is a modernist project, of a modernist era, and as such it is largely non-self-reflective.

Another assumption that I make in this text, backed up when necessary for the arguments herein, is that the reader is conversant with and understands the heritage of interpretive work in sociology, anthropology, and cultural studies. The following chapters, to varying degrees, draw upon an interpretive interactionist framework. They are compiled in an increasingly personal interpretive order, and, accordingly, their styles vary. In other words, though I attempt to blend scholarly, popular, and private interactions throughout, the reader will find the thrust of the different chapters shifting primarily from scholarly to popular to private traditions.[57] In a sense, this evolution of style follows an evolution of thought in which the instillment of the individual writer into the text becomes increasingly appropriate and necessary. This instillment is not entirely a stylistic move, but rather, for me, a public avowal of the subjective—and political—nature of all inquiry. As Jim Thomas writes, "Critical ethnographers . . . celebrate their normative and political position as a means of invoking social consciousness and societal change."[58] As a writer of the text (and, strangely, an actor in it), I cannot, through "scientific" rhetorical device, hide behind the loss of a subject. I am the subject of these pages, ultimately, whether they are veiled in jargon (as the first essays of the text occasionally appear to me to be) or blatantly subjective, as is the final chapter, "Sport as Postmodern Tourism: Warp Speed in Barcelona (Olympism, Ideology, and Experience)."

In utilizing an interpretive interaction framework, I follow Denzin's working, evolving rubric: that interactionists "do not write . . . grand or global theories of societies";[59] that the interrelationships between people are key to a grasp of any so-called "front or back stage" goings-on; that lived experience (and its explication of the particular) remains crucial for the study of how people interact with their environment. Interactionists do not attempt to discover a "reality," but rather to examine the (re)combinant realities that emerge from myriad forms of social interaction.[60] Using an interactionist framework, therefore, I provide a map of my interpretive biases;[61] that map is not necessarily linear, dramaturgical, or unidimensional. Rather, my "map" is like a hologram, dancing between multiple extremes (which may elide or blur), much like Geertz's anthropological reflexivity (and patterned somewhat after his discussion of science and humanism).[62] Geertz demonstrates an

> attempt to come to terms with the diversity of the ways human beings construct their lives in the act of leading them. In the more standard sorts of science the trick is to steer between what statisticians call type-one and type-two errors—accepting hypotheses one would be better advised to reject and rejecting ones one would be wiser to accept; here it is to steer between overinterpretation and underinterpretation, reading more into things than reason permits and less into them than it demands.[63]

Clearly, to venture into this territory with my "map" requires more of the reader than that s/he take my hand and follow along blindly. Readers of this sort of text must become interactively involved (much like spectators of the new sport forms become interactively involved). The instillment of the reader into the text seems to me to be a requisite for an understanding of the text as it resonates within individual experience. In this way, the reader may more readily come to apprehend sensory experience through text. The final arbiter of "truth," in this context, is Geertz's above-cited "reason," or Denzin's "verisimilitude,"[64] or any one of a number of authors' "authenticity" or "truth." The proof, when dealing in things human, is ultimately bound in subjectivity: this is the lesson social psychologists and physicists alike have begun to embed in their research.[65] How we judge the worth of sport spectators', sport scholars', or sportswriters' "stories," then, is a matter for individual scrutiny, not global theory.

And largely because of its temporal compression, nowhere is there a better arena for studying subjectivity in microcosm than in sport.[66] By temporal compression, of course I mean that sensory experiences of a lifetime—joys, anguishes, bitter defeats, come-from-behind "miracles," the meritoriousness of effort, the unevenness of ability—may be experienced in a short time.

That sport is central to western lives is axiomatic in contemporary American society. In this society, we unearth fields of study that concentrate solely on sport: its history, psychology, sociology. We print sections of newspapers devoted to sport, launch general-and special-interest sport magazines, even produce twenty-four-hour television stations whose only *raison d'être* is sport. We watch multinational corporations such as Nike, Reebok, and Adidas—or Coca-Cola and Pepsi—sponsor or tie in with what has become a corporate/athletic complex. We see entrepreneurs open "sports bars," sell special sporting-event apparel, buy blocks of tickets to resell at profit. And such players of sport manage not only to sustain such enterprises, but to ensure that they flourish.

Everywhere we are bombarded—overtly and sometimes covertly—with sport. There are sport games which we willingly attend, read about, watch on television. There are oblique references within popular culture which strike at us tangentially in endless self-referentiality,[67] such as beer advertisements that are recognized as clever imitations of the "real thing," the Super Bowl, which we are instructed to anticipate.[68] These references celebrate, and simultaneously create, new formations, like recombinant folk tropes.

The following two snippets of dialogue from the film *City Slickers* serve to illustrate a sport-nostalgic trope for masculinity in the '90s. In the first, Bonnie questions men's obsession with baseball statistics:

> Phil: I guess it is childish. [But] . . . when I was about eighteen and my Dad and I couldn't communicate about anything at all, we could still talk about baseball. Now *that—that* was real.

Tales of sport's meaning in *City Slickers* circulate within a postmodern western pastiche whose cross-referentiality includes an homage to the opening ("yee-hah") scene from *Red River;* visual references to *Deliverance* and the TV show *Bonanza;* and humorously bizarre juxtapositions of a calf being fed from an Evian water bottle and, in the midst of a (nostalgic) cattle drive, an explanation of how to program a VCR.

In the second example from the film, the three main characters, friends since boyhood, reflect on their past(s) while driving cattle on a "dream vacation":

> Phil: The best day of your life?
> Mitch: I got one. I'm seven years old, and my dad takes me to Yankee Stadium. My first game. We go in this long dark tunnel underneath the stands, and I'm holding his hand, and we come up out of the tunnel into the light. It was huge. How green the grass was, the brown dirt. And that great green copper roof, remember? And we had a black and white TV, so this was the first game I ever saw in color. I sat there the whole game next to my dad. He taught me how to keep score. Mickey hit one out.
> Phil: Good day.
> Mitch: And I still have the program.

It may be that this nostalgic remembrance is confined to baseball, or that, as one middle-aged woman at the 1992 North American Society for the Sociology of Sport Conference challenged me, "I think you're talking about little boys' and men's experiences. Where, for example, do little girls have a similar experience?" That, of course, is a valid point—and there are certainly sociological accounts of females' experience in sport.[69] (Girls' and women's sport experience, especially since Title IX in 1972,[70] has been written—but in keeping with the dominant hegemony of the sporting "culture," apparently, little of it has been noticed.) But the evidence, both popular and scholarly, showing nostalgic remembrance in "masculine" sport as extensive is overwhelming, and is not confined to any specific canons of sport. It is everywhere you look.[71]

However, while such public and popular furor apparently surrounds the "playing" of games, I contend that the actual playing is not central to the experience of spectatorship. Johan Huizinga, whose *Homo Ludens* (*Man the Player*) is a classic in the study of physical culture, contended that everything humans do contains an element of play. Thus, spectators "play" at being spectators; athletes play at their sport, and so on. The actual play—on the field—however, has become secondary to everyone's play at what they do. For example, in a recent article in the *Chicago Tribune,* a senior vice president for marketing and broadcasting for the Chicago White Sox is quoted as saying,

> The stakes have gone up and you just can't sell to the hard-core baseball fan anymore. Your have to sell to the businessman and to the entertainment customer, to the people who spend their dollars on books, movies, plays, restaurants and other leisure-time activities."

> You have to include the casual customer and market the ballpark as fun. It's a place to enjoy the food, the Hall of Fame, the speed-pitch machine, the baseball card booth. You must present a total entertainment package."[72]

Many sport spectators have become "tourists," samplers of easily quantified and recollected snapshots of the game (or collections of those "snapshots," be they in the form of professional athlete cards or ticket stubs to games), whose only requirement is that they believe they have had an authentic experience and can somehow demonstrate that they have attended. They may mark their attendance in various ways: through the collecting of sport souvenirs or memorabilia, in the wearing of sports apparel, in the verbal or written (re)collection of significant moments in their lives, in identification with commodified versions of trend-setting athletes, in excessive spending to travel to and experience the games.

It is as if, for many, the collection of the experience, not the experience itself, has become paramount. This second-level experiencing, of course, is consistent with Baudrillard, Eco, and others' view of a simulacra-intensive world.[73] Markers of the experience serve to replace the actual experience. And increasingly the markers have become American markers, signifiers of the exports of aggressive multinational marketing schemes.[74] Just as a "Been There, Did That"–emblazoned sweatshirt initially serves as a tangible reminder of a tourist experience, so too the collection of tangible markers of experience by sport enthusiasts substitutes for the actual experience.

Television watching of games (virtual reality) has become more substantive than going to an actual game (reality). This compilation of experience calls to mind Walter Benjamin's classic essay "Art in the Age of Mechanical Reproduction." Benjamin saw the originator art as losing its impact when such accurate images and imitations could replicate it so truthfully. In one sense,

sport experiences have become mere replicants of each other, with no originator, no discerning features, like images cast from one mirror into another, *ad
infinitum.*

And yet, there are some sports enthusiasts who embrace the trappings of
the sport experience (as well as the sport itself), and who admit that the
primary experience—the whole sensory, overwhelming experience—of sport
spectating is still satisfying. These people are collectors also: they collect
shards of their individuality largely from sport experience. They identify with
"their" team and, like owners of a fantasy ball club, follow closely anything that
touches on "their" team.

There is, of course, no simple and clear-cut separation between "sport" and
the "surrounding experiences," or context. Similarly, there is no pure sports
fan, or form, absent of surrounding milieu. For example, Donald Hall, writing
of the bonding, reminiscent or originary,[75] which he feels occurs between
fathers and sons through sport, explains the sensory experience of actually
attending a game. Notice his reference to the senses in the description of the
total experience:

> As you look at the scene outside, you'd never believe that anything was new
> at Boston's ballpark. Ancient bars, hamburger joints, and souvenir shops
> jostle each other across from the pitted brick walls. In the streets, vendors of
> hot dogs, pennants, balloons, peanuts, and illegal tickets cry their wares to
> the advancing crowd. The streets carry a sweet, heavy, carnival air, like
> an old-fashioned marketplace. You half expect to run into a juggler or a
> harlequin.
>
> Inside Fenway, late afternoon sun illuminates the grass, making it so bright
> that I squint to see it. I look around at the old park again, green chairs, iron
> girders holding the roof up—and young ballplayers taking batting practice.[76]

Though he alludes to other senses, to Hall, sport—and particularly baseball—is primarily visual.

But, as television sports producers have been keen to notice, sport is also
aural. (And as the above passage indicates, the smell of food, the texture of the
"pitted" walls, the "vendors . . . cry[ing] their wares," and the imagined sense of
nostalgia pervade sport.)

Presently, new technologies,[77] which I view as avant-garde forms within the
sporting context (technological inventions to create a different apprehension
by the "audience"), have forced the at-home viewer closer to the actual experience of attending a game. This simulacrum of sensory experience has, for
many, substituted for any "real" experience—yet, paradoxically, watching a
game on television is "real" experience. There may be nostalgic anticipation
before the game ("You going to watch the 49ers on Sunday? I hope Jerry Rice

[or whoever] plays"), shared appreciation of good play, shared food and drink, and shared re-telling of the experiences after the game of watching/bonding, and of the actual game ("Andy Kaufmann won the game against Iowa with a 3-pointer in the last 1.5 seconds! Did you get to see it?").

▼ ▼ ▼ ▼

In the following chapters, I hope to accomplish several goals. On one level, I hope to demonstrate that the forms of sport and art are inextricably linked, and that the studies of sport and art can profitably borrow from one another. Thus, many issues are raised: Is there a problem with the existence of a canon in sport studies, similar to the one in art theory? Should the "canon" be discussed? Does a postmodernist moment integrate within its fluid borders a modernism that is intolerant of fluid slippage?[78] Is modernism, in fact, clearly dead on the contemporary scene?[79] What has been the impact on sport of collecting, displaying, and sharing? What, in fact, serves to differentiate souvenir from artifact from ethnographic object—and how are these objects found, and thought of, in contemporary sport? The list might go on indefinitely, and in a modernist work those questions might serve as keys to answer. But I do not presume a closed text; I do not presume to answer the questions in a "melodramatic-realist format," whose "story has a happy ending" (or even a necessarily satisfying one):[80] rather, I attempt to examine these questions in very particular moments which may or may not be recaptured either cognitively or experientially. And they may or may not be updated: new evidence supporting or refuting my explorations is continually cropping up in the sports world. Two events from the 1996 Olympics serve as examples. In the first, the producer of the opening ceremonies, Don Mischer, claimed that he was "walking a line between trying to create spectacular entertainment and overproducing things" and that he wanted some secrecy to maintain the "theatrical impact."[81] In the second, NBC explicitly attempted to "humanize" athletes as

> a message from [NBC] President Dick Ebersol . . . promises that telecasts of these Games . . . will be storytelling. That means profiles about the athletes' paths to Atlanta. . . . Asthmatic U. S. swimmer Tom Dolan, millionaire German swimmer–cover girl Franziska Van Almsick and iconoclastic French cyclist Jeannie Longo-Ciprelli, truly disliked by her competitors, all got the profile treatment Sunday.[82]

I leave the issues open, for the reader to explore them, based upon my reporting of evidence and based upon the reader's own experience, and upon any resonances that the text may elicit between text and reader.

Thus, I am not going to explain to the reader, in this introduction, what I feel the chapters do. I do not attempt to consciously separate method from theory from evidence. I have tried to integrate these concerns throughout the text—and now the onus of explication falls to the reader. The reader, in this sense, becomes one of the players of sport as well.

I wish also to show that the reflexive turn in scholarly research is one that can be examined on many levels. For example, the whole of this book demonstrates a change (growth? learning the scholarly discourse? resisting?)—a change from fairly standard formatized and formalized texts (e.g., chapter 3) to what one editor termed "radical ethnography"[83] (chapter 8). Thus, as in the incipient flowering of self-knowledge within sport players, there is an apparent change in style of writing that reflects a deeper change in political stance.

What the chapters are about is quite another matter. They stand independently, yet serve as interchangeable links to a major discussion of the performances of all the players in much of contemporary western sport. Each sporting milieu contains elements of kitsch; likewise, elements of avant-garde, epiphanic markers, and travel and tourism integrate with and touch upon each other in sport. Like good simulacra, these elements ultimately find their place in the minds of their athletes, performers, inventors, coaches, spectators, ticket hawkers, sportswriters, television commentators and producers, and sport tourists.

More specifically, in chapter 2, "Dropping Hierarchies: Toward the Study of a Contemporary Sporting Avant-Garde," I formulate a case for the use of an avant-garde metaphor for sport studies (similar to one that examines non-narrative art or "mindscreen cinema"),[84] which assimilates what I see as the current socially constructed metaphor of choice, the sport-as-drama metaphor.

The next four chapters are case studies of contemporary sport forms, spanning so-called "high" and "low" sport forms. In chapter 3, "Sport as Kitsch: A Case Study of *The American Gladiators*," I examine elements of one programmed sport which may be similar to other contemporary, more highly prized, sport forms. In chapter 4, "Sport as Avant-Garde: A Case Study of the World Wrestling Federation," I reverse the scope to deal with those elements that make contemporary sport, its practitioners, and its audience elements of an advance-guard cultural movement. In chapter 5, I move to a case study of what most sport scholars would consider mainstream sport: the 1992 Super Bowl. Since so many have studied and discussed this sport form so diligently, I used a participant-observer method and writing style—a more self-reflective approach—which better serves to offer readers a sampling of how they, in a spectator role, might have experienced this huge sporting spectacle. In chapter 6, "Sport as Postmodern Construction: A Case Study of Paintball," I continue to open up the writing style, to offer a more experiential take on but one of the many postmodern sport forms currently evolving in the contemporary western world. In chapter 7, "Sport as Constructed Audience: A Case Study of ESPN's *The eXtreme Games*," I engage the notion that audiences, much like sport, are constructed and formed to a proper fit to their subject matter. I delve into an interesting new sport form, the made-for-television international spectacle. And in the final chapter, "Sport as Postmodern Tourism: Warp Speed in Barcelona (Olympism, Ideology, and Experience)," I return to a more mainstream sport form, the 1992 Barcelona Olympics, to explore the phenomenon that is the sport tourist. In a sense, of course, we are all sport tourists, whether venturing from our beds to our televisions, or halfway across the world on an expensive organized sport tour to the Olympics. In the last four chapters, to varying degrees, I note and advance, showing rather than telling, much of what I have discussed earlier, and demonstrate similarities and differences within and between various modern and postmodern sport forms.

TWO | **Dropping Hierarchies**
Toward the Study
of a Contemporary
Sporting Avant-Garde

> To have been in Pasadena, felt the sonic thump of that 2-1
> upset of the Colombians, was to be plugged in—however
> temporarily—to the universe of both the beautiful game
> and its language of emotion.
>
> —Mark Kreidler, 1994

Weave Me Anew: An Introduction

Metaphors provide a sense of bridging from familiar topics to new, innovative concepts. For example, to better situate the processes of sport, those involved in its study have viewed it in a variety of ways. Some of these ways have included sport as a mirror of society, sport as war, and sport as art form. In this chapter, I examine two possible variants of the sport-as-art-form metaphor: sport as drama and sport as avant garde.[1]

I explore the first, sport as a dramatic narrative, as a linear, traditional, restrictive, modernist, and ultimately hierarchical metaphor. Constructors of sport as drama—among them, television producers and directors, radio announcers, and sportswriters—presume that a good story will create a larger audience.[2] In contrast to this approach, most athletes I have known have been too involved in the task at hand, in the pragmatics of participation, to see any larger thread of storyline. Analogously, I argue that many spectators in attendance at the actual game experience a participatory flow, but not necessarily one that coincides with what is televisually constructed. The experience is in many cases cogent, yet not necessarily linear and dramatic.

But athletes and spectators are still of this culture, and remain influenced by the pervasiveness of such produced drama. Sport scholars as well are influenced by this sport-as-drama metaphor, to the point where the metaphors have become more persuasive than the actual sport to which the metaphors allude. Constructors of popular sport discourse—the media, athletes, spectators, and scholars—all influence and are influenced by the pervasiveness of the sport-as-drama metaphor. And, of course, the discourses of each constructor tend to blur together, to symbiotically regenerate each other. They are not discrete categories.

As I watch televised sport, for example, the experience is heightened by my prior knowledge (given to me by the announcer) that Patrick Ewing (of the rival Knicks) has said of the Bulls, "What goes around, comes around." The agon motif is set; I know (or think I know), for example, that extra effort will be exerted (and this is often confirmed, as in "They're really elevating their game tonight!"), and that this—again, I'm told to think—will be a "classic match-up." If I were at the game, the television timeouts, the vendors selling their goods, even the distraction of someone standing up in front of me would lend a disjointed, non-narrative, non-linear, non-dramatic, "dead time" feel to the event. And yet there would be dramatic moments; the game itself might be highly charged with drama, or there might well be singular confrontations of dramatic magnitude or purpose. But the game and its events would as likely be undramatic, and then I would have to find other reasons to appreciate the experience.

While narrative certainly is an important facet of some sporting contests, the tacit (and unexamined) avowal of sport as drama is pervasive. Sport coverage by the electronic media, for example, could be seen as analogous to news coverage.

> Television news [read sport coverage], merely by its format, gives the impression that everything one really needs to know is included. The familiar pattern—a dramatic beginning, followed by more significant, but less dramatic middle stories, followed by a lighter ending—has the comfort of a bedtime story, squalid as it may be. . . . The viewer . . . is treated as a person who wants to be entertained.[3]

More specific to sport, in examining the Joe Montana–San Francisco 49er negotiations, Muller asserts in her abstract that "the dramaturgical perspective is appropriate for analyzing all types of human action."[4] She then proceeds to analyze the media's treatment of this "story" in terms of Turner's "theory of social drama."[5] Furthermore, Harris and Hills note that "sport seems particularly well suited to news coverage using a narrative framework because of its inherent storylike structure."[6] *Is* there an "inherent storylike structure" in sport, or has it been defined as having an inherent structure merely to better canonize what may properly be termed sport?

▼ ▼ ▼ ▼

The utility of the sport-as-drama metaphor (and even a discussion of it as a metaphor) for sport studies naturally allows for its subsumption under the modernist rubric of sport as an art form. Such a schema provides a hierarchical framework, an adversarial, privileged, and deterministic view of the question "What is sport?"

In this chapter, I argue against the exclusive use of the sport-as-drama metaphor, which often, both explicitly and implicitly, informs the sociological research of sport.[7] I indicate how the avant-garde may be used as a metaphor for the study of sport, and I provide specific examples from the media in the United States in the past thirty years to support this theoretical argument regarding the avant-garde in contemporary sport. I suggest that contemporary sport can be viewed in terms of the avant-garde and provide a theoretical basis for the selection of the "sport-as-avant-garde" metaphor. I substantiate the historical art-sport connection (because the most substantial documentation of the avant-garde draws from art criticism) and explore the historical and contemporary use of the term "avant-garde."[8]

The metaphor I propose—sport as avant-garde—is examined in terms of a postmodernist avant-garde movement that has looked at, among other issues, the conflation of static art and organic performance (and participatory) art.[9] This metaphor, somewhat in contrast to the sport-as-drama metaphor, opens up the field of study, demands (re)placement of the "reader" into the text, and coexists with such metaphors as sport as a mirror of society, sport as war,[10] and sport as art.[11] For example, there can be avant-garde in the society as a whole, in war,[12] and certainly in art.

Sport contests are not inherently dramaturgical (indeed, it is questionable whether "everyday life" is inherently dramaturgical, or whether it is, much like the self, "created and presented in the course of interactions . . . through discursive acts").[13] Their linear narrativity is imposed and instilled into them by sport discourse. Sport discourse—the discourse of narrativity—has, in this televisually literate society,[14] become naturalized. The tension of a close contest, while real and palpable during the contest, disappears immediately after it: the effects are transitory, yet live on in memory. And over time they grow in their dramatic feel. In short, the consumers of such a sport contest have become enmeshed in its linear, narrative, and dramaturgical discourse—so that the drama of sport feels, unexamined, as real as sport itself.

The concept of drama in sport may roughly follow a pattern paralleling western art history. Realistic, tension-laden works were considered "high" art—until the impact of the avant-garde was felt. Oppositional artists, attempting to wrest sensibility out of stupor, created new forms. These forms did not necessarily follow linear, rational, narrational, and dramatic lines, but rather played with form, color, texture: the absence of drama, in its traditional sense.[15] It is time to explore a similar trend in sport studies. The lack of tension in a lopsided contest, however, becomes problematic, for the sport consumer and the sport purveyor alike. Not every sports contest is a "masterpiece" (in a classic high/low dichotomy), even though someone may commoditize it as such. (Witness the Final Four, World Series, or Super Bowl discourse, for example. Classics before their playing, they are inventions created to capitalize on increased sales and markets.) Perhaps those sport forms that are not considered "high" sport, as a start, might better be understood in terms of an avant-garde metaphor.

The term "avant-garde" has been alluded to tangentially but infrequently in sport studies. For example, Benjamin Lowe discussed art issues that relate to modernist concerns in the derivation of pleasure from sport.[16] "Avant-garde" was included in the titles of papers given at the "Sport et Sociétés Contemporaines" symposium in Paris in 1983 (but nowhere present in the papers delivered). Peter Donnelly utilized the term "avant-garde" in criticizing the sport-as-a-mirror metaphor when he recognized oppositional forces within dominant sport ideology.[17] Implicit in each of these uses of the "avant-garde" (or, more rightly, the *term* "avant-garde") is narrative: but, as Watten has posited, what of the non-narrative?[18] The assumption that avant-garde work became somehow stillborn and stuck in time and space, so that it opposed only a formal linear structure, is perhaps in error.

Watten provides an interesting postmodernist twist on the narrativity question by discussing formerly marginalized Russian art, art that does not follow a traditional form of narrativity. He makes the point that it is largely their *non-narrativity* which has excluded these arts from discussion. The postmodernist avant-garde creates a window of opportunity for discussion of both artistic and athletic non-narrative.

The seventh game of the 1992 National League Playoffs, won with two outs in the bottom of the ninth inning by the Atlanta Braves over the Pittsburgh Pirates when pinch hitter Francisco Cabrera stroked a clean single and "former Pirate Sid Bream, bad legs and all,"[19] lumbered home just ahead of the throw to bring in the winning run, was clearly a dramatic moment. To a spectator at such an event, the drama would be palpable. There are certainly key moments in much of contemporary sport which *may* offer spectators their "own brand of drama."[20]

While sport as drama as a "master narrative" is rampant in popular, personal, and scholarly discourse, reliance upon the sport-as-drama metaphor limits research to narrative formations, ostracizes the study of non-narrative formations, (re)creates unexamined assumptions of linearity and causality in sport, and perpetuates hierarchy, canonization, and the privileging of scholarly over popular texts.

In this light, I explore three avenues of research applicable to sport studies which the avant-garde metaphor most obviously suggests: (1) the paradoxical and complex individual/group interaction that has emerged in modern and postmodern American sport and society; (2) the emergence of new sport forms due in part to technological advances; intertextually sophisticated sports spectators aware of postmodern parody, pastiche, and irony; more leisure time; and greater mass participation in sport; and (3) the incorporation of the audience/spectator into the lived experience that has become sport in this contemporary historical moment. As we shall see, in the postmodern world of sports, these three avenues often overlap: for example, the installation of new sport forms often demands a basic give-and-take between athlete-as-performer and audience-as-performer.

Us and Them: Individual/Group Interaction

The myriad relationships that exist in sport endeavors have often been studied *en masse*. Yet the constellations of relationships may include those between an individual athlete and other athletes, teams, coaches, sponsors, the media, spectators. Spectators, similarly, have often been bunched into a hodgepodge of non-entities classified as non-interactive viewers. In truth, as Fiske has noted, "oral culture is active, participatory. Because the conventions are so well known and so closely related to the social situation of the community, all members of that community can participate more or less equally in the production and circulation of meanings."[21] Similarly, sportscasters—a group that sport scholars may (and largely have) set aside as on the periphery of sport—can be studied in terms of innovation. Their "cutting edge" self-portrayals can become mythic stories if enough of the community buys into them. In this vein, Home Box Office (HBO) telecast *Play by Play: A History of Sports Television*, which examined in varying degrees the careers of sportscasters from Mel Allen to Lindsey Nelson to Greg Gumbel.

The individuality of these sportscasters was emphasized in the stories selected. For example, Lindsey Nelson asked a clothier to "show me all the jackets you have that you can't sell. Horrible. Just awful. Offensive. That's what I wanted. That's how you get attention." Individual styles, demonstrated in sound bites, were recalled in the distinctive verbal signatures of Mel Allen and Harry Caray ("It might be. It could be. Ho-o-o-ly Cow!").[22] Originality is one of the keys to the senses of authenticity and creativity for these artists of the airways. To imitate Harry Caray's "Holy Cow" might be amusing as a parlor game, but an imitator would be as well received in sports circles as someone in the art world who tried to pass off a replication of Christo's *Running Fence* as genuine and original.

The mix of public and private postures, the collapse and upsetting of the myth of individuality in contemporary society,[23] has, to fans' dismay, risen sharply in the sports world since the 1960s (and was rising steadily before). With the emergence of a potentially lucrative[24]—and enjoyable—NFL/television marriage in the early 1960s, "[then–NFL commissioner Pete] Rozelle became known for advocating short hair in the locker room and for behaving sternly on such 'issues' as players' socks."[25] Yet Al Davis, opposing Pete Rozelle and the rest of the NFL in 1980, claimed that "section 4.3 of the NFL constitution, which stipulated that at least three-fourths of the owners had to agree to any franchise relocations . . . was in restraint of trade and thus a clear violation of the Sherman Antitrust Act."[26] The uneasy distinction between public allegiance to (or disobedience of) trivial rules by players and disobedience of structural rules governing the whole of professional sports by "maverick owners" became problematic. Of course, Davis's players had long before established themselves as anti-hero, renegade media darlings, so the fit with their renegade owner put a slightly different spin on the "disobedience."

The embracing of sports figures by the media has exploded in the '80s and '90s. Michael Jordan, Joe Montana, George Foreman, even Bob Uecker[27]—all have parlayed their individual connections with sport into lucrative advertising packages which include promotional work: endorsement of games, balls, shoes, underwear, and foodstuffs.[28] In fact, the competing shoe companies' campaigns featuring NBA stars have capitalized on the separate media guise that each player has created for himself: David Robinson, the Admiral, epitomizes clean-cut America; Michael Jordan is the creative artiste; Dennis Rodman is a "bad boy," or merely bizarre. And so on. Each star captures a specific niche, and corners a slice of the market.[29]

Their embracing of the commercial side of the media has allowed a certain suspicion to creep in for some spectators: Do these athletes still have the pure and simple love of the game? It seems that spectators will forgive these media virtuosos anything, if only their motives are pure, their results interesting and innovative—as it is with the avant-garde in art. But as Suzi Gablik writes, "Art history, like all history, is woven of many discordant purposes; there is not just one. As John Cage once put it, 'If there were a thousand artists and one purpose, would one artist be having it and all the nine-hundred and ninety-nine others be missing the point? Is that how things are?'"[30] All of these individual entities together—that is, the individuals of basketball, but also all the players in sport: the owners, athletes, entrepreneurs, spectators, media, coaches, and so on—compose sport and bring a richness to our discussion and study of sport.

Amalgams of Change: New Sport Forms

In the west, we tend to idealize art[31]—and sport as well—attributing altruistic intent to obscure and untalented artists; assigning the term "original" willy-nilly before even arriving at a fair conclusion as to what is or is not "original." In this way, reproductions of Ansel Adams's artistry somehow devalue—for the uninitiated and, often, the initiated alike—the aesthetic value of his photography.[32] In 1936, Walter Benjamin wrote, "Earlier much futile thought had been devoted to the question of whether photography is an art. The primary question—whether the very invention of photography had not transformed the entire nature of art—was not raised."[33] Similarly, while sport scholars spend a great deal of time questioning whether sport—or its myriad forms—is of value, the combining of modern sport and the television media may have been mutually transformative.

The ABC television show *The American Gladiators,* for example, contains amalgams and mutations of "real" sport into "made-for-television" sport. In one contest, the running and power of football rushing is combined with a sumo wrestling contest, while another game portrays the upper-body strength of mountain climbing, but with a twist: a "Gladiator" chases the other contestant and attempts to pull him off "The Wall."[34] Contemporary televised sport thus asserts its combined theme: "man" versus "man," added to "man" versus nature. These dramatic themes are amalgamated to produce a new, recombinant form of simpler sports.

Other sports—taken from grassroots movements of the '80s and '90s[35]—have their roots likewise in resistant or recombinant sport forms, yet are in the process of being appropriated and commodified.[36] Witness "sky surfing," which is skydiving combined with boogie boarding, with the added twist of technology: the camera operator's video of the sky surfer's performance is what is critiqued by the judges, who remain on the ground.[37]

To discuss sport forms such as *The American Gladiators,* professional wrestling, or even "sky surfing" solely in terms of the drama metaphor currently in use obviously denies some quite powerful interactions taking place between and among spectators, athletes, performers, contestants—and even officials—at the site. These players' "performances" are not dramatic, yet they are genuine, if only because they are interactive experiences happening to real people.

These interactions are qualitatively different from those of a relatively "passive" theatergoer intellectualizing the moral consequences of Hamlet's vacillations.[38] These interactions are participatory and active, and they are a necessary requirement for the quality of the sport performance itself.[39] The spectatorial element of the sport experience is often skewed with irony, self-deprecation, or self-parody, and can be reflexive. Thus, the sport spectator, having been exposed to television's mark on sport, may turn the camera's gaze in any direction, *unconsciously* completing a participatory element of the avant-garde's project.

While watching televised sports, for example, the at-home viewer is often treated to fans performing for the television camera. One of the most famous of these is Pamela Anderson of *Baywatch* fame:

> Check Pamela's life story. In 1989 some neighbors invited her to a Canadian Football League game in Vancouver. A cameraman put her on the stadium's big-screen TV. The crowd went wild. Pamela happened to be wearing a Labatt's T-shirt that day; the company, noting that its logo had never before looked so good, signed her as a spokesmodel.[40]

> Lee's modelling career took off in a poster and TV ad campaign that plastered her image across Western Canada.[41]

To a lesser, and certainly less lucrative, degree, many fans at large stadiums have learned to perform for the camera. They—and their gigantic images—have become as much a part of the "at game" experience as the smell of hotdogs and stale beer.

Sharing Is Caring: Sport as Lived Experience

One of the major projects of the avant-garde of American modernism appears to be a transference of responsibility for a work of art from its originator to the audience.[42] This transference of responsibility from artist to spectator allows for a creative intermingling between the primary creator and the secondary creator. Thus, the spectator's role in meaning-making may, in fact, become as important in the "art" generated as the role of the primary artist: "Readers create texts as they interpret and interact with them."[43] Sport, as an institution paralleling art, may follow the pattern from modernism to postmodernism that art has initiated—and that sport scholars largely have disregarded. Many sport scholars—and the sporting public—have failed to recognize the dynamic, changing relationship between sport and society, choosing instead to produce nostalgic texts that reproduce the separation of audience from performer and, in Denzin's terms, reinforce an Oedipal logic that privileges males in sport, and reinstitutes the audience as scopophilic gazer, as voyeur.[44]

Through study of the installation of the reader into the text—i.e., the multiply shared responsibility between athlete, sports organization, and spectatorial elements—we can begin to understand the complex of interrelationships forged within sport. The lived experiences of spectators, athletes, and organizational members are complex, have changed profoundly with time, and should be studied as "universal singulars."[45]

As such, individuals' stories—Denzin calls them "exemplars"—serve as examples, but not generalizations, of core, unified, shared experience with others. The complexity of individually lived lives, of course, begins to play out when one shares certain characteristics with one cadre, other experiences with another group, and so on. Thus, as a fairly simplistic example, an individual sport spectator may be deeply involved in supporting "his" Dallas Cowboys (because he was born in Dallas, before moving at age four), marginally interested in the Pittsburgh Steelers (because he went to college in Pittsburgh), and nostalgically yearning for the Chicago Bears (because his father always rooted for "da Bears"). And this is only in professional football—imagine the interplay of "ownership" and belonging in all sports! Rich gradations of individual and group voices must be heard and examined in order to begin to determine how the sport experience interplays with individuals—and with groups.

From a strictly marketing standpoint, the dramatic angle of creating audience and fans is only one of many ways that the sport experience may resonate. The study of how fans bond with teams, regions, other fans—and how they become disenfranchised—should, if one is examining it from a pecuniary standpoint, be one that examines spectators' experience. And more and more often their experience is not linear, but rather sensory; not objective, but rather subjective; not easily structured, but rather somewhat convoluted and complex.

Given all this, however, the mark television has made on sport is legendary. Some technological advances have forever changed the quality of a sport experience for fans, athletes, and even those involved in "the business" of media. As Jim Lampley says (again utilizing the drama metaphor),

> Over the years, television has dramatically enhanced its coverage of sporting events. With the latest audio technology, we are now privy to conversations we would *never* hear—at the game. With an array of graphics, we learn pertinent facts, and with cameras stationed almost everywhere it's almost like having a dozen pairs of eyes. Being at the stadium is its own special experience, but when you're at home, in your living room, watching it all on television, sometimes that's the best seat in the house.[46]

It was the mission of forward-thinking sports programmers on network television (particularly in the United States) to immerse the viewer in the sensory appeal of the sports covered.

The motives were not based merely on economics: "Producers and directors have been searching for the ultimate camera position, the most unusual angle, the most compelling point of view," says Jim Lampley. Producers and directors are, in HBO's estimation, "the visionaries [who invented] . . . the slo-motion replays, the hand held cameras, the you-are-there audio." Clearly, some sort of artistic mission was at work, because "cameras moved the viewer from the stands to the playing field, so that we could almost taste the action, and nearly touch it."[47] A bathing of the senses was one of the primary motives. And while the initial impulse to find alternate forms of technology may have been to better "tell the story," the result has been that use of these technologies has created an MTV-style sports/media flavor in contemporary sports programming. The sharing of primary and sensory experience—of the "lived" (filmed) experience of athletes on camera, with sweat flying, the satisfying plunk of a ball putted into a cup, the loneliness of a Hawaiian Ironman triathlete as she gaped at the barren stretch lying before her—imitated reality exceedingly well. Competitive technology was the driving force behind this "imitated reality."[48]

When "the slo-motion replay became the *super* slo-motion replay, *magnificently re-capturing a part of the present* we may have missed" (my emphasis),[49] the ability of the spectator to interrogate, appraise, regard, reflect on, and evaluate that which was viewed, formerly confined to things artistic, was now possible within sporting endeavors. But it was a simulacrum, a reality of text over concrete experience, and the slo-motion and super slo-motion were just further exemplifications of hyperreality.[50]

But the same thinking—"let's involve the spectator more"—continues to prevail. Announcer Dick Enberg of NBC-TV, a self-admitted neophyte in golf announcing, was given the task of anchoring the network's golf coverage for 1995. According to Rudy Martzke, executive producer Tom Roy justified this move by saying, "Our golf philosophy has shifted . . . from machine-gun shots to more storytelling to *get the viewer to develop a rooting interest* in the golfers. And the best story-teller in the business is Enberg"[51] (my emphasis). "Storytelling" drama and dramatic tension do involve the older viewer, but clearly the numbingly standardized packaging of televised sports into neatly compartmentalized two- or three-hour dramas misses much of the point of sport as experienced by on-site sport spectators. And the more visually savvy younger viewer becomes bored by such linearity: that is one reason why golf, catering to an older audience trained in linear narrative, has returned to the "storytelling" that sells best. Conversely, some of the "newer" sports—such as the ESPN *eXtreme Games*—are presented in just the "machine-gun" approach—visually—that Roy disparaged for golf. Audiences are taught the conventions; they are thus *made* to participate.

Compelling Images: Metaphors as Directions of Study

The way we speak betrays our sensibilities toward a subject. Sport studies in North America has produced public, private, and scholarly discourses that range the spectrum of theoretical approaches and methodologies. Some work currently being done by sport studies scholars and the sports media, for example, consists of descriptive analyses, fond reminiscences, and biographical sketches.

Each of these, in turn, creates and utilizes its own particular metaphoric language to facilitate discussion. All three of these approaches, however, might use terms such as "growth of the league," "building character," "overcoming obstacles," "changing with the times," "up to the challenge," and "perseverance" to indicate rising and falling action and denouement—dramatic, conflictual language. Such figurative language—the language of growth, conflict, and resolution—seeks to produce as well as illuminate understanding by likening a group, a movement, or a person's life to a drama. Westerners follow the rise and fall of action as if it were ordered, as if causality were assumed—as if progress were assured. Indeed, sport in recent years has been studied largely in terms of this dramatic metaphor—this is reflected in scholarly discourse as well as in the popular culture.

As examples, Rader cites the fact that Walter C. Hagen "helped erase social discrimination in golf"[52] (this idealistic-sounding statement is belied by other work which points out that African Americans "remain guests within a predominantly white culture . . . [which formerly] allowed [them] a space in which to develop cultural events apart from the white community")[53] and that "[Gertrude] Ederle's swim represented victories for women, German-Americans, the United States, and the efficacy of practicing traditional virtues."[54] Statements such as these create and provide storylines that reflect use of a dramatic, linear, and causal metaphor.[55] *Post facto*, such statements may be marginally credible; but they imply efficacy where there might, in real time, have been none. In reconstituting the (recent or long) past, we make it sensible, ordered, logical.

In the *New York Times*'s "Sport Pages" (ironically housed in the "Living Arts" section), Anderson demonstrates the pervasiveness of the sport-as-drama phenomenon in popular culture as a lead-in to the 1991 World Series:

With his two 1–0 *masterpieces* after an 18–8 record that included three crucial pennant-race triumphs, Steve Avery is the pride of the Braves, the *lead* in baseball's most charming *storyline*: the kid pitcher that older sluggers can't touch. He's also part of baseball's most stirring *subplot*: the kid pitcher taught by his father who didn't make the big leagues.[56] (My emphasis)

Another example: Yankees pitcher David Cone, hoping to pitch in Game 4 of the 1997 American League division series with Cleveland, announced that he was not healthy enough to compete. The *New York Times's* headline for the article, using the drama metaphor, read "A Tearful Cone Exits the Stage as Gooden Re-enters."[57]

▼ ▼ ▼ ▼

In the print—and electronic—media, there are countless examples of such dramatizing of sport. But the point I wish to make here is that the conscious use of terms such as "storyline" and "subplot" indicates the writer's willing acceptance of and complicity in the construction of the sport-as-drama metaphor. The writer is not merely falling into a socialized trope; he is consciously referring to the shared "knowledge" that sport is ordered and orderly, and that at least in sport, we can count on logic pervading.

● Sporting events, of course, *do* have beginnings, middles, and ends. They *may* have rising and falling action—as well as resolutions. They *may* be linear in structure. Or they may not. Athletes—who become characters in the constructed dramas—are personalized, especially by announcers working in the electronic media, and the events are oftentimes recorded as microcosms of larger life issues. Thus we are told that a college basketball championship game (in the Final Four) is emblematic of two kinds of basketball: street, inner-city, athletic, improvisational—and, by implication, black—basketball (Tarkanian's Runnin' Rebels of the University of Nevada, Las Vegas), versus controlled, disciplined, cerebral—and, by implication, white—basketball (Duke's Blue Devils).

As spectators we are implicitly given the instructions to care deeply about this or that event, for its outcome *could* change our lives. This singular emphasis on the dramatic element, however, not only *reflects* how sport operates, but may *determine* how a society views sport (not coincidentally, this tends to determine how individuals and societies view themselves). Such mechanisms, which often operate covertly as socially accepted master narratives, become more explicit through the (c)overt use of metaphors.[58]

Victor Turner has described the concept of "root metaphor," which closely aligns with the idea of master narratives. Such metaphors become determiners of how a culture views itself, and play into the hegemonic formations of social control. The language we use becomes not merely accepted, but rather expected and unquestioned. For example, Turner points out the Marxist metaphor of "social orders 'forming embryonically' in the 'wombs' of preceding orders, with each transition akin to 'birth,' and requiring the assistance of the 'midwife,' force."[59] With the birthing metaphor in place, the benign and natural sense of Marxism then becomes something more easily accepted by those who struggle to understand it. Turner's idea of metaphor also may prove fruitful to scholars in micro-analyses of historical and sociological moments in poststructural American sport.

But extended metaphors are best judged by proper fit, and the currently extant metaphor—largely unexamined—for late-twentieth-century sport is drama. While popular writing has used the sport-as-drama metaphor extensively, so too have sport scholars. There exists, for example, in Sage's *Power and Ideology in American Sport* the indication of a hierarchical tension between "trash" and "traditional" sport.[60] Such categorical bipolarities delineate sport as falling under a dramatic rubric that inscribes limitations upon the very nature of sport itself. In the past century, at least, drama has been viewed in the bipolar hierarchies of "high" versus "low" culture,[61] and sport drama particularly. For instance, "[Lipsky] highlights the mounting dramatic tension which is often created by means of journalistic characterizations of opposing teams or particular sports stars prior to important athletic contests."[62] The metaphor of drama has come to represent and signify sport for the public, sport scholars, and media alike.

Sport has come to be signified by the dramatic: anything less (or more) than a dramatic contest is less-than-sport. Thus, sport promoters do everything in their power to create a dramatic tension, even if one does not exist. The thinking is that more audience will clamor for more dramatic contests. But while the catering to a massified audience creates more audience, the so-called spontaneous dramatic tension has become commoditized as well.

Unfortunately, under closer examination, such a monolithic metaphor as drama in sport breaks down: the drama of sport is scripted and is quite often, within parameters, predetermined.[63] Those involved in sport generally deride—in fact, punish—anyone, spectator or athlete, who presumes to determine an outcome in advance. For example, athletes have been banned from sport for consciously predetermining the results of a contest[64]—or for any other "offenses" which even touch on predetermination of results.[65]

As well, the dramatic effects of the sporting behaviors of World Wrestling Federation athletes are generally claimed to result in theatrical non-sport,[66] or at best "trash" or "marginal" sport. To type athletic contests in this way denies the importance of any participatory element for spectators. This denial of the WWF as sport may, ironically, align with the drama metaphor, promoting elitism while denying popular involvement in sport, and inhibit research into a potentially fertile area.[67] Sport scholars and the public alike seem to feel that if a sport is too successful at reproducing the dramatic elements, it becomes a parody of sport. So there exists a very narrow margin of acceptability for contemporary sport: play up the (traditional) theatrical elements, but not too far. This kind of narrowness—and narrow thinking—seems exclusionary, and it re-creates existing power differentials among and between sport forms.

On the other hand, the metaphor of sport as avant garde is vital and challenging, one that I feel reflects a more accessible interplay between "actor" and spectator. While Lowe painstakingly synthesized modernist notions of both sport and art; while Best and Wertz carried a lively intellectual debate from the *Journal of Aesthetic Education* to the pages of the *Journal of the Philosophy of Sport* in the late 1970s and mid-1980s;[68] and while others have continued to discuss the aesthetic/artistic/sport relationship,[69] a viable metaphor needs to emerge that will cut across these epistemological boundaries, to transcend such esoteric issues.

Sport as avant-garde is a metaphor, as is sport as drama. As a metaphor, it carries some of the same problems as any metaphor.[70] As avant-garde, however, sport is an art form, but not an art form in the sense that Lowe and others conceptualize it.

Rather than fashioning itself after and fastening itself to only one art form (drama),[71] this metaphor follows a broader avenue of inquiry. The avant-garde metaphor is inclusive of the linear temporal structure of "traditional" drama as well as that drama, performance art, and staged spectacle that might be termed "non-linear." It is multidimensional and multifaceted, much like contemporary sport. It is based upon theorizing of the modernist and postmodernist turns in architecture, visual art, literature, music, and performance art. Thus, by use of the avant-garde movement, I seek to describe contemporary sport. This tack, paradoxically, serves to lessen the burden of value-laden notions of "high" (e.g., the Olympics) and "low" (e.g., dwarf bowling, demolition derbies) culture, "elite" (e.g., yachting, polo) and "mass" (e.g., bowling, pool) sport, "drama" and "spectacle,"[72] audience and participant, as well as hegemonic and marginalized sport practices, and in fact attempts to collapse these categories. The collapse of the heretofore oppositional categories of "vanguard culture" and "mass culture" encompasses the fact that "there are few distinctions one can make at the levels of form, content, even, possibly, ideology between current vanguard and mass-cultural work."[73] In postmodernism, avant-garde art forms are becoming pastiches, as are contemporary sport formations.

That ideology between elite and egalitarian art (or sport) forms is converging is, of course, a particularly political statement. For example, István Deák discusses the Activists, a pre–World War I Hungarian avant-garde artist's collective:

Many of the Activists came from the working class themselves, making their identification with the interests of the masses more genuine, if not less romantic, than the earlier, more genteel Hungarian movements. Their artistic credo was quite simple: each creation of a modern artist was a political as well as aesthetic act. They also felt *the old distinctions between "fine" and "utilitarian" art were false and artificial,* thus laying the basis for the tremendous development of the political, and later commercial, poster in the hands of these artists.[74] (My emphasis)

The realignment of art with life for the Activists was not unlike the postmodern critical artist's position of seemingly participating in culture in order to reject it. As Auslander writes, "Postmodernist art does not position itself outside the practices it holds up for scrutiny. It *problematizes,* but does not *reject,* the representational means it shares with other cultural practices."[75] The avant-garde of the postmodernist moment, while it is of the problem, is also at the cutting edge of this problematization.

The modernist avant-garde has been exemplified by Marcel Duchamp's work—perhaps especially by his Ready-Mades—which "negates the category of individual production."[76] One historical example is a urinal turned upside down, titled *Fountain, by R. Mutt, 1917.*[77] Ready-Made "sculptures" neither used original materials nor prepared their audiences for the experience to come. Rather, Duchamp's (and the artistic avant-garde's) innovation, like most creative endeavors, had its roots in the combination, permutation, and juxtaposition of disparate ideas, materials, and technologies—or in the appropriations and reworkings of such combinations—for ironic ends. And they involved audience for their effects to be realized: the contributions of audience to the very *creation* of the art was of critical importance. Sport figures' making of themselves—a sort of "the body as Ready-Made"—certainly carries out this theme. Somewhat in contrast, drama plays to an audience, but does not invite the audience into the play itself; the audience is passive, expecting to be entertained rather than actively involved in creating the entertainment. Such pastiche in sport might be exemplified by the WWF's appropriation of other sport forms' marketing strategies, gimmickry, and iconic personalities.[78] And, of course, the WWF's appropriation is not limited to one direction. The WWF has served as a model for imitative "legitimate" sport marketing practices.

Paving the Way: Avenues of Research

How might all these ideas work within sport studies? The metaphor of the avant-garde within sport may better allow scholars to examine the ways in which sport, sport figures, and even those seemingly on the periphery of sport, including audiences, have negotiated space for themselves in late-twentieth-century culture. For while art criticism explores new modes of seeing (and ways of understanding those new perceptions), new modes of criticism in contemporary sport lag behind the very diversity of sport as it is practiced in late-twentieth-century America. The forms of contemporary sport have outstripped former, modernist, definitions of sport, and demand a cogent understanding of them.

For example, one classic modernist definition (in sport studies) of sport reads: "We formally define sport as a structured, goal-oriented, competitive, contest-based, ludic physical activity."[79] Further explication of this definition demonstrates that to be classified as sport, an activity requires an uncertain outcome as one of the components of ludic activity, thus perpetuating the sport-as-drama metaphor, thus perpetuating the canonization of certain sport forms over others.

Uncertain outcome to whom? one wonders. One of the criticisms of professional wrestling as sport is that the outcomes of the contests (and contestants) are predetermined.[80] The same can be said of a mismatched basketball game (the Dream Team at the Barcelona Olympics), the pre-seeded finals in swimming or track meets, or even many Super Bowls, including the 1992 Super Bowl between the Washington Redskins and the Buffalo Bills. To an audience, such "certainty of outcome" does not exist, since they are not privy to critical inside information. But more to the point, appreciation of a performance does not require uncertainty of outcome when the audience itself becomes implicated in the very act of creating the performance.

In terms of sport studies, this definition might be considered a modernist, "all or none," linear, exclusionary, hierarchical one. If such a restriction of form were used in art circles, cubist, dadaist, and surrealist art would be excluded from the art canon. Studies dealing in color would be relegated to a "not art" category, without regard for the meanings of juxtaposed colors, asymmetry, or balance. The entry of an avant-garde element into art sidestepped such definitional difficulty by embracing all art forms—without, it must be added, nullifying the subjectivity of personal taste.[81] Personal tension, thus, was retained without public constraint.

Simply utilizing this definition (and, by extension, the metaphor of sport as drama) privileges certain sport forms over others, without regard to their individual meanings to spectators and participants. Thus a more contemporary and inclusive definition of sport—which allows for a metaphor of sport as avant-garde to subsume the sport-as-drama metaphor—might be something like Sansone's: "sport is the ritual sacrifice of physical energy."[82] This broader, more inclusive definition is liberating simply because it allows for examination of sport forms that scholars may have traditionally relegated to a "low-sport" category (and thereby dismissed). By privileging certain sports over others at the definitional level (and using the metaphor of sport as drama), a primary denial of popular and populist sport has tainted the study of the "sport canon." It has created taboo topics. As Sansone writes,

> The difficulties involved in devising a definition are frequently mitiga
> the liberal application of personal prejudice. If one is attempting a defi
> of sport and is oneself a sportsman—as so many who have written ɑ
> sport proclaim themselves to be—one tends to eliminate from consideration
> activities (which "others," perhaps, may regard as sport) that are somehow
> distasteful, inelegant or otherwise unworthy of inclusion in the company of
> such noble activities as those one practices oneself.[83]

Of course, a more radical (and perhaps intriguing) approach might be to discard all definitional attempts as modernist and exclusionary. But this might not deal with issues of, among others, nihilism, the problematic of the cusp of modernism/postmodernism, and privilege.

The combination of a new electronic technology with a nineteenth-century brand of hucksterism has surely wrought sport forms never before seen. A conservative sport establishment may distance itself from proclaiming some of these as sport, yet popular culture, often at the forefront of such movements, demonstrates very little definitional ambivalence or vacillation.[84] Of course, other institutions are less hesitant to argue. In an article in *Newsweek* decrying the onslaught of "crash TV," author Harry Waters describes the sport television situation thus: "In the checkered annals of made-for-TV 'sports,' 'American Gladiators' makes the demolition derby seem like high tea at the Savoy."[85] Questions of whether an activity is or is not sport, in fact, do not appear to be relevant to many people: if an activity is participated in, it is worthy. (However, this public stance ignores the political ramifications of privilege.) An avant-garde fitted to modern American sport, especially to the spectatorial elements within professional televised sport since the early 1960s (when professional football and television began to share in the lucrative commercialization of both industries), may provide valuable insights into the shared meanings between spectator, media, and athlete.

Just as art scholars return to the sources of their fascination and listen to the voices of the avant-garde artists whom they study, so too is it important for sport studies scholars to return to the prime movers in sport. To listen to the multivocal texts of such practitioners—folk experts, in a real sense—is to participate in the enaction, construction, and generation of culture,[86] which is, of course, an enactment of the avant-garde's project.

Winds of Change: A Conclusion

Many studies of sport nowadays involve discussions of modernism, postmodernism, bureaucracy, and institutionalization, all of which have been examined in art discourse. Gablik writes about contemporary art:

The old values of individuality, indispensability, and spontaneity are re-placed by new ones, based on obedience, dispensability, specialization, plan-ning, and paternalism. The goal is security: to be part of the big powerful machine, to be protected by it, and to feel strong in the symbiotic connection with it.[87]

Gablik is emphasizing the decline of the modernist project in art.

I have argued that for sport studies, it is imperative that we take note of a similar decline in the modernist project in sport. Sport and the study of sport may be on a modern/postmodern cusp. We need to notice these changes in terms of a postmodern avant-garde, one whose project understands and seeks to uncover the interdependence and symbiotic nature of sport and society.

The technological advances of the past thirty years clearly have served to bring the art, aesthetic, and sport worlds closer together. The relationship between art and sport (and sport and the media) appears to be deep-seated, institutional, and even, perhaps, ominous. Metaphors such as "sport as avant-garde" may provide some insight into where sport as an institutional practice is going, but perhaps may best serve as warnings of what might occur or of what might be avoided. It is important to remember, however, that the avant-garde of postmodernity is fragmented, multivocal, and tinged with a sense of parody and irony which was not necessarily a condition of the project of the avant-garde of modernity.[88] This postmodern avant-garde is one that paradoxically rejects and embraces bureaucracy, its own seriousness, and commercialization. As Denzin writes of cinema (and it can be said of postmodern sport),

Reflexive cinema is duplicitous. The very agency that purports to be under-mining its own agency is in control of this cinematic apparatus which is doing these tellings. So the apparatus attempts its own epistemological privileging as it critiques from within its selfsame representations of reality. The machine that mocks the copy controls the copies that are made.[89]

In terms of research on sport, we need to take note of, and account for, many more forms of contemporary sport in our studies. We need to include those sport forms that are subtly "mocking the copies" of other sport forms, to better understand what is at work. Sport is a glistening and omnipresent facet of postmodernity, both a vanguard and a rearguard which both is informed by and informs the culture. Consumerism and bureaucracy, for example, are woven into sport and vice versa.

Mass production and commodification have become inextricably linked, though temporally separate, in contemporary sport. In other words, to survive as spectator sport, a given sport needs to reach a mass audience, and it then becomes indelibly commodified, tied to a dramatic nostalgia (temporally sepa-rate) that mythologizes individuals within it.[90] The very act of commodification does not necessarily, however, suggest that a postmodern avant-garde is absent: in a complex society, subversive acts often are worked from within, and apparently superficial change such as individual stances on commodification in sport may have profound effects.

The art criticism work of Linda Hutcheon, who explores the use of parody that skews postmodern projects,[91] and that of David Kolb, who describes the codings and shades of meanings inherent in irony in architecture,[92] offer important ideas for sport scholars. One point each makes independently is that recombinations and recodings are taking place constantly in relationships: in the cases I have presented here, between athletes and spectators, who are by varying degrees, in individual, particular ways, self-aware.

In sport studies, scholars need a metaphor consistent with that which is being studied. I have tried to demonstrate that the "sport as avant-garde" metaphor, at the very least, will move the sport studies field a step closer to the study of non-linear and linear movement, which is continually regenerated, constantly reborn, multivoiced, and particularized.

How we study sport must become more a question of interest to sport scholars, for just as the labels we use suggest the parameters we allow ourselves to study, so too do the metaphors and methods we use determine our results. Thus we find that the study of sport has been divided into the study of back stage and front stage, sport spectator and participant, or high and low cultural forms. These very terms pre-construct bipolarities that reflect a bias toward the sport-as-drama metaphor. The use of a metaphor such as the avant-garde has no prior bias, for the avant-garde may turn in any direction, may utilize any of a myriad of tools, may even create new forms. By its very nature—its resistance to labeling—the avant-garde allows for change. The avant-garde limits the researcher only in that there are few culturally constructed barriers (which may in itself be a prior bias, but it is an encompassing rather than restrictive bias).

Through the study of sport as avant-garde, the totality of the sport experience can be examined. Through examination of the shared and diverse lived experience of athlete and spectator, sport—and its players—may be able to better tell us just what it is, has been, and will be.

The problem in the study of sport is not in sport; it is in us, in our reaction to sport. That which is most agreeably embraced, or that which is reprehensible, may serve to allow us, as spectators and participants, new insights into ourselves. It is only in our apathy toward (or dull acceptance of) any sport form that we deny our humanity, our ability to interact with the aesthetic form embedded in sport.

Thus, the use of the "sport as avant-garde" metaphor may provide sport scholars with a tool that broadens research avenues rather than constricts them. This metaphor may allow for—indeed, may demand—such organic concepts as "innovative," "processual," "sport as contested terrain," and "sport as living history," as opposed to the previously cited static terms used by the "sport as dramatic narrative" metaphor: "growth of the league," "building character," "overcoming obstacles," "changing with the times," "up to the challenge," and "perseverance." Such terms deny the conflictual and uncertain nature of sport, often implying sport to be synchronic rather than diachronic, studied as a slice in time rather than as an integrated, processual, contextualized study of the ebb and flow of relationships.

THREE | **Sport as Kitsch**
A Case Study of
The American Gladiators

Contemporary American televised sport reaches more individuals more profoundly than does on-site sport. The intertextuality and interplay between on-site sport and televised sport has increased as television viewers' and sport spectators' numbers have increased. In fact, promoters of sport intentionally create markers that effectively establish the links between televised sport and on-site sport. And the pervasiveness of sport in children's lives—both live and televised—has a great impact on their socialization into and through sport. The influences of television on socialization patterns of children, for example, have been well established.[1]

Mainstream, high-level sport (thus, more visible sport), such as the quadrennially anticipated Olympics or professional football and basketball games, reaches worldwide television audiences of millions. For football fans, in fact, the lure of televised professional football has become so seductive that "many disgruntled fans leave a live game complaining that they could have seen it better on television."[2]

Some non-mainstream, "marginal" sports, popularized by a mass audience, have similarly enjoyed their increase in mass-market status by means of heightened television exposure. WrestleMania (WM) VII, an annual pro wrestling "event," was predicted to be a sell-out at 100,000 in the Los Angeles Coliseum, but because of limited seating capacity, it could pull in a maximum of only 16,000 at the Los Angeles Sports Arena.[3] In contrast, the televised pay-per-view "Wrestlemania IV (at $19.95 per view) drew 909,000 homes and Wrestlemania V (at $24.95) drew 915,000, while Wrestlemania VI (at $29.95) drew 825,000."[4]

This phenomenon of mass consumerism of televised sport has created a much different feel for sport than in the past. There are television time-outs, efforts to make the game more comprehensible (witness the explanation of new sport forms—or even the more subtle intricacies of the more common sports—by sport commentators), even attempts to make the ball (Charley O. Finley's suggestion of an orange baseball was not driven just by color loyalty) or the puck (Fox Network's use of a "comet" puck for television viewing) more visible.[5]

Where baseball began at a nearly grassroots level, initially deriving almost solely from participant enthusiasm, a new sport (such as indoor soccer or beach volleyball) in the late twentieth century, in order to reach a mass audience, is extremely dependent upon the support of television. Or so, at least, sport promoters believe. There of course is an intertexuality involved between the participating television enthusiast and the non-participating enthusiast, but television producers—through various means—have accounted for many audiences almost simultaneously. In this chapter, I will explore some of the ways television audiences may be drawn into participation in the new televised sport.

The bureaucratization, rationalization, and institutionalization of modern art and sport have created a "Catch-22" in sport.[6] Televised forms of expressive sport (sport driven by the contestant's intrinsic "needs"), by definition, are largely excluded from spectatorship,[7] while spectacle sport forms (sport driven by rewards) have become the standard by which sport is measured.[8] The western ideal and ideology promote expressive sport—yet spectacle sport, to some extent by virtue of the medium in which it is transmitted, has taken over. Ideally, from the producers' (and sponsors') points of view, all sport will reach mass audiences. And the producers and writers of sports programming continue to stress the expressive aspects of spectacle sport. But television has also *created* new sport in hopes of consolidating the two goals.

The American Gladiators (*TAG*), an American Broadcasting Company television show, is an example of ready-made sport, of marginal sport created and produced by executive fiat.[9] On this program, contestants vie for cash prizes against physical obstacles, against each other, and against human resistance in the form of the "American Gladiators." It is, in a sense, a game show in which physical ability is more important than knowledge and luck. In fact, Fiske discusses quiz shows, indicating a hierarchy of knowledge wherein "power and cultural capital [is exemplified by] the 'factual,' 'academic' type used in shows such as *Sale of the Century* . . . *Ford Super Quiz,* and *Jeopardy* . . . less academic, more everyday [knowledge] . . . in shows like *The New Price Is Right* . . . is democratic rather than elitist in temper."[10] *TAG* Contestants can win cash prizes, just like their quiz show counterparts, but to do so they are not required to demonstrate much cognitive knowledge. Rather, these contestants must exhibit physical prowess—which may well be a 1990s exemplification of a societal acceptance of multiple knowledges.[11]

The very marginality of *TAG* as an emerging sport form may well exemplify, perhaps metaphorically, modernist and postmodernist concepts. To a modernist sensibility, *TAG* either succeeded or failed; to a postmodernist "reader," *TAG* may have succeeded or failed on various levels. Its marginality to the "mainstream," for example, may have attracted "marginal" viewers at the same time that its similarities to the "mainstream" brought in viewers who expected old-time sexist sport.

However, in terms of the collision and blending of bipolar opposites,[12] it might be that marginal and mainstream sport share more similarities than differences. Concepts of art theory heretofore limited largely to literature and other of the arts may be readily applied to sport. The presence of an avant-garde element in art is one such concept, but as Clement Greenberg pointed out in 1939, for every avant-garde there is a rearguard element of kitsch.[13]

In this chapter I examine and rethink both mainstream and marginal sport in the western tradition—and their alignment with the traditional aesthetic of "high" and "low" culture.[14] Further, I trace the concept of kitsch in contemporary art and marginal sport by detailing a few striking kitschian elements in *The American Gladiators*. Finally, I propose sport as performing art to be a highly mediated, amalgamated, and contemporary version of so-called mainstream (and perhaps even traditional) sport—which has created space for itself on the postmodern sport scene.[15]

The Place of Marginal Sport

Many popular sports (among them English bear-baiting, cockfighting,[16] bare-knuckle boxing, circus strength tests, New England oxen and horse pulls, and All-Terrain Vehicle races), though often marginalized as sport by traditionalists involved in sporting culture, have a long and storied status in both England and the United States.[17] One of the major ingredients of popular sport forms that have not become commoditized is their transitory, evanescent nature. Events live on in people's minds, but they pass by largely unrecorded and unremarked upon, so that their importance appears to be marginal. When such marginal sports do begin to reach a larger audience, they become, by definition, less marginalized. They move, as on a continuum, toward mainstream status.

The presence of such marginal sports programs on television, however, is a relatively recent phenomenon which has not received a great deal of examination. Such network offerings as professional wrestling, *Rock 'n' Wrestling,*[18] roller derby, Super Sports, Celebrity Sports, as well as local celebrity sport contests—on local programming—have long been a national and regional television staple. Yet such programs have received only passing commentary by media experts and sport sociologists—an expected response, given the very marginality of these programming choices. But in a postmodern world, these diverse audiences and their demonstration of "plurality of experience"[19] in a heteroglossic world[20] are the coming thing. No longer will sports entrepreneurs put all their marketing eggs in one basket.

If the dichotomy between mainstream and marginal sport holds, *The American Gladiators* certainly would be considered marginal sport. Indeed, many might question whether it is sport at all. It contains elements of what Sage terms "trash" sport,[21] but it also presents elements of mainstream, so-called legitimate, sport. It is simultaneously a game show (where "contestants" vie for "$150,000 in cash and prizes") and a sporting contest. For example, an exchange between Mike Adamle and Larry Csonka, co-hosts of the show, compares *TAG* to professional football:

> Adamle: "This draws parallels, at least to me anyway, of the NFL play-offs. Fair analogy?"
> Csonka: "Certainly, a couple of old pros remember when the play-offs, when there was a lot of money involved, it was a lifestyle. . . . So we're looking forward to a fine exhibition of *sporting talent* today."[22]

Thus, the show ironically panders to both its marginality to sport (somehow skewed by marketing as uniqueness) and its nostalgic recollection of legitimate sport. *TAG* also seeks—and encourages—a large, highly vocal and dedicated audience—not unlike the audience for professional wrestling—which understands both the seriousness and campiness of the proceedings.

Indeed, *The American Gladiators* has a live show that tours the country. This live tour serves several purposes: (1) as with the circus, there is pre-event publicity that builds the attendance and sophistication level of the fans (the exposure to the live show presumably creates a larger television audience as well); (2) "contestants" are chosen to compete against the Gladiators during the upcoming live show; (3) the merchandising of American Gladiator artifacts (easily replicable kitsch items) brings in money and, again, serves to promote the television show.

I attended tryouts (October 7, 1991) for contestants a month before the "live" show in Champaign-Urbana. There were several physical tests that "wannabe" contestants had to pass: one minute of fingertip pushups (women had to complete at least 35, men 55), a timed sprint, and a timed "suicide" (shuttle run). Anyone who made it through those preliminary rounds (and most failed at the fingertip pushups)[23] continued on to head-to-head Powerball. Powerball is one of the games that actual contestants play, both on the tour and on the television show. In Powerball, two contestants start from opposite ends of a "field," taking one ball at a time. Their goal is to stuff the ball into one of five baskets, four on the outside, one on the inside. A "goal" in the inside basket gains them five points; a goal in an outer basket is worth three points. Obviously, potential successful contestants were familiar with the rules—and strategies—of Powerball.

The announcer told the crowd that the contestants were vying for a chance to eventually go to Atlantic City to compete. But they also could win an "American Gladiator watch from Armitron, a one-year supply of food supplements from GMC, as well as [an] American Gladiator home fitness machine—retails for over six hundred dollars." The recombinant forms of self-referential selling became, of themselves, elements of kitsch.

Sales of American Gladiators (AG) items at the actual event were brisk. The American Gladiator–logoed merchandise consisted of items within just about anyone's price range (except the very high end of the scale): $1 American flags, $1 programs, $5 helmets, $6 pins, $7 posters, $12 "Only the Strong Survive" T-shirts, $15 baseball hats, $20 AG logo T-shirts, $35 AG sweatshirts. Many pre-teenagers and teenagers stood in line to buy merchandise.

▼ ▼ ▼ ▼

Historically, terms such as "junk," "trash," "pseudo," and "mainstream" sport have been couched within a rubric of aesthetics that implies "high" versus "low" culture. Additionally, the apologetic is often advanced that merely to study a cultural phenomenon such as televised sport implies common, low, mass culture (as if the terms were equivalent). There are qualities assigned to points along the spectra, and these qualities generally translate into stratification, privilege, and political action: stratification because canons tend to create distinction; privilege because the differences become polarized to the extent that sources of access and resources of money create a have–have not distinction; and political action because, for example, implementation of school curricula (which is driven by—and drives—budgetary considerations) is, to a large degree, an extension of the power relationships that exist at the grassroots level.

Of course, within the sporting realm, a general, unspoken continuum exists, along which live professional football, with a great deal of spontaneity implied, may be considered an example of "high" cultural sport, and the more highly staged sports demonstrate "low" cultural sport. The logic of this continuum is questionable at best: professional football, with its highly ritualistic behavior, is certainly "staged." It is merely staged more solemnly, with more pseudo-religious fervor, than those sport forms that have been marginalized—and have somehow marginalized themselves.[24]

Recent theorists have proposed that the existence of such polar dichotomies as "high" and "low" culture may be reductionistic, indeed simplistic. One characteristic of a postmodern condition, in fact, may be the very absence of such clear-cut distinctions.[25] There is, of course, a growing subculture of post-modernisms as well as postmodern theorists. Each has the attendant differences of interpretation, yet most who abide by a "'commercial' or co-opted postmodernism"[26] will agree that dualistic thinking—whether of the popular or elite, high or low culture, avant garde or kitsch—has evolved into, for want of a better term, a polyphonic form consisting of continuum thinking.

Thus, the term "marginal sport"—descriptive of that sport at the fringes of highly bureaucratized, formalized sport—seems preferable to the disparaging terms "trash" or "junk" sport. It is less judgmental. Within marginal sport, there are elements of mainstream sport, yet there are more elements of spectacle than of self-expression.[27] The deprecating terms "trash" and "junk" sport appear to fall into the cultural trap of class stratification, dividing sport along class lines much as the English club system evolved an amateur-professional stratum at the turn of the twentieth century.[28]

Aesthetics, Art, Sport, and Kitsch

The delineation between high and low culture has not proven terribly fruitful either in the study of architecture, in the valuation and apprehension of art,[29] or in the analysis of various realms of sport in contemporary society. While Lowe treated elite sport in terms of classic, modernist art (and its attendant aesthetic posture), he failed to provide convincing arguments to account for the appeal of participatory and mass sport. His attempts to drive interest in the sport-art parallels, to see the body as object and subject simultaneously, to house sport studies in a classic aesthetic, to enjoin others to return to the study of sport in broad cultural terms, all established a solid foundation for an art-sport relationship.[30] But while explanatory of so-called "high" sport culture (e.g., the Olympic Games and elite quality performance—mainstream sport), Lowe's work—and its classic aesthetic metaphor—does not well represent participatory, folk, massified (or marginalized) sport.

Thus, a major problem with studying sport in terms of classical (modernist) aesthetic theory may be that such theory has failed to come to terms with late-twentieth-century (postmodernist) theory. The kinds of value judgments in classical aesthetics imply a hierarchical framework between, in this case, sporting endeavors, which may not exist quite as solidly in the popular mind.[31] In a postmodern sense, of course, such a prioritized discrimination is unnecessary; indeed, it becomes problematic when describing avant-garde, postmodern processes.[32] A quality of their essence is their very irreducibility.

Such value judgments aside, to delineate electronically mediated sport as a contemporary art form, to place *The American Gladiators* and its kind of folk-sporting endeavor within an artistic and historical postmodernist framework, and to blend the postmodernity movement in art with a sense of the postmodernity within sport—all appear to be fruitful avenues of discourse. Furthermore, by specifically exploring contemporary sport in light of the concept of kitsch, forms of sport such as *The American Gladiators* may be seated within an interactive process that may be inclusive of more historical voices and moments. There are echoes of mainstream sport within *TAG;* there are conscious reverberations with, for example, the stereotypical Roman gladiatorial contests. The intersections of kitsch with sport—as demonstrated in *The American Gladiators*—provide an entry into a broader study of the sport-art connection. Thus, the study of a small, non-representational sample of televised sport such as *TAG* may begin to establish relationships between televised and massified sport and art, relationships that have primarily been limited to the realm of art and literature.

▼ ▼ ▼

The term "kitsch" most likely derives from the German *verkitschen,* or "to make cheap."[33] In 1939, Clement Greenberg described kitsch as a rearguard reaction to "Western bourgeois society['s] [production of] something unheard of heretofore: avant garde culture."[34] When the "far-out" avant-garde work was displayed and became remarkable, there was a countermovement that denigrated the very sincerity of the avant-garde artists.

The avant garde sought to replicate the very *impulse* of creation, rather than to re-create already formed works.[35] In contrast, kitsch wallows in re-creation: in fact, its very dependence upon mass consumption (and the economic benefits derived from such consumption) serves as an integral part of its definition.

Since "kitsch" is a term considered to pertain primarily to art and things artistic, the link between such a concept of bad art or self-consciously woeful taste and popular televised sport must be forged within a mass-culture rubric. For just as surely as Baudrillard views a transplantation by J. Paul Getty of European "culture" to America as an absurdist kitschian re-creation, as an "unintended humour" bordering on the hyperreal,[36] the varied conditions of televised sport in this country have elided from the real to the hyperreal, from an individual to a collective doctrine, from big business to self-conscious kitsch.

The very nature of television has changed the rules of sport, and these new rules are inextricably linked with kitsch: it is no longer athlete as heroine or hero, but rather athletic body as commodity or icon. This change is similar to the attitudinal changes in art (read kitsch) brought on by the inevitable yet paradoxical proliferation of mass consumer art by the early-twentieth-century avant-garde.[37] With so many replaceable bodies lining up to replicate athletic moves, one could argue that the very system of sport is replete with kitsch. That may be why, to the non-interested observer of televised sport, one game seems quite like any other.[38] Archetypes, which are in and of themselves a type of kitsch, then satisfy viewer expectations: thus we see the actual Gladiators on *The American Gladiators* representing—vaguely—nondescript archetypes of athletic prowess.

Matei Calinescu looks at kitsch in the following three ways. In the passage below, if the word "sport" is substituted for "art," and "performers" for "artists," the parallels between kitsch in sport and kitsch in art are remarkable:

> To begin, we may consider kitsch as a product of a certain category of [performers] who, addressing themselves to a well-defined audience of average consumers, apply definite sets of rules and communicate varieties of highly predictable messages in stereotyped "aesthetic" packages. From this point of view, kitsch is a *style*. . . . [Secondly, we may] take into account the specific kitsch elements that appear in the process of mass production and diffusion of [sport]. Such elements are clearly unintentional (that is, they are not planned in advance by the producers of kitsch but are rather the fatal consequences of modern technology's intervention in the [sport] world). The third possibility consists of considering kitsch from the vantage point of the consumer who, willing to accept the "aesthetic lie" of kitsch and who, conditioned by the sheer quantity of pseudo[sport] and instant beauty with which he is surrounded, can perceive even genuine works of [sport] as kitsch.[39]

Placed within the modernist artistic movement, the existence of kitsch is nevertheless neither *precisely* defined nor reified. Furthermore, though Calinescu delineates kitsch in three ways—that is, the previously mentioned style, hyperreal elements, and worldview of kitsch—to more precisely define kitsch is as slippery as to attempt to define its counter, the avant-garde. But we can describe elements of a sport endeavor, and then pronounce them kitschian or not.

There are moments of kitsch; there are "kitschy" objects, generally identified *post facto*. Yet kitsch is not completely indefinable: Calinescu argues that "kitsch may be conveniently defined as a specifically aesthetic form of lying," and its presence is inextricably related to the "modern illusion that beauty may be bought and sold."[40] Moreover, kitsch is "mechanical and operates by formulas. Kitsch is vicarious experience and faked sensations. Kitsch changes according to style, but remains always the same."[41] It is the changing according to style that makes the precise definition of kitsch so slippery.

In any case, the glamorization of modern art and literature and the lived experience of high-culture aficionados have their parallels in modern-day sport. Just as some artists of the late nineteenth and early twentieth centuries found that their "talents" could turn a prettier profit if quickly replicated (thus tracing one Calinescuian branch of kitsch, the "hyperreal" replication of so-called classic art forms), so too have late-twentieth-century athletes—increasingly consciously—provided their bodies as monetary fodder and cultural barter material. Their movements, motivated extrinsically much like some artist's forms which preceded them, may have become mechanistic and predictable, and worthy of parody.

Yet there is a difference between public display and private discovery, a difference between innovation and the learning of previously constituted creative moves. There is a great difference between "mak[ing] the familiar strange . . . [and] mak[ing] the strange familiar."[42] For example, Michael Jordan's split-second reactions to defensive attempts describe creativity; children's schoolyard imitations of those recorded moves, exact to the placement of the tongue outside the mouth, exemplify learning. In this sense, Michael Jordan's moves might be classified as avant-garde, while the children's attempts could be only unconsciously kitschian. Especially since the spatial and temporal elements of Michael Jordan's moves can never be exactly replicated, the children's imitative behaviors are not creative, but rather derivative. Michael Jordan's oeuvre describes creative work;[43] the children's imitations describe kitsch.

Kitsch and *The American Gladiators*

What are some examples of kitsch elements, style, and worldview of the early, seamed presentations of *The American Gladiators*? Analysis of one specific text of the program (aired on ABC TV on November 10, 1990), live attendance at tryouts (October 7, 1991) and at one live show (November 5, 1991), and observation of subsequent programs provide the basis for the specific references that follow. However, many of the examples cited are synecdochic in nature, so that specific examples are representative of general themes, and the general is representative of the specific.

First, and most obviously, the games or contests are not new, but rather consist of components or amalgams of well-established sports. Like any good kitsch, they are derivative of something else. For example, "Powerball" demands agility, strength, and power—all components of many of the mainstream, modern, male, western sport forms currently seen on TV—for contestants to score goals against Gladiators.

In "Break Through and Conquer," contestants attempt to rush with a football twenty yards past a tackling Gladiator, then get in a small ring with another Gladiator and, in imitation of a western stereotyped version of sumo wrestling, attempt to displace their opponent from the ring. As homage to the rich invented tradition that is sumo (with its attendant rituals and deeply idiosyncratic subculture), "Break Through and Conquer" falls disastrously short.[44] (The fad of bar patrons donning inflatable sumo "costumes," "grappling around in blow-up or padded body suits,"[45] and challenging each other to matches[46] is yet another example of spectator/players who are "willing to accept the 'aesthetic lie' of kitsch"[47] and play—in many senses of the word—with it.)

In "The Wall," contestants get a ten-second head start, begin climbing a nearly vertical wall (à la mountain climbing), and then are pursued by Gladiators who attempt to pull them off the wall. This parody of mountain climbing—the agon of humans versus nature—has been playfully skewed to incorporate agon with other humans. All of these *American Gladiators* sporting events, then, are forms or amalgams of legitimate sport parodied, skewed, incorporated, or carried to an extreme.

Modern production techniques, which have become a trademark of modern televised sport to the point where they are evaluated in television sections of newspapers,[48] are co-opted for *The American Gladiators*. Since it is a prerecorded television show, scopophilic gazes that use "another person as an object of sexual stimulation through sight"[49] may be edited into and included in the program.

Such "gazes" include fragmented close-ups and fade-outs on body parts, including female Gladiators' breasts and buttocks; stumbling and awkward post-game interviews; instant replays of mistakes or victoriously raised fists. If the moments of triumph or verbal exultation are ever spontaneous, they lose their spontaneity by means of slo-motion and close-up techniques. These are "planned" voyeuristic moments, if they may be termed that—moments that are carefully edited to imply voyeurism rather than to capture voyeuristic moments in the athletic events.[50] Their very presence in the finished product—and the camera's lingering on them—implies a kitsch *style* which speaks to an assumed male gaze, kitsch *elements* which have become conventions for sports television, and, taken together, a kitsch worldview.

The Gladiators have glitzy show names that are common nouns rather than adjectives combined with proper nouns. Instead of the personalized, heroic-sounding names of the bare-knuckle boxers of a modern yesteryear (e.g., Hen Pearce, the Game Chicken; or Bill Richmond, the Black Terror),[51] the Gladiators have names such as Nitro, Gold, Malibu, Thunder, Zap, Laser, Blaze, Ice, Gemini, and Diamond. In later shows, these pared-down names are used by the announcers as verb forms or as metaphors for the agonistic element in the show. Thus the announcers tell the audience, "In this event our contenders face the firepower of Blaze."[52] In later shows, contenders are "Iced" or "Zapped." The names are meant to stereotype the Gladiators, to establish in the audience's mind some sort of coherent personality for each one.

And yet the Gladiators (particularly the female Gladiators) appear predominantly to be fetishes—objects to look at rather than to be identified with. This dominant reading is intensified by use of replays and super slo-motion shots, which Morse characterizes as "the deliberate slowness which is the attribute of perfect machines, automatons and robots which are doubles of and exchanged for the human body."[53] While the Gladiators are presented in super slo-motion, they are also presented quickly and unrequitedly; Barry Brummett and Margaret Carlisle Duncan write of such presentation: "objects are presented and withdrawn in such profusion and with such speed that they cannot all be possessed, so the desire remains unfulfilled and, thus, continual."[54] It is worth noting, however, that even the Gladiators, generic non-people with generic non-names, have engendered a rather avid following among the fans.

From the opening sequence, *The American Gladiators* attempts to hark back to the image of Roman times and some sort of 1980s brand of nationalism. Examples include the very title of the show, with its campy reference to gladiators, reminiscent of the *circus maximus* (or at least its alignment with the Modern Olympic Games); the Live Tour's announcer saying, "Those who are about to do battle salute you!" and "Let the games begin!"; Mike Adamle's "Welcome to our arena" instead of "Welcome to Universal Studios"; shots of a frenzied crowd, which is in fact the studio audience made to resemble spectators in *Ben Hur*; opening-sequence graphics of a generic stars-and-stripes nationalistic shield/emblem; split-screen images of former contestants and Gladiators performing in slo-motion, in both color and black and white, accompanied by Bill Conti's (of "Rocky" fame) martial music, which again draws on the Hollywood image of martial Roman films; quick subliminal references to a presumed common enemy,[55] as in "the Ayatollah of smackola." Finally, Adamle's "Let the games begin!" echoes pagan ritual and a populist notion of Olympism. This manner of misappropriated and misplaced nostalgia, the elements of the show, is pure kitsch; the manner of stylistically subtle references to world affairs and the ready creation of pseudo-enemies is racist kitsch.[56]

Finally, there is sexist kitsch in *The American Gladiators*. Try as the producers might to demonstrate equal status for men and women on the show, the mixed signals of interviews and camera angles belie a male chauvinism, kitschy in nature, that is "a facile assumption of the rightness of things,"[57] and that demonstrates a worldview that reflects the sexist world of commodified sport.

This sexist kitsch—the previously mentioned examples of scopophilia included—serves to deny empowerment for women[58] while it protests just the opposite. As Margaret Carlisle Duncan has demonstrated in much of her work, women athletes' accomplishments are quite often undercut by verbal or visual trivialization.[59]

Dehumanization through such ambivalent signals presumes an audience with a shared ideology. But an ideology of audiences—not a single, monolithic audience—uncovers the lie. Examples of comments directed at female contestants in *The American Gladiators* included "You're overcoming fear," "You're learning about yourself," "You're tiny in stature, quiet when you compete," "I understand you have a parakeet, Tweetie," "Don't worry, honey, you'll be a success," and "Human Cannonball: hard on the body *and* on the makeup." In contrast, comments directed toward males included "It's more than a game for you—it's a cause," "That's what they call a meat grinder—and he got ground," and "You take a beating and keep on competing."

Furthermore, the media have allowed for an objectification of bodies, particularly female. The camera lingers on the female Gladiators' and contestants' bodies, often showing segmented and fragmented views of various body parts. The fetishization of the female body, as previously denoted, creates objects of desire for viewers. This, of course, contributes further to sexist kitsch.

Conclusion: Kitschsport as Performing Art

Through the electronic mass media, sport figures seemingly have become more accessible to sport fans than ever before. Paradoxically, their images tend toward homogenization and planned obsolescence. That is to say, it is often difficult to distinguish one sport personality from another, and by the time a fan does this, a favorite athlete will have been replaced by a younger, less expensive version.

Yet identification with athletes is a requisite for fan approval: in *The American Gladiators,* the announcers repeatedly remind the television audience that Rico, one of the contestants, is a crowd favorite. There is an American Gladiators Fan Club, based in Studio City, California. There is "a Nintendo video-game version of *Gladiators* . . . trading cards of the 10 gladiators . . . [and] American Gladiators Juniors vitamins for young gladiator wannabes."[60] In 1991, Mattel announced that it would "manufacture a line of toys based on the syndicated American Gladiators."[61] There is the nationwide tour, during which contestants are threshed from pretenders. Additionally, there was the *American Gladiators 2000,* a children's version of the adult show.

Such fan identification is imperative for the success of televised (and localized) sport. In other words, the objectification and fetishization of the athletes' bodies and selves creates a bond with the other which becomes a bond with the self. Or, as Duncan and Brummett state, "we move from a preoccupation with things to imagining ourselves integrated with those things."[62]

In *The American Gladiators,* the announcers identify contestants with personal statistics and interview them as they would sport personalities, or any other celebrities. Thus we see a dominant trope of scientificity intruding into made-for-TV sport: "Margaret McCargo of East Orange, New Jersey, a communications major at Upsala College," is then quantified with a neat graphic detailing her name, height, weight, age, home, and occupation. When Margaret the contestant does not win, the kitsch-speak is bathetic: "You'll be back," intones Larry Csonka, while Margaret's eyes remain downcast. "Twenty-one years old—you have a bright future ahead of you, Margaret—as an athlete . . . and as a person."[63]

Such technological and directorial intrusion is blatant on a show such as *The American Gladiators;* thus it is easier to discern elements of kitsch, good intent with pseudo-sport results. The technical intrusion is rougher, less slick,[64] than the making of more "mainstream sport" broadcasts. Yet mainstream sport, as it is filtered through television, is no less prone to such kitschsport. The men's U.S. Olympic marathon qualifying, broadcast from Charlotte, North Carolina (2-17-96), had high production standards, yet utilized voyeuristic techniques to produce the "story." When the eventual winner, Bob Kempainea, began vomiting during his race, the announcers consistently referred to it, the cameras (and producers) made sure the audience could see it, and it became incorporated into the story that was woven around the event. Moreover, the awarding of $30,000, $40,000, and $100,000 to the third-, second-, and first-place finishers by, respectively, UPS, Bell South, and Nation's Bank—and their blatant advertising—became a kitsch attempt at legitimizing the entry of money into what was formerly "amateur" sport.

Sport is no longer just sport for individual expression. Rather, it has become spectacle, with a jaundiced eye on the profit margin.

Currently, the merging of cultural forms such as televised sport and the hyperreality (through objectification, narcissism, and fetishism) of sport figures may have created a trend toward kitsch in marginal sport. However, legitimate sport may contain kitschian elements as well. The terms "Howard Cosell," "Joe Namath," and "Wrestling" were labeled in 1975 as kitschian, and pro football was predicted to be Futurekitsch.[65] By virtue of the fact that it has become highly mediated, egalitarian, and popular, sport, by definition, contains elements of kitsch.[66]

Perhaps, then, *The American Gladiators* is merely filling a late-twentieth-century need for mediated kitsch. Certainly the show, though an extreme example, is emblematic of a current trend toward self-conscious replication, hybridization, and even mutation of mainstream sport forms, and of the ideology of the individual.

If art has tended to postmodernism, and sport, like dance, can be considered a performing art,[67] then gazing at *The American Gladiators* through both a modern and a postmodern lens may be appropriate. Though the barriers between such abrupt bipolarities as modernism and postmodernism have eroded somewhat, there still exists an interplay between postmodernisms and modernisms. Thus the concepts of avant-garde and kitsch, though commingled, may still remain viable notions for the study of contemporary sport.

FOUR | **Sport as Avant-Garde**
A Case Study of the World
Wrestling Federation

Once we focus on actual experiences and practices, it is clear
that there are similarities between these alleged postmodern
experiences and practices and many of those designated as
modern (in the sense of *modernité*), and even pre-modern.

—Featherstone, 1991

[Lyotard] asks us to regard [postmodernism] as the latest
episode in the evolution of the avant-garde.

—Rojek, 1995

Just as aspects of *The American Gladiators* represent elements of kitsch, so
too they represent what kitsch became reactive to: the avant-garde. The interplay between elements of kitsch and elements of the avant-garde is, throughout sport, one of the keys to understanding the fluidity of sport forms. Thus,
when we see the Wall on *The American Gladiators*—where competitors scale an
indoor, constructed wall whose difficulty can be adjusted in accordance with
the expertise of the competitor—and view it as kitsch, we also must see
elements of *The American Gladiators'* use of the indoor climbing wall as innovative, even avant-garde, particularly as it relates to the increase in numbers of
participants in sport climbing.[1] In fact, as the number of sport climbers has
increased, there has been a concomitant increase in the media's display of sport
climbing: witness ESPN's *The eXtreme Games* (1995), with the "rock climbing"
component as one of the events.[2] When there is kitsch, there is avant-garde:
one has only to look for either element within contemporary sport.

We see the numbers of novice (and expert) climbers—who now train in-doors in inclement weather, who vary the difficulty of the walls they attempt, who maximize their "learning" experiences by using safety harnesses—increase in proportion to the television exposure of their sport. Technology, to some extent, has driven the avant-garde aspects of sport. But there are also innovators, individuals and groups whose "avant-garde" approach to a sport has produced epiphanal change in the sport. And while scholars may disagree on the exact elements of the modern and postmodern avant-garde and kitsch (some even disagree that there is a postmodern avant-garde, for example), most agree that there still is a tentative interrelationship between the two.

Television certainly has enjoyed such a dual status, embodying both avant-garde and kitsch in promoting and sustaining sport. Perhaps sport, in some now-nostalgic pre-television era, was once a pure and primal event in the lives of participants and spectators alike, but with the advent of television and a resultant snapshot recognition and contextualizing of images, sport players[3]—all known sport players—have turned or are in the process of turning into commodities.[4] The values of televised sport, in fact, have tended more toward entertainment and commercialization than to any accurate depiction of sporting events. Production values based on garnering an audience, decision-making by directors of televised sport to incorporate sensual aspects of sport in order to create a "you are there" feel for the audience,[5] and the unfolding of a "storyline" have become the industry standard for producing any major or minor sporting event. Prior to an event, the production crew discusses dramatic storylines, the telling of which lends greater cohesiveness, continuity, and coherence to the televised sporting event.[6] The "unpredictable," "uncertain outcome" stories of sport are thus pre-packaged and pre-interpreted for viewers' consumption.

Nowhere along the continuum that is postmodern sport is the tenuous balance between a pure re-creation of the athletic impulse and the pandering to a public's clamor for athlete/sports figure-as-commodity more obvious than in professional wrestling.[7] Yet professional wrestling, ridiculed by many sport players as non-sport (as, indeed, an exemplar of the kitsch in sport), contains avant-garde elements as well.

In this chapter, I seek to place "marginal" (or marginalized) televised sport within a non-classical aesthetic. I see the World Wrestling Federation athletic performances as exemplars of a late-twentieth-century moment precariously bridging the last gasps of modernity and the grudging acceptance of a postmodern condition.[8] I will trace the concept of the avant-garde in contemporary art (and sport), and demonstrate that a populist notion of the avant-garde accommodates both mainstream and so-called marginal sport, while (much as in the idea of kitsch) collapsing the concepts of "high" versus "low" culture. Using examples drawn from the World Wrestling Federation's August 1991 pay-per-view SummerSlam™, I will detail elements of an avant-garde element in as modest a sporting event as professional wrestling. Finally, tracing mediated images of body-as-commodity in the WWF program, I hope to demonstrate that the use of pejorative terms such as "mainstream" and "marginal" sport is quite beside the point, since televisual incantations and intrusions—exemplified by the existence of an avant-garde element in the WWF—have irrevocably changed the essence of all that currently calls itself sport.

The Avant-Garde

Though this remains a contested point even in art circles,[9] I see an existing avant-garde element in both modernism and postmodernism. The avant-garde of modernity, by its very nature, is oppositional. It utilizes mainstream culture as a foil, often ironically becoming reified in and absorbed into mainstream culture itself, only to reinvent itself, to rise from the ashes and oppose former, now mainstreamed, avant-gardes. The modernist avant-garde is ever-changing, seeking new mutations for old forms, providing blatant or subtle commentary on artistic and cultural formations, breathing new life into suffocated traditions.

Steeped as it was in the modernist tradition, the avant-garde became enmeshed in counterpointing massified culture (which became, by definition, "low" culture) with what has come to be termed "high" culture.[10] Kenneth Clark alludes to the avant-garde—and its uneasy relationship with massified culture—when he admits an aesthetic creation that is "created by a minority: yes, but accepted by the majority unquestioningly, eagerly, and with a sense of participation."[11] By extension, then, modernism's minority elite is represented by the avant-garde, only to be freshly opposed by a new avant-garde.

But the notion of an avant-garde need not be so restrictive; nor need it be abandoned with the abandonment of modernism. The notion of the avant-garde of postmodernism is one that continues to be oppositional, yet opposition takes many forms in a post-industrial world. Arguments proposing the death of modernism, and by extension the death of the avant-garde, within contemporary society have been made to fit existing theory, rather than theory's reflecting intuitive, popular, or empirical knowledge.[12] In language reminiscent of Aldous Huxley's A Brave New World, writers urge us to throw off the shackles of modernism, forget past building blocks (either good or bad), and emerge, blinking and stunned, into a suddenly crystalline world, devoid of past polarities and oppositions, brimming with pluralist secularism.[13] At the same time as we are to forget history, postmodernism is said to embrace and envelop the past, indeed to skew it with parody, pastiche, and irony.[14] Postmodernism recodes previous messages, so that the culturally literate individual is reinforced with nostalgic pleasure when recognition registers.[15]

However, as Andrew Benjamin has written, "Pluralism involves the recognition that judgement has to take place despite the absence of universal criteria for judgement. . . . Pluralism does not deny the existence of unities."[16] Marjorie Perloff, in insightful studies of the historical avant-garde[17] and of the persistence of avant-garde signs within a contemporary technocratic society,[18] writes convincingly of the temporal flow between a modernist and a postmodernist avant-garde. So in the public consciousness (and now in the scholarly literature), despite recent reports of its demise in this brave new postmodern world, the avant-garde remains a multivoiced and fertile concept, one that "understand[s] difference as differential."[19]

The very concept of an avant-garde is a social construction, so it comes as no surprise that by saying a postmodern avant-garde exists, it may indeed be so. One reason may be a temporal period between the innovation and the installation of new concepts.[20] Yet another factor may be the omnipotent eye of an electronic medium: the polar oppositions conceived by an avant-garde/mainstream opposition create greater tension, more diverse oppositional readings, and more dramatic effect, which in turn lead to higher audience ratings—and more lucrative corporate sponsorship. Of course, there is a point at which saturation of the market can occur, as well. Holubitsky, citing Mike Perrino of Edmonton, speaks of this as part of the cycle of fads: "He sees fads dying when an item becomes a commodity to be bought, sold and speculated on, driving values through the roof and beyond the reach of those who play the game—the kids."[21] Likewise, televised marketing must be careful to retain the tenuous balance between avant-garde (representing "high" culture) and kitsch (representing "low" culture). The trap of the historical avant-garde is definitional: as Huyssen puts it, regarding the pop avant-garde of the 1960s (and sport might be classed in such a way), "despite such cooption through commodification the pop avantgarde retained a certain cutting edge in its proximity to the 1960s culture of confrontation. . . . The attack on the institution art was always also an attack on hegemonic social institutions."[22] Avant-gardes work as oppositions, yet the oppositions that they foster have different meanings within different contexts. In conservative sport, for example NBA basketball, a highly commoditized Dennis Rodman serves as no less an avant-garde icon than did Andy Warhol in the '60's.

However, drama is the dominant metaphor for television: rising action and falling action are at all times privileged. Thus the media work to commoditize presidential candidates, to build them up (that is a story), to tear them down (another story). Tension is key. For whatever reason, such seeming oppositions (as between the avant-garde and the mainstream) and real paradoxes (as between and among commercial interests and the avant-garde) are thus fostered and sustained in popular minds by the media.

For example, televised sports are no longer strict reportings of a game or sporting event; rather, they are framed to tell a story, to provide a classic rise and fall of action, to create tension through (real or imagined) conflict situations, and to satisfy through proper denouement. They are, despite vehement protestations to the contrary by those involved in sport, filled blocks of time given structure linguistically and symbolically;[23] they are human interest stories and profiles; they are continuing embattlements between and among groups stratified by geography, age, gender, race, and class. (And now the battles have extended, apparently, to corporate-stratified groups. As reported by *Sports Illustrated,* Nike chairman Phil Knight was quoted in the *New York Times* [7 February 1996] as saying, "We see a natural evolution . . . dividing the world into their athletes and ours. And we glory ours. When the U.S. played Brazil in the World Cup, I rooted for Brazil because it was a Nike team. America was Adidas.")[24]

The avant-garde, as Jochen Schulte-Sasse sees it, serves a purpose that invigorates art (and, I argue, other institutions such as sport):

> Most American criticism has lost sight of the goal the avant-garde set up for itself. Avant-garde artists were not just reacting to society with feelings of ennui, angst, weltschmerz, and a host of other pseudoexistentialist passions of the soul. Avant-garde artists weren't merely reacting to society with last-ditch efforts at breaking up and dislodging prevalent styles. American theories of modernism—like their French models—have emphasized the pathos and not the praxis of the modern artist. We should come to see that avant-garde artists were actively attacking the institution of art. Their effort was not to isolate themselves, but to reintegrate themselves and their art into life.[25]

Avant-garde artists sought more personal control in the face of a burgeoning art bureaucracy; so too have enterprising athletes attempted, in some cases through subversion of the institutions of sport, to paraphrase Schulte-Sasse, to "reintegrate themselves and their [sport] into life."[26] Certainly the politicization of Olympic sport may be a well-known example: the Black Power salute given by John Carlos and Tommy Smith at the 1968 Mexico City Olympics was an attempt to break down the arbitrary distancing between sport and life.[27]

The term "avant-garde" is itself burdened with historical, cultural, and aesthetic baggage.[28] Arising from the artistic modernist framework, the aesthetic avant-garde was a nebulous, politically motivated group whose raison d'être was a return to the primacy of experience: it followed that this artistic avant-garde attacked the institutionality and rising bureaucracy of the postindustrialist art world.[29] Simultaneously, as Dunn puts it, "*cultural* avant-gardes . . . function[ed] within a broad terrain of social and political relationships."[30] The postmodern avant-garde, then, is an avant-garde that pushes culture in a new direction, an "Anglo-American avant-garde" which is "less theoretical and self-conscious, more instinctive and empirical."[31]

Thus this kind of avant-garde (in the sense of "the advance group in any field, esp. in the visual, literary, or musical arts, whose works are characterized chiefly by unorthodox and experimental methods")[32] may form as an oppositional or, in the case of sport, an anticipatory group. When a group anticipates future trends, it can be broadly stated to be of the avant-garde. There is none of the self-congratulatory hoopla that surrounds statements of cause-effect relationships: anticipation does not necessarily drive change, but it certainly coexists with it.

The postmodern avant-garde is no longer an avant-garde dedicated solely to opposition. Contemporary avant-garde is not so easily labeled. It is a multifaceted attack, driven on many levels and at a multiplicity of sites, using the weapons of parody, irony, commodification, and pastiche. It turns the very vehicles of oppression into modes of oppositional discourse. Huyssen writes,

> The avant garde, then, only makes sense if it remains dialectically related to that for which it serves as the vanguard—speaking narrowly, to the older modes of artistic expression, speaking broadly, to the life of the masses which Saint Simon's avant garde scientists, engineers, and artists were to lead into the golden age of bourgeois prosperity.[33]

The *cultural* avant-garde to which Robert Dunn alludes may be, in fact, a *cultural* realization of Saint Simon's (1825) role of the vanguard for the *aesthetic* avant-garde.[34]

As such, the avant-garde, to Paul Mann, remains "the outside of the inside, the leading edge of the mainstream, and thus marginal in both senses: excluded and salient."[35] How can this be? The avant-garde, in this sense, simultaneously depends upon the mainstream culture even as it rejects and skews the mainstream culture. While the postmodern avant-garde may be outwardly complicit in its acceptance of hegemonic culture, its subtle acts of opposition may, in fact, be more profound than outright opposition through a (modernist) artistic undermining.[36]

The postmodern avant-garde works on many levels and forms cultural resistance in small, personal, and popularly accepted, as well as popularly embraced, ways. By working within the so-called hegemonic establishment, by subtly skewing the normative way of seeing, a cultural avant-garde may realize more profound results than by directly and openly resisting. Ironically, of course, the moment the avant-garde's desires become mainstream, that particular avant-garde movement is dead.

In art, the postmodern avant-garde continues to realize its primary modernist function: to attack filtered experience and to create immediacy and creativity through shared experience between creator and spectator. The same can be said for an avant-garde element in sport. In spectator experience and the shared and created development of individual personas in professional wrestling, the attack on filtered experience is nearly genuine, and the sense of immediacy, of participatory and pseudo-cathartic experience for spectators dedicated to the spectacle, is truly real.[37]

Avant-Garde and Sport

Innovation, singularity, parody, and crisis are integral elements of a postmodern avant-garde. More than that, an attempt to elicit spectatorial emotions—that is, an effort to recapture the creative impulse, shared by players and audience alike—is at the heart of the contemporary avant-garde's project.[38]

Environmental artist Christo's *Running Fence* consisted of twenty-four and one-half miles of running fabric, steel cable, and steel poles. This project involved public agencies and private citizens who participated in leasing requirements, land surveys, and public hearings.[39] His work certainly emphasized the process involved in artistic creation; one of its major accomplishments, certainly, was a reawakening of individuals to their own creative potential. The static, actual display of *Running Fence* was only one of the components that made the work artistic: "the dialectic between presence and absence" creates a tension which reinforces the importance of what normally might be termed "absence."[40] The actual preparation of his works ("Running Fence was in place for only two weeks in the middle of September 1976")[41] involves

> various documentary forms (plans, maps, photographs, collages) which generate for the work, in the social and cultural imagination and virtually independent of its creator, a power and force of its own. In its unrealized manifestations Christo's work proceeds as a series of *projections,* which *exceed* their eventual embodiment—and survive it as a record of process.[42] (Emphasis in original)

With Christo's oeuvre, a basic tenet of the postmodern avant-garde, that of spectator involvement (so that "spectators" become actual players in the enactment of the process of making art), is realized.

In a postindustrial society, it is no longer sufficient to see contemporary sport—or, for that matter, art—exclusive of media, bureaucracy, or economics.[43] Symbiotically linked, television and sport have forged a marriage that could be replaced only by more lucrative bonds.[44] Organized sport is no longer pure and unsullied—if it ever was—by cultural effects. Thus, the cry in reference to professional wrestling that "It isn't sport: sport has to have an uncertain outcome" or some such prescriptive, traditional definition, is quite beside the point.[45] All (post)modern televised sport is staged and produced for spectator consumption. Modern mediated sport is primarily entertainment, and athletes are likewise primarily entertainers.

Witness, for example, the privileging given to entertainment. This sport-as-entertainment model has become legend in the Super Bowl: in a sidebar to an article detailing the 1994 Super Bowl halftime show, Bob Cannon quotes Jim Steeg, "the NFL's executive director of special events," as saying, "It's important to draw more than football fans. Otherwise, you don't get 135 million people watching it when your normal audience is 60 million."[46]

Similarly, on a taped World Wrestling Federation show, Vincent McMahon, the head of TitanSports, Incorporated (which owns the WWF), sermonizes several messages: that the WWF is sport (and its "performers" are role models and athletes); that, like all of contemporary sport, the WWF has been touched by the outside world—and particularly by drugs; that the WWF's drug program will reestablish it as the clean, family-oriented, positive-value entertainment package the WWF has always been. In an "editorial" type setting, McMahon says,

> From other professional sports emerge a number of stars who become superstars, and espouse the message, "Don't do drugs." We applaud their effort. However, here in the World Wrestling Federation, we have *many* superstars, some of whom have even become superheroes. All of whom recognize their responsibility as role models, to "Just say no to drugs." Therefore, it should come as no surprise to you that the WWF has one of the most comprehensive drug testing, education, and rehabilitation programs in all of sports. This program will now be expanded to include testing for anabolic steroids. In short, the standards of excellence the athletes in the WWF live by will become the standard bearer for all professional sports for years to come. That's why when you see this symbol [WWF], you can be assured of drug-free sports entertainment that you and your entire family can be proud of.[47]

Despite its obvious campiness and kitsch aspects (and irony: Hulk Hogan had recently been accused of steroid use), there are, as McMahon intimates, some avant-garde, innovative aspects of the WWF which more mainstream sports emulate. One, of course, is the blatant recognition that athletes are, to some degree, entertainers: they exist for "The Show" (as in Major League Baseball); the entertainment they provide, while generally related to their physical prowess and skill, is also linked intertextually to product endorsement; as entertainers, they can be role models, but they may also be anti-heroes (as in Charles Barkley's pronouncements that he is not a role model).

Further evidence that the postmodern athlete is an entertainment entity filling a contemporary space for icon-as-commodity: in a strange pastiche of ritual, sport, and lifting of racist taboo, the Grand Champion Selection Committee recently awarded a non-Japanese sumo wrestler (Chad Rowan, from Hawaii) the title of *yokozuna*. The reaction from marketing overseers in the United States included Ralph Cindrich's remarks (paraphrased in *USA Today*) that "some team might pay as much as $200,000 to try him at nose guard or defensive tackle," Lloyd Kolmer's comment that "you could submit him right away to Slim-Fast," and Bob Dorfman's prediction that "a lot of Americans will be chowing down now to get up to 500 pounds."[48]

Indeed, the instillation of sport-figure-as-commodity maintains its tenuous balance between a creation of fan interest and a reactionary fan revulsion at sports figures' seeming greed. In other words, individual sports figures must be wary of overexposure to the public.

Likewise, to be effective, the avant-garde forms oppositions with the mainstream culture. The effective avant-garde sport figure, within this commoditization culture of modern-day organized sport, must align within this type of economy structure.[49] Yet, as with some artistic avant-gardes that have incorporated commoditization, the sell-out by avant-garde sport figures is only apparent: while they embrace the commoditization market economy, they also work to retain their innovative, avant-garde aspects. It is a tenuous task, and certainly there is more at stake for avant-garde artists than for avant-garde athletes, if only because both modern and postmodern culture tend to privilege art over sport (in a hierarchical structure reminiscent of the "high"–"low" art dichotomy).

Sporting Avant-Garde in Professional Wrestling

The role of sport figures as representative of a postmodern avant-garde may be delineated in at least four ways. First, sport figures may subvert the mainstream system to suit their own personal ends, enjoying lucrative careers and post-careers through self-promotion and aggressive self-marketing.[50] Dennis Rodman is but one of many examples of athletes who have aligned themselves this way. As he said in the spring of 1995, "I don't give a —— about basketball anymore. . . . It's like the Back to the Future ride in Orlando, like virtual reality. I'm already out of life in the NBA. I'm just living my life the way I want to. I'm not an athlete anymore. I'm an entertainer."[51] The sport lifetime of some professional athletes is incredibly short,[52] yet star-status athletes may utilize networking strategies to extend their involvement with sport through media or advertising.

The second way that athletes may be part of a sport avant-garde, as an adjunct to the first project (subversion of the mainstream system), is in working, as Birringer paraphrases Linda Singer, to oppose "the intensification of regulatory regimes centered on phantasmatic sites of erotic danger,"[53] so that their very position and status decenters a mainstream regulation of the body. Dennis Rodman's tattoos, body armor, and hair style and color not only work to establish his own space as a commodity, but also work on the level of providing access to others for deregulation of their own bodies. His accepted "outrageousness" reduces the "regulatory regimes" at the very least in sport. But behaviors oppositional to such "regulatory regimes" in postmodern sport started, as avant-garde sport behaviors, in professional wrestling. The outrageous tattooing, loud colors, and decidedly theatrical behaviors that Rodman imitates began with wrestlers such as Gorgeous George, continued with the likes of Mr. T, and continue in the present with wrestlers such as the Natural Disasters, Macho Man Randy Savage, and Ultimate Warrior.

Third, sport figures may be innovators who, through "stylistic" or real changes of performance, influence the play of others for years to come. Playgrounds around the country may feature derivative, kitschian, and mainstream moves of such formerly avant-garde styles as Dr. J's glide to the basket or Michael Jordan's protruding tongue.

Finally, sport figures may create such spectator interest as to affect the growth or awareness of their sport through increased fan identification and participation. The chopping motion that Atlanta Braves fans utilized throughout the 1991 major league baseball season is but one example.[54] The participation of the fans did not detract from the "sportive" nature of the games; on the contrary, one commentator announced that the fans were "like a tenth player out there."[55]

In the World Wrestling Federation, all four types of avant-garde are at work, either separately or simultaneously. The promotional tactics of Vincent McMahon have produced "a showbiz package so flamboyant that it makes the Macy's Thanksgiving Day parade look like a Russian funeral procession."[56] How, except by degree, are such tactics different from the tactics herein described? "It was that kind of a 'Wavy Lay's Rockin' Country Sunday' halftime show. Pity poor commentator Jim Lampley, who had to enunciate that phrase countless times in introducing this garish spectacle. The potato chip company, out to plug its latest rippled oil-and-salt concoction."[57] The Super Bowl half-time show has learned from entrepreneurial sports entertainment corporations. Just as entertainment workers learn their trade from each other, so too do the various players of sport. But the intricacies of commodification and the intertextual weaving of product and "non-product" sports programming have become increasingly complex. Likewise, the advertising campaigns for successive Super Bowls have become increasingly costly: in Super Bowl XXX (1996), for example, "NBC executives say they were able to get a 20 percent increase over the $1 million ABC got" for each thirty-second commercial.[58] And the ads are progressively "quirky": "Frogs croak for beer, a goldfish plays dead for a soft drink and a city slicker leads a cattle drive in a snazzy four-wheeler during what may be the most widely watched TV show of the year."[59]

As an ongoing example of product identification, lucrative packaging, and self-promotion, however, the World Wrestling Federation has few peers. The promotion of Hulk Hogan has created a cottage industry in its own right. The names Hulk Hogan, the Hulkster, and Hulkamania, unashamedly trademarked by the Marvel Entertainment Group, Incorporated, are found on Hulkster Superstars of Wrestling™ Ice Cream Bars, WWF Trading Cards, the Hulk Hogan Python Power Bandana ($5.95), stickers, WWF™ Superstars Official Sticker Albums, Hulk Hogan posters ($5.95), Hulk Hogan Python Power Painter's Caps ($7.95), stuffed animals (a Hulk Rules Teddy Bear for $19.95; a WWF Hulk Hogan Wrestling Buddy for $19.95), Hulkster Rules Hand-Cut [but mass-produced] T-shirts ($15.95), Hulk Styled T-shirts ($15.95), a Hulk Rules Wall Hanging ($9.95), fabric art, a Hulk Hogan Pillow ($14.95), beverage mugs, sweaters, a Hulk Hogan Jacket ($29.95), a Little Hulkster Infant Set (T shirt, diaper cover, and socks for $17.95), Hulkamania Friendship Bracelets ($2.95), Hulk Hogan Shorts ($17.95), Hulk Hogan Slippers ($9.95), a Hulk Hogan Belt Pack ($9.95), backpacks, WWF Superstar "Water Pumpers" ($8.95)[60] in short, nearly any item that can carry a name, emblem, or "Hulkster Rules" slogan. In addition to the merchandising mentioned, Hulk Hogan the wrestler (original name Terry Bollea) has branched out into advertisements for Right Guard deodorant (he stands on a beach, paintbrush in hand, in front of an easel—the stereotypical artist's pose—while the audience is informed, "A true artiste should be known for his inspiration, not perspiration"), toys, and vitamins; a recorded 900 telephone line ("Hey, Hulkamaniacs, here's your chance to hear from the Hulkster! Every day you can hear a new power-packed message from ME, or you can play my HULK HOGAN™ WWF Wrestling Challenge, where I'll be in your corner as you wrestle against the baddest dudes in the WWF"); and movies (*Suburban Commando*). In 1992 he grossed "an estimated $5 million . . . , much of it coming from . . . outside-the-arena enterprises."[61] It is a multilevel, intertextual advertising barrage—and it has worked. Other sports stars, coming from more accepted venues of sport, have emulated his success.

The initial and continuing success of Hulk Hogan was unprecedented, even for the hyperbole that has become professional wrestling. Similarly, professional wrestling itself may have served as the inspiration for other sport narratives: recall the theatrics of "Cassius Clay, consciously mimicking the bravura of a wrestling heavy [Gorgeous George], [who] transformed his considerable boxing talents into Muhammad Ali, a folk hero the public loved and hated."[62]

The division between "highbrow" sports such as football, boxing, and baseball (the "major" sports) and "lowbrow" sports such as professional wrestling is eroding, at least in popular culture. Just as high and low cultures have tended toward collapse within a postmodern, multi-narratorial framework, so too have the concepts of mainstream and marginal sport. And much of this collapse runs tangentially with the lead provided by professional wrestling. It is no more a marginal or trash sport than less popular sports such as major league baseball (especially after the decline in attendance after the baseball strike of 1994).[63]

What professional wrestling may be, though, is self-conscious "sports entertainment" which allows spectatorial participation, much as avant-garde art allowed spectator involvement and apprehension. The co-construction of texts by spectators of professional wrestling is participatory and active. But so is the construction of texts by the audience of, for example, professional (or semi-professional) hockey. Fans gesticulate, yell obscenities, and generally behave quite differently in this "sacred space" that is sport.[64]

As another example of the shared participatory nature of postmodern sport, the WWF pay-per-view WrestleMania VI was sold to 825,000 homes at a cost per home of $29.95.[65] That "attendance" is equivalent to eight Rose Bowls, at nearly $30 per attendance. Pay-per-view has not been financially feasible for the Olympics, yet it is a lucrative winner for the WWF. (And "mainstream" sport is scurrying to learn to adapt the technology to its own devices.)

Ironically, the WWF's downfall, to purists in sport, may be in its admission of the theatrical nature of its presentation.[66] The key word, in fact, may be "admission," for a good case can be argued for the intentional theatricality of every televised major sporting event. Yet the very admission of theatrics is something mainstream sport seeks to hide. With few exceptions, the desired mode of presentation for televised mainstream sport is a seamless, slick presentation. The confrontation of audience as audience, however, is critical to the WWF's very sense of self and success. Within the WWF SummerSlam™

program of 1991,[67] for instance, blatant story threads provided continuity between bouts as they interwove with the actual physical activity.

The stories were stereotypical. There was Big Boss Man versus the Mountie, with the loser suffering a night in jail; there was Virgil, a black wrestler who formerly was in a servile relationship with his opponent and who, the audience was informed, by winning could become "a millionaire overnight"; there was the recapitulation of "Desert Storm," with the "Match Made in Hell" featuring Sgt. Slaughter™, Col. Mustafa™, and Gen. Adnan™ versus Hulk Hogan and the Ultimate Warrior; and most bizarre of all, there was the parallel "Match Made in Heaven," the marriage of Macho Man Randy Savage™ and Miss Elizabeth™. The narrativity of professional wrestling, blatant and kitschy, is mirrored, however, in the televising of more mainstream sport forms.

In a similar fashion and during the same year, for the televised "Escape from Alcatraz" triathlon,[68] viewers followed the travails of one woman, given a year to live by her doctors, whose "story" was to finish at all costs; they also witnessed the rivalry between Mike Pigg and Scott Tinley; and television audiences learned several other contestants' stories. From pre-event show to the actual event to the post-event show, the viewer is informed what to watch, given backgrounds against which to contextualize the game, and even shown spouses of the athletes.

In professional wrestling, the strokes are broader, the gestures more theatrical than in mainstream sport.[69] But the same production values apply equally to mainstream and so-called marginal sport. Professional wrestlers have, in a sense, been innovators for televised sport, not only providing the athletes with models of how to create audience, but also providing directors with new visions for presentation. Indeed, long before the *NFL Media Relations Playbook* was published,[70] professional wrestlers used the medium of television to enhance spectator interest, to create individual stories of each wrestler that would resonate with a portion of the audience. Regional markets have led to lucrative profits—for savvy promoters, directors, and wrestlers.[71]

Finally, the way in which the avant-garde is perhaps most profoundly wrought in professional wrestling is through spectator involvement. For many spectators, professional wrestling satisfies many conditions of sport, not the least of which is "It has to have an uncertain outcome." To most spectators watching professional wrestling, though they suspect what might or might not happen, the outcome is uncertain. Through guided, but individualized, narrative discourses, spectators are freed to create their own story.[72] The athletic acting out of prescribed movements has no impact upon this: fans will cheer for the villain one moment, for the hero the next. To many fans of professional wrestling, the outcome of the event is less important than enactment, embodiment, and participation in the stories. In a constant reworking of their own narratives, spectators may then satisfy one of the major goals of the avant-garde: to attack filtered experience and to create immediacy and creativity through shared experience between creator and spectator.

Conclusion: Athlete as Entrepreneur

The intricate use of parody by a contemporary avant-garde may provide one with a point of delineation between the postmodern and modern avant-garde. As Linda Hutcheon puts it, citing Christopher Butler,

> While all avant-garde forms are intended to be elitist by nature and therefore have traditionally been the province of the anti-bourgeois (at least in Europe), today's particular postmodernist modes are more eclectic, egalitarian, and accessible. Certainly parody demands of the (real and inferred) parodist much skill, craftsmanship, critical understanding, and, often, wit. . . . But the reader too must share a certain amount of this sophistication, if not skill, for it is the reader who must effect the decoding of the superimposed texts by means of his or her generic competence.[73]

A critical mission of the postmodern sporting avant-garde seems to be bringing the all-important reader back into the work. In the WWF, the reader is an audience made up of children, parents, grandfathers, and grandmothers, who can be heard yelling things like "Oh, c'mon Jake! Don't let that fat pig hit you!" and "Your mama don't even know how to take a bath!"[74]

A striking difference between the modern and postmodern avant-garde is the temporal lag between the creation or appreciation of the minority elite's work or conceptions and their acceptance by a majority, mainstream audience. Thus, an instantization of image by electronic media and its reception by an audience may serve to compress, temporally, such an avant-garde, aesthetic process. Or this quickening of image recognition may hasten the formerly gradual acceptance of the avant-garde by the majority.[75] Paradoxically, the avant-garde may (and usually does) become the very institution it seeks to attack. In this full-circle event, Kenneth Clark's minority elite and the majority have become confounded so that popular culture artists may, in fact, be assumed to represent the avant-garde, the so-called "establishment," or the rear-garde, depending upon spectatorial interpretation, point of view, and worldview. Thus, an avant-garde Hulk Hogan, much like Andy Warhol, works independently within a populist framework and remains enigmatic, a self- and publicly constructed cartoonist (subject) and cartoon character (object) whose impact, profound or not, is remarkable.[76] The parody, ultimately, becomes one of self- or other-embodiment. And the lines between control of the self and control by others are, in this postmodern moment, fading fast.

FIVE | **Sport as Epiphanic Marker**
A Case Study of
Super Bowl XXVI

Why do we write? Is it to convey knowledge and experiences to unseen readers, as a sort of educational mission? Is it to demonstrate our own knowledge and insights, a type of ritual display behavior? Or do we write to continually inscribe ourselves on lived life, to ensure our own immortality, realizing that writers such as Plato and Shakespeare, though dead, still manage somehow to speak to countless humans across the ages? These questions lie behind the impulse to write, but they also impinge upon the process of what we choose to write.

When I sat down, deliberately, to relate my experience in Minneapolis, Minnesota, at the twenty-sixth annual Super Bowl festivities, actually to commit it to the page, I was faced with a dilemma: the experience itself and my field notes and home video were like big blobs of paint on a blank canvas. They were unartful. They were non-narratives, with no apparent linearity, no dramaturgical sense. They occasionally ran together, once in a while made sense to me, but as a mishmash probably would be of no interest to scholars, the public, or even Alyssa and Nicholas, my two children. I couldn't see the stories I told as being cogent whatsoever. I had to chew on the experience a bit, reconstitute it into something that would make some kind of sense.

The experience itself—that is, of traveling to Minneapolis; of the tastes, smells, feel, sounds, and sights of the Super Bowl environs; of the attempt, almost while in the midst of the experience, to make sense of it all—required my mediation. My exploits and field experience would be difficult to convey, since experience and reality generally have few discernible patterns while we are immersed in them.[1] But then, "all forms of writing and interpretation [are] being made problematic" within ethnographic discussion[2]—indeed, within all of the postmodern world. I would have to inscribe a pattern, a form, a written logic, upon the raw chronological but non-linear experience. By virtue of such tinkering, I would forever change the experience: if I inscribed sequential order to it, privileging, for example, chronological sense over thematic sense, it would make my experience seem ordered by time; if I inscribed intuitive order to it, my experience might seem ordered by whim. Any possible singular representation of my experience would thus seem "the right" reading of my experience. My representation would become a "second-order reflection on the reality of a sign," as Denzin says, "when the sign (image) depart[ed] from preformatted representations."[3] But of course our experience is a fluid thing, changing in interpretation depending upon our circumstances of telling it.

The very act of writing it down on paper serves to decontextualize the experience itself. This concept is akin to Denzin's claim that the "double and triple reflexivity that 'neo-TV' and the video-text permit . . . reflects just how far the simulational, hyperreal mode of experiencing reality has gone in the contemporary age."[4] I could argue that the experience of actual playing—Nickelodeon's postmodern use of a commercial that urged children to experience "actual reality" in favor of "virtual reality," with the accompanying image of kids dribbling a basketball, comes to mind—has been replaced by viewing on-site, which, of course, has been further replaced by distance aided by technology. In watching sports on television, the spectator is at one more degree of removal from the actual experience, just as the on-site spectator is removed from the actual experience of actually playing in the game.[5]

To write about the experience of watching people get ready to watch others play (and to have the reader interpret that writing so that a modicum of fidelity to the experience is conveyed) becomes another level of removal from the initial experience. It is simulational, yet of course participatory. Just as sports fans create themselves in new and amazing ways for the Super Bowl, the reader becomes an active maker of sense, an active participant in sharing (and creating) the experience. As Denzin writes, we may be "watching ourselves watching ourselves watching ourselves watching them."[6] But *conveying* this maze of reflexivity further removes it from the original experience. Narrational conventions shape the way writing is conveyed—and help to form how it is received.

Naturally, in writing this chapter, I was faced with many options.[7] In my first draft, I told my "story"[8] chronologically, demonstrating my travel to, arrival at, and departure from the site. This linear arrangement recalled Van Gennep's *Rites of Passage,* and brought me into contact with Victor Turner's chapter "Pilgrimages as Social Processes."[9]

Van Gennep's explication of the seasonal nature of ritual—as I read it, an application of chthonic, naturalistic cycles to human endeavors—works with the Super Bowl on two levels. The first is the "January thaw" ritual, the vestigial celebration of renewal and rebirth implicit in the coming spring (and nowhere as profoundly obvious as in the curious juxtaposition of football with a chilling Minnesota winter). The coming together of people in seeming celebration during midwinter reminds them of better times.

This January thaw celebration was reinforced in Minnesota by the midwinter ritual and attendant discourse related to the construction of the Ice Palace and nearly six-hundred-foot-long Ice Slide, in conjunction with the St. Paul Winter Carnival. The discourse surrounding these winter events—with the omnipresent Super Bowl hovering nearby—is telling. In a pre–Super Bowl show, Regis Philbin discussed the Winter Carnival with Bill Rust, the architect of the Ice Palace and Ice Slide:

> Regis: "What is the celebration basically all about? I know it's a celebration of winter . . . "
> Rust: "Right. It's a celebration about winter, and, uh, how proud we are of our heritage in Minnesota. But then Volcanus Rex comes in who represents Summer and he dethrones King Boreas . . . "
> Regis: " . . . and tells him it's time, uh . . ."
> Rust: " . . . right. Tells him it's time to go and we want summer now."[10]

The vestiges of seasonal rituals still exist, even if the players of the drama must become cartoonish and representative, playful tropes like Volcanus Rex and King Boreas.

The second level at which Van Gennep's schema might work is at the level of the spectator and the spectator's travel to the Super Bowl site. Pilgrimage rituals have remained viable and plausible reasons why groups of individuals may travel en masse to sacred, but invented (and sometimes nomadic), spaces.[11] There is separation from the home (in this case, predominantly Washington, D.C., or Buffalo, N.Y.), and re-integration with other spectators (or the "football team as 'family,'" symbolic of home) at the site. Then the process reinstills itself so that the spectators can return home, changed by the experience, yet still the same. Similarly, the rite of "going to a Super Bowl party" works at this vestigial level for spectators throughout the world.

Although I hesitate to agree with scholars who find direct relationships between religious and secular ritual, some Super Bowl fans are involved in this sort of modern-day ritual of pilgrimage as a bonding experience with other fans who share, at the least, an appreciation for their team. Of course, most of those who attend the Super Bowl are not representative of the cities that field the competing teams: many spectators remain affiliated with corporate sponsors. Despite this cleaving of the classical nationalistic bent of team support, the Super Bowl strikes me as an event at which the gathering of groups small or large is a *requirement* for attendance.

Even when a spectator views the event alone, he or she is deliberately incorporated (usually through media strategies) into the *communitas* of "football fan." I envision some fanatic Buffalo Bills or Washington Redskin fans experiencing, in concert with others of the same frenzied bent, a sense of communitas which leads to profound change. Fans certainly savor this belong-ingness—and some, who exhibit their sentiments through non-permanent "scarifications," such as body and face paint, use the regular patterns of sport seasons to distill—indeed, often to define—their existence.

But the pilgrimage metaphor breaks down somewhat when you look at the absence of a legitimate crisis point for most fans. The crisis might be construed as the actual playing of the game—a symbolic crisis, to be sure, and one that Baudrillard would reckon as a legitimate simulacrum-crisis.[12] But for the most part, the non-permanence, playfulness, and benign nature of the sport experi-ence belies true crisis.

As well, there is a non-human interface between the event and spectators (travelers), as indicated by the presence of pseudo– "football shrines," such as the oversized televisions in the downtown malls. Through huge speakers, these sites pontificate about the historical significance of, for instance, Joe Namath's "upstart" Jets' beating the established Baltimore Colts. The speakers echo the auditory insolence of the American Gladiators' and the World Wres-tling Federation's live shows. These auditory Super Bowl sites, unsupervised by humans, are set up on the streets of Minneapolis, and they electronically greet the pilgrim to the simultaneously sacred and secular areas. Furthermore, they serve as reminders of the transparency and playful nature of this type of sporting pilgrimage, a pilgrimage to a postmodern spectacle. Discussing the sacred and secular anomaly, Erik Cohen states, "For [modern secular exist-ence], transcendence can only be playfully imagined, but can no longer claim reality. . . . [Such a view] erase[s] the distinctive quality of secular 'recreational' tourism as against religious ritual or pilgrimage."[13]

As evidence, sacred culture, purposely conflated with secular culture, plays upon a historical Roman (Latin) theme as the St. Olaf Catholic Church in downtown Minneapolis displays a sign reading "Consalutamus Advenientes Ad Supremum Craterem XXVI" (We salute/welcome travelers/adventurers to Super Bowl XXVI). This sign is accompanied by silhouettes of two footballs, lest anyone misread the church's Latinate "sacred," albeit appropriated, greet-ing to sport travelers.

The bizarre juxtaposition of such formerly sacred markers—the signage of a prominent Catholic church—with a marker such as the Super Bowl—a hy-persecular event—gives one pause. Does this mean that sport really has become a form of religion? As Wallace classifies religion, there are many anal-ogous requisites to both sport and religion.[14] Certainly some fans approach the Super Bowl with a similar fervor (and may have even internalized such a theme), yet Cohen again warns those who believe in an "analogy between religious ritual and ludic tourism" not to draw parallels between this aspect of "modern secular society" and the religiosity of "traditional societies."[15] Sport tourists embody a lack of depth which betrays their alliance with such a "modern secular society."

The Super Bowl as a playful and secular "pilgrimage" might work for a few fans, but as a pilgrimage site it certainly does not work in the sense in which "traditional societies" view pilgrimages. Moreover, the financial and commercial aspects of the commoditization of the Super Bowl intrude upon the sport-as-pilgrimage metaphor. For many fans, the purity of purpose that seems critical for the occurrence of a true pilgrimage is largely absent.

I did not discard the discussion of pilgrimage, yet I moved on. In my second draft, I mentioned the pilgrimage aspect, but I emphasized the commoditization of the game, the selling of the so-called "sporting experience" as genuine and authentic. Rather than being a chronological recollection, this was a thematic tale, a tale of economics in which large corporate bodies' marketing schemes have interfaced with sport, made it into a nostalgic product whose effects trickle down to the everyday, commonplace level and signify fascination with things tangible.

My second draft was not confined to the Super Bowl. The commoditization aspect is everywhere: when the Montreal Forum was to be replaced by the Molson Centre (named after Molson Beer), Gerald Redmond complained,

> Gone is the feeling that hockey for hockey purists is all that matters in this building.
>
> Corporate boxes have been added. The clock at centre ice tells fans who are among the most knowledgable in the world, when to cheer.
>
> The boards are covered with ads, music blares and millionaire players make plays that once would have had them playing for the senior Royals, not the Canadiens.[16]

The commoditization of games has replaced what Redmond sees as a more pure aspect—the enjoyment of sport for its own sake. But Redmond weaves his own twist on the sports nostalgia angle: he talks of four generations of Redmonds and their different expectations of the sporting experience. In San Francisco, another aspect of commoditization has been realized: the purchase of Candlestick Park by the 3Com computer technology manufacturer (and subsequent renaming of the park to 3Com Park)[17] evoked a mild response on the part of fans and media who disputed the change on the simple grounds that they would lose their memories of Candlestick. In Montreal, the president of the Montreal Canadiens, Ronald Corey, along with Molson Cos. Ltd., anticipated fan response: "'The user of the building is the fan, and we want to have a great building for the fan,' Corey said. And the fan meant the *hockey* fan. Not the basketball fan or rock-concert fan or roller-hockey fan or arena-football fan."[18] But the commoditization of Super Bowl XXVI included having the game share the spotlight with a "Bud-Bowl," an "invited guests only" Budweiser tent outside the Metrodome, and many oversized M & M, Coca-Cola, and beer inflatables hovering over downtown Minneapolis.

It should be obvious that this commoditization aspect is not new, or merely an aberrant product of the eighties, as some observers would have it. In a nostalgic "historical" piece written for the 1993 Super Bowl about the history of the Vince Lombardi Trophy, two angles emerge. The first is that along with the "authentic" and singular trophy, made up each year by Tiffany's for the Super Bowl winner, a replica is made "just in case the unthinkable should happen. Tiffany's makes that copy available for display, at its various stores and conventions, throughout the USA."[19] Simulacra before the fact of presentation.

The second aspect of the trophy's history (since its first incarnation at Super Bowl V in January of 1971) is the fabricated nature of the nostalgic commoditization. The "thinking that went into commissioning and unveiling the trophy" included, according to Don Weiss, the NFL director of planning/operations, someone suggesting "'Why not have it stolen, announce a reward, then suddenly have it rediscovered in the nick of time?' . . . We discarded that idea; we thought it was a little too tacky."[20] Surely many fans' experience includes collision (and collusion) with "sport" as commodity, either overtly or covertly.

This covert, insidious aspect, which Mills terms "the result of manipulation, of management, of blind drift,"[21] ends in unease on the part of individuals who are not able to "determine what it is that imperils the values they vaguely discern as theirs."[22] Commoditization has become expected, a "velvet noose"[23] that gently and comfortably restricts movement, resistance, and struggle, and results in a conformist malaise—or, as Foucault might have it, that results in a disciplined and docile society made up of those who willingly enter into the process of self-regulation.[24]

In this second version, I recounted, at the local level, the many merchandisers whose shops were uncharacteristically open on Super Sabbath, whose stock had been significantly modified to pander to the Buffalo and Washington fans, so that there were items in the maroon and gold of Washington or in the blue and orange of Buffalo.

I demonstrated that the avant-garde and kitsch aspects of such entertainment find their concrete expression in a range of products, from hand-painted ornamental earrings of the teams' logos and close-cropped, blue-and-red-painted buffalo haircuts, to mass-produced team-inscribed items ranging from relatively inexpensive shot glasses costing three dollars to glamorized rainsuits selling for more than three hundred dollars. Looking over the selling of the Super Bowl reminded me of looking at the WWF and American Gladiators displays: items in every price range, needless items whose only apparent value was that they carried some written inscription tying them in to the event itself. This is desperate stuff.

Sport, professional or otherwise, is packaged as entertainment, as something to be consumed, and, as Veblen put it so long ago, as something to be conspicuously consumed—especially for wealthy enthusiasts. "Millionaires, rock musicians, film and sports stars,"[25] "NFL stars such as Walter Payton, Lawrence Taylor, Ronnie Lott, Warren Moon, and Carl Banks . . . media personalities like Roy Firestone, Leslie Visser and Downtown Julie Brown [who were in town and watched the Jan. 23 Detroit Pistons-Minnesota Timberwolves' game],"[26] and people such as "Dr. Dale Helman, Monterey, Calif., self-described high roller," who "needed a $10,000 tax writeoff" so bought "four tickets to the game . . . [for] $1,550 a ticket"[27]—these people most certainly attended the game. They were there to be seen as well as to see. But the former-athletes-turned-broadcasters fall into this group as well: Terry Bradshaw, Dan Fouts, Randy Cross. Their presence adds nostalgic glamour to the proceedings, and intensifies the stakes through their "expert" status. Thus, the makeup of the players changes for high-end events such as the Super Bowl, but the characteristic nostalgic, kitschian, avant-garde, and commoditization tropes still draw in the players to postmodern sport.

I thought about the cost of attending the game itself. With prices ranging from $440 to $1,795 per ticket,[28] many people are shut out, but a few symbolically representative "lucky" ones may attend by winning a ticket in a contest. On Super Bowl Sunday, radio station KLXK, 93.7 FM, offered "two tickets to give away—who knows, you might make it to the big game!" Strangely, this has become the only way that many sport fans have a chance to get close to the actual contest. Of course, this *deus ex machina* solution is consistent with a myriad of social solutions that momentarily assuage current problems: the most glaring comparison is to the proliferation of state and national lotteries, which, during times of economic crisis, seem the only apparent way to extricate oneself from debt. The chances of non–"high-rollers" getting to attend the Super Bowl are, of course, quite similar.

But there are even more bizarre ways to attend the big game, as evidenced by the following human interest story: "Super gesture/ Larry and Karen Thompson are going to the Super Bowl. The parents of John Thompson, whose arms were ripped off in a farm accident and restored in surgery, received free tickets."[29] Why? one is compelled to ask. Was this an example of meritorious behavior, where the donee received the gift because of outstanding effort or accomplishment? The parents of a teenager, not the teenager himself, went to the Super Bowl. The kitsch borders on schlock.

Clearly, only a select few are privileged to attend.[30] Others become symbolic representatives—processual congregations, as Anthony Wallace uses the term, who "come together as a group"[31]—for the television audience in the competing teams' cities and throughout the world. The actual attendees thus serve as synecdoches, in which the individual is representative of the whole of the society. As such, particularly for television purposes, individuals representative of different constituencies must be reflected in the on-air samples.

The sport fan, like the sport tourist, comes in many forms, with many intentions. Some may see sport—in this case football—as a modern-day form of religiosity, and their annual travel to one of the shrines as a form of secular pilgrimage. The icons these sport tourists pick up are both sacred and secular; sport as religious experience has become confused with sport as commodity. Thus the salt and pepper shakers they buy in Minneapolis go into their Super Bowl "shrine" at home—and serve as a part of the representation of what the Super Bowl meant to them.

In fact, there is a whole line of research that sees such events as the Super Bowl as redirected contemporary religion.[32] The interpenetration of Wallace's "minimal categories of religious behavior" into the sport setting encourages the use of the sport/religion analogy: among them, "addressing the supernatural," "dancing, singing, and playing instruments," "the physical manipulation of psychological state," "exhortation," "reciting the code [of the belief system]," "simulation: imitating things," "feasts: eating and drinking," "congregation: processions, meetings, and convocations."[33] For example, in Wallace's terms, sacrifices and offerings are made to the "powers who populate the supernatural world."[34] Outrageous ticket prices—in Veblen's terms, "the struggle [of accumulation] . . . a race for reputability on the basis of an invidious comparison"[35]—become ritualized practices which "may be rationalized as a sacrificial service to the supernatural beings themselves."[36]

In a sense, then, buying season tickets from seemingly All-Powerful owners may serve to satisfy this sense of sacrifice. Similarly, a few of the "offerings" granted to victorious athletes include parades after the Super Bowl for the returning teams, ticker tape, words of praise, keys to the city, solemn pronouncements, perhaps even the fairly new practice of dousing the winning coach with a bucket of iced Gatorade. These kinds of offering and sacrifice to the gods tie in well with Sansone's broad definition of sport,[37] in which it becomes a "ritual sacrifice of human energy."[38] In this sense, the whole of sport itself takes on a certain religiosity.

But there is a subtle aspect of charisma to this "worship" of the "gods" of sport. Chris Rojek, in discussing Max Weber's view of charisma, writes,

[Weber] identifies charisma as the bestowal of exceptional and perhaps even supernatural qualities by an assembly of people upon an individual or group of individuals. . . . Charisma inheres in leisure practice under capitalism in the form of "the fan club," "the star system," and the various cults that surround famous people or groups. Empirically, it can be studied in such cases as the rise of successful sporting personalities, authors, actors, and pop stars. These individuals are seen as superhuman, and sometimes their followers endow them with magical powers. The late John Lennon complained that in the heyday of the Beatles, the group was often besieged after performances by cripples wanting to be touched. More generally, the phenomenon of wanting to see and touch a famous person is widely understood in modern society.[39]

Thus, identification with sport stars takes on a sacred aspect so that the stars themselves—and those now-commoditized items that are representative of the stars—become fetishes for fans.

There are similarities between the ritual aspects of contemporary sport and the rituals of religion as studied by anthropologists—and yet it is clear that *most* sport fans still know that there is a difference between the sacred and the secular, between pious and profane. It is clear, as Sansone states, because "the connection between sport and religion, like that between ritual in general and religion, is not an essential one."[40] It is clear precisely because advertisers and marketers continually play upon and intentionally blur the lines of distinction (assuming a culturally knowledgeable audience), with resounding success.[41] But it is also clear in a Bakhtinian sense, so that sport fans intentionally turn the established world order inside out.

This may overflow dangerously, however, indicating that fans themselves can lose a clear sense of the distinction between the pious and the profane. Occasionally, such a blurring has resulted in serious consequences. The 1993 celebration-cum-riot (on February 9, 1993) in Dallas after the Cowboys' victory in Super Bowl XXVII is just one example of joyous celebration that metamorphosed into destructive force.

While the events and context of games enamor many spectators, other fans may profess to enjoy the actual game itself.[42] But some may want to be onsite to be seen; some may enjoy the hoopla and sporting experience; some may genuinely feel that they are supporting "their team" when they purchase team logo goods. In a sense, "their team" represents their extended family. The preceding reasons for attending games are not by any means, of course, mutually exclusive categories. And yet it seems that this kind of categorization tends to imply only singularity of purpose, a static state of sport tourists who are easily duped by the sport tourist discourse.

In my third draft, I explored some of this sport tourist discourse, following Wenner's use of Bormann's "fantasy theme analysis" to determine the interplay of fan, discourse, and a reality-fantasy context. As Wenner puts it, "The rhetorical vision of a sports program such as NBC's Super Bowl pregame show can be understood in terms of the fantasies chained by the group participants . . . and embraced by the audience that has chosen to enter the fantastic reality by becoming members of a larger fantasy group."[43] The fans' willing suspension of disbelief becomes an integral point in their participation in the world of sport tourism. Thus, individuals consciously enter into a social world in which they may become valued members. As in much of membership study (sport psychologists call it "group cohesion"), the attractiveness and value of the group make group cohesion greater or lesser.

The stance of joining in on fantasy certainly exists for some fans to some degree both at the site or while watching television, and ties in with the idea of symbolic congregations. Yet the actual "being there" aspect of on-site attendance reduces the spectator's exposure to media packaging while creating a manic sense of not seeing the "real" Super Bowl (which has become an electronic simulacrum). Fantasy chaining thus provides a comfort zone for spectators. Indeed, I saw many dazed travelers, themselves being filmed, sitting down in front of giant multiple-screen televisions to witness the media's treatment of their own experience: their fantasies re-enacted on screen, as is proper and fit. They continued the fantasy chaining by videotaping their own "memories," to be recounted later in the privacy of their own homes with their own audiences. Such video souvenirs have become commodities for the postmodern sport tourist.

Thus the "suspension of disbelief" for sport tourists breaks down a bit. Sport has taken on the aura of real reality. Rarely does one question the fabricated nature of played sport: the arbitrary rules, distinctions, rituals, or the socially constructed nature of the very enactment of such rules. Some of the glue that holds sport as a construct together consists of groups of people not "suspending their disbelief" but rather learning to believe fervently in the rightness of sport.

My fourth draft went further, I think. I demonstrated that sport is a performance, a performance marketed as "sports entertainment," but nevertheless a performance. Unlike self-conscious performances, however, such as Balinese dances,[44] mediated sport has managed to retain an aura of self-consciouslessness. Of course, production values and crafting play a large part in such seamless, slick presentations.[45] But that sport and its "tourists" are not interdependent,[46] that the games would continue *exactly the same* even if there weren't sport "tourists," is a fabrication, a pretense to extend the feeling of authenticity for the "tourist." It is as if the sport tourist is a voyeur gazing at a pure form of performance, with the performers unaware of the spectators' gaze. But of course the spectators' presence (and gaze) is implicated in many aspects of sport, not the least of which is the performance itself. The presence of co-actors and audience has, in fact, constituted a large part of the North American sport psychology research agenda ever since the 1890s, when Norman Triplett surmised that a dynamogenic factor facilitated performance.

The interrelationships of all of the sport players—among them, fans, coaches, directors, athletes—are what make sport, to many, such a fascinating social institution. In fact, as Ron Roizen, who is a part-time sports official, wrote to the Sociological Aspects of Sports Discussion group on the Internet,

> I've tried to write down some thoughts about coach-official conflict but haven't yet come up with a satisfactory effort. One thing that bears noting is that the game might actually seem a little flat or dead if such conflict NEVER OCCURRED. Somehow the coach[es'] emotional outbursts to officials . . . [are] a lightning rod for the game's affect.[47]

Similarly, all of the "players" of sport—officials, tourists, vendors, athletes—are "lightning rod[s] for the game's affect."

In my fifth draft of this chapter, I attempted to build on the third and fourth drafts by getting to some of the specific touristic discourse in sport. The difficulty, of course, in examining sport discourse is that it is invisible, a fabric of ideology so deeply inlaid in our society that it often escapes serious discussion.[48] As discourse, it is insidious. It is unlike, say, Third World touristic discourse, wherein tourists may consciously and willingly "suspend disbelief"[49] in order to enter into the spirit of any of a number of tourist/native illusions—and the illusions are so very foreign to the tourists. The discourse of the Super Bowl, on the other hand, is self-congratulatory, it is celebratory of business, it is "serious" in the midst of seeming frivolity—and it is a familiar, safe, "naturalized" discourse.

So with this draft I look at how we may remember[50] big sporting events, what they might signify in our lives, how that discourse affects the sports fan who has become privileged to attend in person or through the media. I borrow from Norman Denzin's explication of epiphanies, in which he describes four types of epiphanies: the major, the cumulative, the illuminative (minor), and the relived epiphany.[51] Though Denzin has generally used this structure to describe "problematic experience," I use "epiphany" as descriptive of a similarly life-shaping event, but one of a possibly more positive nature.

Tangentially, the "vernacular moment" in art appears related to this kind of epiphany in its intersection of public "help" and private "woe." There exists a creative vernacular moment, a turning point of sorts, where there is "a sort of double movement, between desire and destruction, financial reward and aesthetic impoverishment" for the artist.[52] I submit that spectators—in fact, all of us—create their own self-stories, made up of problematic and pleasurable epiphanies. We are all artists of the self, avant-garde artists of the self. And the looming shadow of sport in late-twentieth-century America is, in effect, an overwhelming *Zeitgeist* that provides an enormous canvas for our self-creations.

Thus, in 1985, Donald Hall savored this remembrance of an epiphanal sport moment: "In 1948 I watched the one-game play-off between Boston and Cleveland for the American League pennant, won by Cleveland as Lou Boudreau lifted a fly ball into the left-field screen and a line drive into the right-field bleachers—or was it the bullpen?"[53]

This kind of remembering, in which the details matter less than the feel and totality of the experience, I consider to be "positively epiphanic" for Donald Hall. It encompasses singular—as in a "first game" scenario—as well as cumulative—as in following and supporting a team since childhood—experiences. Spectacle sports events—and it is difficult to avoid them anymore if you are interested in sport—may become positive epiphanies for the sport fan. The sharing of experience that once was going to the Montreal Forum or Fenway Park with Dad may nowadays be realized by going with Mom, Dad, or grandparents to see Hulk Hogan take on the Ultimate Warrior.

But these positive epiphanies also become indicators of having been there. As Dean MacCannell uses the term "marker," it is "information about a specific sight."[54] Thus, in his context, a marker is a representation of a sight (or site), including written "travel books, museum guides . . . descriptive brochures" which may serve to elicit touristic expectations.[55]

My use of "marker" is slightly different, though inclusive of expectation-producing sport-event programs and pre-game media literature. I use the term to locate in memory a special time for some fans. This kind of marker is primarily temporal, though as a relatively transitory, illusive device it may itself be marked by a tangible memory-jogger, which triggers recall not only of cognitions, but also of sensory affect. John MacAloon speaks of this concept when he writes, "Several of my informants recall significant events in their lives by spontaneously placing them in reference to the Olympic Games."[56] Indeed, this "marking" is a key concept in the nostalgia music market, where marketers hope that songs from years previous call forth fond memories for the audience.

The tangible marker thus resonates with a sport nostalgia that is embodied in the (re)collection of such "reminders" as player cards, logo clothing, videotapes, and so on. Donald Hall, in the previously cited example, ties his nostalgic memory of the 1948 American League playoff game to a Boston Red Sox game a year later, when he first introduced his grandfather to Fenway Park.

When the concepts of epiphany and marker are combined, then, an "epiphanic marker" in sport becomes a recollected peak moment which the sport fan uses to (re)shape his or her constitution of self and to serve as a signifier for the occurrence of previous life events. The epiphanic marker serves to recall and (re)collect not only the sport event in great and illuminative detail, but also the affect and context of one's life at that time, and the sensory elements that surround that event. But the epiphanic marker also serves to continually (re)construct the self in terms of such experience.

Advertisers have capitalized on such nostalgia and have even parodied it. As an example, there is the television commercial for Pizza Hut in which a group of men sit around reminiscing about the time in high school that one of them kicked a winning field goal. The next scene is years later, the field goal is farther out, the myth expands, and their wives laugh at the retelling of the story.

The Super Bowl, like much of postmodern sport, is steeped in nostalgia, and uncritically allows for the provision of markers and opportunities for marker acquisition for the (un)suspecting fan. Bizarre and memorable combinations often occur, and they serve to burn into memory, to memorialize the moment, as if they have become a provided photo, the image of "differentness," of oddity, of an oxymoronic massified uniqueness. The stories are unique, yet they serve as synecdoches for the total, confusing experience.

For example, my markers of the 1992 Super Bowl: one San Franciscan, interviewed over the radio, flies into Minneapolis to see if he can buy a scalped ticket. He says he won't pay more than the going NFL rate for it ($150). If he can't get it, he will just watch the game at a bar somewhere in the Minneapolis area. As I drive north, I see, taped to the side window of a car with Illinois plates, a sign reading, "I NEED 1 TICKET." At a convenience store in the Wisconsin Dells, I overhear a man on the phone: "I think I can get one for two hundred and fifty." These people are going, it seems, for adventure, to have a story to tell, to "see what will happen next" so they can add it to their biography. (Who am I to talk? Are my reasons for going—to "do" research on postmodern sport forms, of which the Super Bowl is but one example—any less bizarre?) The ticket stub from the actual Super Bowl,[57] the photograph taken while one poses next to the Native American protesting the use of "Redskin," the ten-dollar souvenir program—all qualify as tangible markers of the recollected epiphanic marker.

There is more evidence that multinational corporations, national sponsors, local business representatives—everyone involved, in fact—are literally and figuratively buying into providing the penultimate pseudo-experience for the fan. The Roman numerals of Super Bowls (in this particular case, Super Bowl XXVI) ground the game itself in a mythos of pseudo-historic nostalgia. Indeed, game footage, "great player" profiles, and human interest stories gleaned from the Hall of Fame continually bombard the tourist to the Super Bowl by means of giant four-by-four televisions (sixteen screens in all) which replay those "magical moments" of Super Bowls past (which have, ironically, existed only since the mid-1960s).

But the fan has been set up for this, in an intertextual rendering of media/sport nostalgia. Super Bowls and Super Bowl pre-games have capitalized on a historical aspect of the event. Wenner reports segments of "yesteryear," the 1966 Kansas City Chiefs, and Vince Lombardi at the Super Bowl XX pre-game show. Similarly, the use of former professionals Merlin Olsen, Ahmad Rashad, and Bob Griese as reporters adds a nostalgic element to the proceedings.[58] There is reference to when these former stars played, much like Mike Adamle's reference to Larry Csonka's NFL past on *The American Gladiators*. As well, the 1992 show included segments, interspersed throughout, entitled "Football: The First Time," in which current Bills or Redskins players were profiled in terms of their first experiences playing football as children.

Fans—or segments of fans—are invited to participate in such discourse-sharing and history-making. Through shared recollection, a kind of "where were you when" game, fans become immersed in the nostalgic resonances of a Super Bowl. By steeping itself in a collective nostalgic past, the NFL has re-created a safe temporal haven for many fans, as well as a safe spatial haven for a representative few.

For many, the Super Bowl represents, at the very least, a midwinter party at friends' homes. The very recollection of who gave what party for which Super Bowl triggers further recollections of that period of our lives. But it is an uncrowded space: everyone is invited into the temporal kind of space, and all can easily fit.

But to actually attend a Super Bowl! One elderly man from Kansas, who had never before attended a professional football game, much less the Super Bowl, perhaps best exemplifies the importance of representative attendance at significant sporting events. His eyes dancing, he told me, "Even though I don't follow the teams, I couldn't pass up tickets to the Super Bowl, now could I? It's the Super Bowl, after all!" For this man, Super Bowl attendance was a marker of elevated status, but it also became something he could savor and embellish upon in later years. It was an epiphanic marker to him, if only because he felt he had finally achieved one signpost of the American Dream.

I must step aside as participant-spectator for a moment, and draw attention to the fact of myself as author. In this chapter, I have tried to introduce the category of epiphanic markers in sport and to understand and experience the processual nature of writing.[59] The various "drafts," obviously techniques to explore a variety of voices and perspectives of the Super Bowl, served as open texts which may be entered into and dialogued with, like the Super Bowl itself, at several levels. Writing is not only process: it is (re)constructed, at every possible level, from field note notation to noticing of exemplars to the actual thinking, writing, and (re)writing process.

I introduced multiple drafts in this chapter to provide a multivocal text (within one author)—not to imply that any of the five drafts I described (or even the sequence in which they are offered) is necessarily more correct than the other. Through this text, I wish to indicate that the scholar-ethnographer ultimately must de-privilege him- or herself, and recognize that shared power and insight, far from being nihilistic, may join a new, fertile ground of research in concert with new Others.

This "open[ing] up [of the] institutionalized practices of reading and writing to different voices of this society" is clearly one of the primary next steps in ethnographic research.[60] But this, in my view, is only a tentative first step. To privilege previously unheard voices means to shake up the hegemonic order of things, and to offer new explorations of phenomena that formerly were considered manifestly obvious. It means to see, as the avant-garde artist does, the ordinary in extraordinary new ways. Thus, within the tiny (albeit enormous) universe that is the Super Bowl and its spectatorship, the changes that reflective study may foster begin with spectatorial awareness. There is one caution in this. Tzvetan Todorov writes of the

> frequent misprisions of Bakhtin's interpretation of Dostoevsky; the notion that, in Dostoevsky, all positions are equally valid, the author having no opinion of his own. . . . Such is not the case; in these novels, characters can enter in a *dialogue* with the author: the structure of the relation is what is different, not its content.[61]

This is the prison in which scholars frequently find themselves: they forget to listen. The dialogic, unlike the monologic, does not "objectivize all reality. Monologue pretends to be the *last word*."[62] In dialogue, there is no last word: there is only continual reciprocity—and this the ethnographer must continue to strive to acknowledge.[63] Ethnographers working in a postmodern world have experimented with various methods to give voice to those groups or individuals who have heretofore been marginalized. One possible approach introduces the next chapter, which is a discussion of participants in and the birth of the new sport form of paintball.

SIX

Sport as Postmodern Construction
A Case Study of Paintball

> Victorious forces first achieve victory and then conduct battle;
> losing forces first conduct battle and then seek victory.

—Sun-Tzu, *The Art of War*

A Story

He was dressed in black: dull black Levis, unshined black combat-type boots, a black T-shirt with dark lettering proclaiming his allegiance to Harley-Davidson motorcycles. He was tall and thin, with a protuberant Adam's apple that, I later saw, quivered when he was excited about a shot he'd made. But he exuded confidence, remained off to himself—and he glided when he walked.

Earlier, during the day, I had spoken to him as he stood next to his car in the "safe" parking lot, while he calibrated his paintball equipment. He said he'd brought a thousand paintballs; clearly he planned to spray a lot of paint that day. He carried his own gun, an imposing-looking long-barreled monster that was as close to an automatic as could be. After several games of paintball, we usually took a break, during which everyone generally congregated with their friends, replaying the good hits and positionings. I was a loner, and not much liking it. He was a loner, too, but he reminded me of a 1990s version of Shane—a loner of necessity, because of a grudging sense of duty. A stereotypical rugged individual, born of the Reagan era.

The group leader called us all to head up the hill to what was known as Quang Tri Village. The walk was strenuous, the climb steep. Scrub pine, oaks, and manzanita provided cover for small animals. With every step, we kicked up dust, and with our face masks on, it became difficult to breathe. At the top, the group leader told us to set our guns on the ground. When he was sure that everyone had complied, we were told that we could remove our masks and breathe deeply. My chest heaving, I gasped for air, knowing it was gauche and showed me to be a novice, yet unable to resist the sweet air of the Sierra foothills.

Shane stood off to the side, relaxed, barely breathing. He somehow fit in with the landscape: shallow breathing, aware, taller than the rest of us, watchful. The hunter. He was our tribal Hollywood revisited.

In the first game at Quang Tri Village, I was in the "attacking" forces. Shane was a village defender. At the whistle, we spread out, trying to surround the village from below. We intended to surround them, then make our way up the hill. The defenders were confined to the village perimeters, and could hide in makeshift plywood huts. The object was for us to "kill" them or for them to survive for fifteen minutes.

I scurried to the right. Someone from the village called out, "There's one in white down there going left." That would be me: stupidly, I'd shown up in a light gray long-sleeved shirt to play this "hide-and-seek" game.

There was so much deep brush that I knew they couldn't hit me even if they shot: the balls would splatter on the trees and shrubs before they got to me. So, with a certain impunity, I crawled off to my right, finally crouching behind a two-foot-diameter oak tree that split just about at shoulder height. The view was clear; I could see one hut about thirty feet above me. I was completely hidden behind the tree trunk, so I rested my gun in the crotch of the tree and waited.

After about five minutes of silence, Shane pulled out to my left and above about fifty yards, from behind the hut, and shot off about twenty rounds of paint. He showed me his noble profile, fully exposed as he shot confidently. I raised my gun barrel, aimed just above his shoulder, and squeezed off one shot. I could see the paintball arc up, then drive into his upper abdomen. He looked down in amazement, not even knowing where I was, since I'd shot only one ball, and yelled, "I'm hit!"

Later, after I'd divulged my position by firing four shots, I was spooked out by dozens of paintballs, finally getting shot myself. I strolled down to the safe area, and saw Shane.

"I'm the one who got you," I said, not really caring whether it was bad form. I told him, as if I were recounting a good play in football, how I'd done it.

"Payback's a bitch," he said. And smiled. Next game, when my team defended the village, Shane flanked to my left side, drilling me in the hip with four quick shots. His laugh echoed among the scrub manzanita.

After that game, as we walked back down the hill to the neutral area, Shane spoke excitedly. "I started up that little river bed, then you pinned me down."

"Yeah, I was emptying my gun: I'm done for the day, figured I'd use all my paint."

"Well," he continued, "I crawled back down, then cut off to my right. Meanwhile, another guy was firing back at you from where I had been before."

"So I couldn't tell who it was. Nice move."

"Right. So then I managed to flank you on your left when I took out your backup. You stood, I popped you."

"Four times to be exact." I showed him the paint splatters; we laughed. He was no longer merely a self-made archetype. He was no longer Shane, but just another player, one I could recount the game with—not a "loner," but, like me, only alone. I would have to reconsider my first, superficial, assumptions.

A Genealogy

In the mid- to late 1800s, many of the sports with which we now culturally identify emerged from informal, usually cosmologically significant rituals to become highly structured, organized, and more secular games.[1] Allen Guttmann, using a Weberian model, has demystified much of the emergence of modern, masculinized, participatory sport.[2]

There are certainly some similarities (which reflect a modern-postmodern overlap)[3] between the processes of nineteenth-century sport development and late-twentieth-century sport development. However, the process by which such games became commoditized and became sport one hundred years ago is unlike the process by which physical activities emerge into sport nowadays. In this chapter I explore the current process of sport reification, and indicate, with the specific exemplar of paintball, how this process can occur in contemporary sport, thus influencing the development of sport consumers, who are otherwise known as participants. The development of sport players as consumers is integral to the reification of sports in the late twentieth century. Furthermore, a sport such as paintball is valuable to study, I think, primarily because of its emergent, contested, and transitional nature.[4]

Much of contemporary sport either is already reified or is in such a state of infancy that its direction is unclear. Paintball, on the other hand, like a butterfly emerging from a chrysalis, contains and displays raw (and often unsophisticated) elements of the struggling effort to make it viable—as a sports commodity. This is reflected in the less-than-slick production values of the telecast,[5] the grassroots nature of on-site participants and regulators (owners, entrepreneurs, referees), and the uneven discourse emerging from paintball's promoters and enthusiasts. The televised productions of paintball certainly can be categorized as what Laclau and Mouffe term "new cultural forms linked to the expansion of the means of mass communication. . . . This media-based culture also contains powerful elements for the subversion of inequalities."[6] But while the televised—and actual—forms of paintball may create space for a new egalitarianism in postmodern sport, the opposite may also be true. Laclau and Mouffe say that "the effects are ambiguous," including "massification and uniformization."[7] As Baudrillard says, discussing his concept of the hypermarket,

> Another kind of work is at issue here, the work of acculturation, of confrontation, of examination, of the social code, and of the verdict: people go there to find and to select objects-responses to all the questions they may ask themselves. . . . Thus all the messages in the media function in a similar fashion: neither information nor communication, but referendum, perpetual test, circular response, verification of the code.[8]

The agency of the members of sport players thus comes into question: Are they dupes, being manipulated by a cynical media, or is there a more complex set of relationships at work?

Some current sport formations exhibit characteristics of postmodern sport.[9] There are certainly similarities between deeply ensconced, dominant, mainstream (and predominantly modern) sport forms (such as baseball, hockey, football, basketball) and this newly emergent contemporary, postmodern sport. In fact, one of the points I wish to demonstrate is that the dominant sport forms, powerful icons in and of themselves, have been selectively reproduced—utilized, commodified, and pastiched—by postmodern, contemporary sport forms.[10] The borrowing of styles, techniques, and methods, in fact, can be multidirectional, so that modern forms tend to take on styles of the postmodern and vice versa.

Furthermore, in mainstream sport, the sport-as-drama ritual has emerged as the dominant metaphor and, in fact, become emblematic of and synonymous with sport itself. The construction of sport as drama has transformed the expectations and game experience for the (mediated) spectator. Thus, we can discriminate the on-site sporting experience in which one apprehends only occasional clear moments of unity and insight from the at-home experience in which one *feels* that she or he is experiencing unity and insight constantly, through the course of the televised contest. Susan Birrell and John W. Loy, drawing from Marshall McLuhan, categorized this distinction as a dynamic of "hot and cool media."[11]

But, of course, varied spectatorial experiences *may* indicate or influence how we view sport. They may demonstrate how our perceptions of "what is sport" change over time, and what that process means. If sport is inherently dramaturgical, that is one thing: the process of drama—an impulse in the arts as old, perhaps, as humankind—may find a modern-day example in sport. But the drama that has been linked with sport is, of course, socially constructed drama.

Nevertheless, the element of dramaturgy in sport has ramifications for our current views of sport: Is contemporary sport, like much of drama, predominantly a commoditized form of entertainment? (If so, should Olympic athletes of school age—the workers who bring in so much money for their sport institutions—be paid to play?[12] Should athletes' educations follow a vocational school model, a liberal arts model, or the terminal degree model of fine arts programs?) Can there be originals of sport, or are its myriad forms (I call them mutations or amalgams of sport) merely a sort of sport simulacra, regenerating forms of a "proliferation of myths of origin and signs of reality"?[13] Does the televising of postmodern sport tend to create an MTV look to current sport forms, to the exclusion of the actual activity itself? In fact, are there any actual activities? In short, what does it take to produce a sport that will "make it," one that will thrive in contemporary society, and how does production of that sport mesh with our conceptions of what sport is? Does the amalgamation of sport forms, which incorporate earlier instantiations of sport, fall into Baudrillard's sense of simulacra, or are there, in lived and actual reality, new productions of forms?[14]

Another Genealogy

If we accept two postmodern premises—one, that experience and its representation are individual (that there are, in short, polyvocal texts available to be appropriated and shared by both producers and receivers, and that the very categories "producers and receivers" are problematic),[15] and, two, that "the author [producer] is not solely responsible for the content of the discourse he produces: the receiver [audience], at least as imagined by the author, is equally involved in the *process:* one writes differently for different audiences"[16] (my emphasis)—then, by extension, we can begin to understand some of the complexity of dealing with audience creation of and participation in the cultural formations of currently emerging sports.

The emergence of North American sport forms such as football, basketball, and baseball has been well documented.[17] Less well examined, for reasons I have explained in previous chapters, are what Sage calls the "trash sports"— the sport forms whose intent ranges from "promot[ion of] show business personalities and the programs they represent" to "pseudo-sport events" (the generally accepted but marginal sports) whose purveyors' intent is not "pure."[18] In the case of pseudo-sport events, however, the questions remain: Does their pseudo-sport status lead "naturally" to their not being sanctioned by a governing body, or do governing bodies not sanction them, which in turn leads to their pseudo-sport status?

I believe that views of sports (including their degree of "purity") are socially constructed, and that power battles (some might call them "critical mass" battles) create imbalances that fluctuate among certain sports at different historical moments. Thus, the Amateur Athletic Union of the United States (AAU) appropriates certain sports as sports and only considers others: Hackeysack™, a brand name but also the name by which participants play the game, is relegated to a miscellaneous category, under the "World Footbag Association"; croquet, basketball, even underwater hockey are considered sports, while paintball and laser tag are not.[19]

Guttmann provided a framework for looking at the "modernization" of sport forms. He determined that there were seven aspects of modern sport that mark it as different from previous sport forms: secularism, democratization, specialization, rationalization, bureaucratization, quantification, and record-seeking. Bureaucracy has only recently begun to reach much of postmodern sport. While the six other aspects that Guttmann details are present in postmodern sport forms to varying degrees, in many cases the sports themselves do not appear to be lucrative ventures; thus, the very foundation of sport bureaucracies, profit and recognition, is absent from much of incipient postmodern sport.

Many sponsors of these sport formations are clamoring for recognition, for with recognition comes money and power; yet if the sport corners only a small niche of the massive sport market, it is deemed a failure by many (modernist) business-oriented sport promoters—and consumers. Its "demise" is almost assured.[20] To "make it" as a contemporary sport means to be financially viable. So, by implication, those aspects of the "sport canon" that are more spontaneous, grassroots, and less financially viable are less privileged (by scholars, the media, the public: that is to say, culture) when compared with the more stable, mainstream, established, and reified sport forms.

To be sure, the initial impulse to promulgate a sport business may be altruistic: I enjoy doing this sport; why don't you try it? Such contemporary emergent or oppositional/alternative and largely intertextual sport formations as the NFL Run to Daylight,[21] the American Gladiators, Roller Games,[22] Gladiators 2000, arm wrestling tournaments,[23] sumo wrestling at bars,[24] the Gus Macker 3-on-3 basketball tournament,[25] and disc golf[26] are not just written about or televised, but rather are defined as sport only after having been written about or televised.[27] Though some of these sports have been made for television (the so-called "pseudo-sports" of which Sage speaks), the borrowing from both "made-for-television" sports and mainstream sports is making many postmodern sport forms into a blurred category.

This sanctioning—or perhaps anointing—of sport activities by the media appears to be a critical component of exclusion or inclusion in what we know as sport. In fact, sociologist John Loy, discussing definitional terms for sport, occasionally jokes that "sports are what are on the sports pages." Sports in the 1990s may have become "what is on television."

Many postmodern sport forms contain portions of dominant, mainstream activities, pastiches of the more highly "sanctioned," reified sports. The activities themselves are segmented, decontextualized from their originals. They are occasionally patched together awkwardly, and eventually made to seem natural (through a mediated "trial and error")—like the mainstream sports from which they draw.

But in the beginning, in their incipient forms, attempts to standardize them seem hollow and fabricated. For example, to make these sports appear dramatic—as we have seen with the *American Gladiators* live show—the announcer shills like a huckster at a carnival in announcing the score or introducing the contestants. It seems that the sports players of these sports are trying too hard. Hype is everywhere.

Much of viewers' uneasiness is due to the fact that the narrative attempts—much like those reported by Duncan and Hasbrook for televised women's sports—are still raw and do not match the visual images in producing drama. Such "incongruence between the narrative and visual coverage,"[28] known in this case as a form of ambivalence, lends credence to the premise that while women's televised sports are undercut (and thereby devalued), so are these new, relatively powerless forms of contemporary sport undercut and devalued. The result in either case is that the very production values of such broadcasts send messages to the audience that these activities are less-than-sport.

For example, the "sport"[29] of the NFL Run to Daylight (for NFL running backs) becomes visually decontextualized segments: "The Sprint," a forty-yard sprint; the "Sled Drive," in which the contestants push two blocking sleds; "Rapid Fire," a test of pass-catching; and "The Maze," which is a combined-skill test of running, jumping, blocking, and agility. One might argue that each of the skills tested may come into play in an actual football game; yet the skills are broken down, almost in a football-drill order, ostensibly to assess the strengths and weaknesses of each athlete. In this manner, the body's skills are fragmented. The performance is less a flowing, sequential, potentially dramatic one than it is a series of component, disparate chunks of performances.

Upon closer examination, however, the "sport" nature of such traditional (and powerful) icons of sport forms as NFL football itself may break down: To what degree, for example, is the Super Bowl (which some claim as the pinnacle of sport forms) sport and/or spectacle? How has the specialization of even mainstream sport created decontextualized participants who enter the game only during specific situations? During the 1980s, the San Francisco 49ers used situation substitutions effectively, but how, except by the magic and seamless flow of television, could those athletes be considered anything but decontexualized effectors of the coaches' game plans? Many athletes (and sport players) have become role players, specialists who perform only some of their former functions.[30]

Similarly, events on *The American Gladiators* are amalgams of other sports, as in the "Break Through and Conquer" segment: a shortened, narrowed football field and broken-field running segues into a sumo wrestling match. As another example, the Gus Macker 3-on-3 basketball tournament is a scaled-down version of 5-on-5 basketball, a mutation of the dominant sport form, and it provides greater opportunity—and now media exposure—for basketball players who are less than NBA quality.

But the main point I want to emphasize that is common to all of these contemporary sport formations I've just mentioned is that they continue to be—or aspire to be—symbiotically related to the print or televisual media:[31] a business strategy, including the creation of a market, drives their success or failure. While their presentations may be different—they are attempting a postmodern, MTV style of televisual presentation of sport—they remain embroiled with the media.

There are, however, other sport forms that, for one reason or another, do not primarily seek such an interdependence with the media. (Yet it is important to note that the "grassroots" nature of these sport forms is only one of many contemporary sports instantiations: there is a range of efforts, dominant, residual, oppositional, and emergent, which make the playing, marketing, and selling of these sport forms resemble a continuum, rather than a binary, of choices. Thus, the highly hyped, highly visible sports may or may not be emulated.) One example of such a new emerging sport form is paintball.

A Postmodern Game

Paintball is a contest promoted as "capture the flag" using paint pellets as the tags. The game is held between two groups of individuals who bond together for the duration of the contest. Its ideology requires that players use strategy to attack the opposing forces. The game is as old as sport itself, harking back at least to the Middle Ages, when the military sport "behourd" was practiced between groups of military pretenders.[32] According to Van Dalen and Bennett, behourd was a

> military sport to improve techniques in handling arms. . . . it appears to have been a mock battle in which one group attempted to defend a small fortress while the others attacked.[33]

Furthermore, there existed the grand tourney or mêlée:

> The tournament proper was the mêlée in which many knights fought under conditions similar to war. Regulations attempted to limit all the activities in the program to blunted weapons (arms of courtesy), but sharp lances and swords did come into use and were particularly common in the mêlée.[34]

The impulse for this pseudo-agon game, for baby-boomers, may be nostalgic—a remembrance of playing at war as a child, or recollections of actual wartime in Korea or Vietnam. For younger participants, the cultural memory to contest with others still promises some semblance of satisfaction.

To the uninitiated, then, the game of paintball imitates war. But those who play paintball have told me, "We're not warmongers like everybody thinks." In fact, some promoters decry this popular image of paintball. For example, the editor of *Action Pursuit Games* states:

> The uninitiated public, the media and the television/motion picture industry have a distorted image of the game we love. They think we're training for combat; preparing for the end of civilization. Others think our game is violent and propagates violence.

> Unfortunately, members of our own industry help foster this violent image. There are several stores and fields with "War Game" as part of their names. Many fields use props such as "tanks" and "missile sites" to add to the "realism" of their games.[35]

Many promoters—and players, too—would like to distance themselves from such negative connotations and instead substitute the "active promotion of our sport as a safe, non-violent, and non-malignant recreational and professional activity."[36] Thus, much of the discourse that paintball enthusiasts engage in works to reduce the distance between this violent image and a more acceptable attitude toward the sport. One player wrote,

> I find it funny the way I'm looked at as strange by even some of my fellow players because of my enthusiasm for the sport, but am I any different from baseball card collectors or league players? Season ticket holders? And how about those caps & jerseys? The only difference is we [paintball] haven't been around as long. They've got their favorite sport, we've got ours—let's show it.[37]

Nevertheless, paintball the game is designed after small-scale war, played by "squads" of five or ten or twenty, rather than by full companies or regiments.

As in many postmodern sport forms, there exists a multiplicity of motives and belief systems, a sharing of Laurel Richardson's "*doubt* that any discourse has a privileged place, any method or theory a universal and general claim to authoritative knowledge"[38]—even within a fairly homogeneous group such as paintball aficionados. It seems, however, that the assumption that "the more traditional a male's sex-role values the more he would participate in this 'macho' game" simply is not borne out.[39]

Generally, the object of paintball, for those unfamiliar with the "game," is to overcome the enemy and capture the flag using military stratagems. It is a territorial game, a land-acquisition game, in which the flag serves as symbolic capital, representative of the opposition. When I played, we never "captured the flag"; rather, it was a game of "them versus us," where we attempted to eliminate the other team, and vice versa.

Paintball is a game as old as war, yet with a twist: paint pellets instead of bullets are the weapons of choice. In keeping with sanitary ideas of modern warfare, paint, which can be washed off, indicates a hit player. No one dies in actuality, but rather in simulation. There are fieldmasters/referees who monitor the game, rendering judgment calls when necessary; in tournament play, "ultimates" oversee the fieldmasters. The judges are former or current players, not unlike most sports officials.

As an activity that is promoted as a form of recreation, paintball is highly auto-communicative. In Canada, the International Practice Shooting Competition (with real pistols) is similarly a highly "auto-communicative ritual" that exists for its participants' own sake: it has a "highly individualistic nature, relatively small following (virtually all spectators are competitors), [and] lack of media attention."[40]

But many paintball promoters hope to branch out, to create more mass appeal, to engender a higher media profile. For example, the editor of *Paintcheck International* writes, "I doubt that there are any among us who do not enjoy the burgeoning prosperity and mass appeal that international paintball is bringing to a sport that not too long ago was indexed under 'cult' status."[41] This, I've found, is not a feeling shared by all players. The shop owners, of course, want more and more participation, and seek to cultivate new customers. But only to an extent. The "cult," "underground" status of paintball, at least regionally in Idaho, is still prevalent. The most accessible avenues of most sport businesses are not being followed: there are no yellow pages advertisements, no newspaper ads, rare television commercials. "Most of it's by word of mouth," said one paintball shop owner. "Still, I get four hundred to six hundred players a month. That's as many as I can handle."

Of course, the possibility exists that this cult aspect is a regional difference: California and New York are the centers of promotion for the sport, and the business people I spoke with from California treated paintball as more everyday, more ordinary, than "cultish." This "underground" versus "mainstream" status of the sport begs further examination. It also may be, though, that the paintball operators who do not advertise are merely poor business people.[42]

Nevertheless, there is an underlying attitude of tacit admiration for the "underground" status of the sport on the part of many owners (and players). I asked an owner if there were any games available nearby, and the answer was, "Oh, occasionally. There's always renegade people trying to get up a game." "Where can I get in touch with them?" I asked. "They're in and out. You just have to be around, I guess." But another owner said, "There's a lot of outlaw fields. But us: we've got insurance, licensing, the whole bit."

Still another field in northern California uses a catchy subtitle for its outdoor field: "American War Games." The actual playing fields consist of such evocative names as the "Strike Force" maze, "Hamburger Hill," "Cemetery Ridge," "Pork Chop Hill," and "Quang Tri Village." It is a conscious strategy to align the sport with evocations of war and battlefields from the past—and from a fantasy, mediated, nostalgic past.

So a multiplicity of reasons and motivations play out into ranges of machismo, bravado, strategy, and recreation;[43] a constellation of marketing strategies reflect these perceived motivations for play. There are many paintballs, and there are many paintball players. Each individual brings a certain attitude about the play to the game situation. I have not yet, however, discovered the "survivalist" attitude which seems to be a stereotype propounded for promotional purposes. That is not to say that the macho aspects do not exist, but rather to demonstrate that if there is organized opportunity for play (paintball) to turn into practice for war, I have not yet uncovered it.[44]

The use of historical icons—generally icons of previous wars fought by the United States—is one of those promotional attempts that lend a feel of historicity to the playing of paintball. However, just as bowlers at a city bowling alley most likely do not realize that they are playing a historically seated sport/game (which has its antecedents in, for example, the upper-class games of lawn bowling and boccie),[45] many paintball players (especially younger players, born after the Vietnam War) are not even aware of any specific historical referents to war. Yet the promoters' impulse still is to lend a subtle "feel" of macho/war, combined with Caillois' mimicry/ilinx, to paintball.

The Play of the Game: Before, During, and After

The purpose of the game at Quang Tri Village was for one team to defend the perimeter and huts (which were the "village"), while the other team, at the base of a large hill, attempted to "kill" all the defenders.[46] If any "villagers" were still "alive" after fifteen minutes, they won. Clearly, the slant of this game is toward a war game, yet during this play (and subsequently) I found little of the macho aspect I initially expected. It was fantasy war, with out-of-shape, mostly disorganized players struggling to remain "alive." Players were given a five-minute safety speech and were warned to "never take off your mask while you're on the fields." We signed liability release forms. The game itself was matter-of-fact, and became individually strategic (though the strategy went unsaid: for example, firing repeatedly would give away one's own position) but rarely group-organized.[47]

In fact, the televised versions of paintball—where teams are pre-organized, and work together—have followed a format in which the team "captain" usually kneels down to whisper his (usually they are males) team's "strategy." Reminiscent of a quarterback drawing a play in the dirt, these "strategy" explications are amazingly simplistic and betray either a psychic knowing within the team membership or a lack of depth in strategic planning. The game itself involved a lot of running, ducking, sliding, and other anaerobic effort. Games lasted fifteen to twenty minutes, at which time the teams were switched by the fieldmaster, and another game began. No physical contact between players was allowed. Safety was constantly stressed.

Reading the magazines, however—slick magazines with titles such as *Paintcheck International, Paintcheck, Action Pursuit Games,* and *Paintball Sports*—you get an impression that belies the "safe" nature of the sport. There are ads for Battle Boy Goggle Bags™,[48] for a Sheridan Paintball Gun in which the copy reads "TAKES A LICKING AND KEEPS ON KICKING BUTT,"[49] for paintballs named "Stingers,"[50] and for "a Squadbuster grenade with a 30-foot-plus marking zone." Most of the "recreational" players I encountered were playing for the first time; there was no reference to specific equipment, gear, or strategies from these players. But the few more dedicated players I spoke with clearly were knowledgeable about the sport and about the more subtle aspects of it.

There are also articles such as the one titled "Fun with Scenario Games: Attack on Peenemunde."[51] It appears that the paintball fanzines are geared toward enthusiasts who invest in equipment and play on a fairly regular basis—who, in short, follow and imitate a "watered-down" professional model for paintball. But the fanzines also include tongue-in-cheek pieces, intended to verbally replay games while creating a bit of an insider feel:

> Game four is when I felt that it was time for a little strategy, so I delivered the infamous speech given by Bill Murray in Stripes. Newly inspired, and feeling like cold-nosed, American soldiers, my team began marching down the field together singing "boom-chugga-lugga." After about 15 minutes or so, our flag's in the bag—the pink team's bag that is. Thanks to Keith Rappaport, pink, once again, claimed their third victory. I've since learned to keep my nose out of strategy planning (maybe I should have tried a speech from Apocalypse Now).[52]

As well, the paintball fanzines bear a striking similarity to macho-wannabe magazines, such as *Soldier of Fortune:* they all contain the same hyperbole, nearly identical cover layouts (and use of a stenciled title font), and comparable article layouts and slants. But *Soldier of Fortune* seems to take itself seriously, while the paintball fanzines appear to be more humorous, more self-parodic, and more postmodern in their tone.

Certainly not yet a mass-appeal sport (though even this is debatable—there is now a World Cup Paintball competition, first broadcast during 1995 on ESPN I and ESPN II), paintball is hyped by its players and producers variously as a "growing sport" and a "new, adrenaline-addicting sport that is sweeping the world: an adult version of capture-the-flag."[53] In both the outdoor and the indoor games, it seemed more like "hide-and-seek" to me, but that might be another issue. Paintball comes in many specific game forms, which are dependent upon the field and terrain (and the attitude of the players),[54] even though the public stereotypically perceives it to be a survivalist model of what war is. Typically, one person I talked to explained the sport as "just another war game, since we aren't at war now: the boys have to have something to kill."[55] It is fantasy war, war simulacrum, intentionally reproduced for mass consumption—and, to a degree, willingly participated in and reproduced by many players who enter into the play of it with their senses of irony intact.[56]

This is a burgeoning industry, uncertain of its direction: should it, for example, buy in with the NRA lobby,[57] or find its own, more benign future? Should paintball supplies be sold in the game/sport sections or with the ammunition in Walmarts and other discount department stores? Should it promote the dangerous, vertiginous aspects of the sport, or should it go the route of family entertainment? Should it follow the masculine model of sport as it is explained by Postow,[58] or might this be an opportunity to promote an androgynous model of sport? (In fact, however, one woman player from Idaho said, "Mostly men play. It's kind of a sexist sport. Many women are interested, but it can be intimidating. It's kind of a military type of game.")[59]

Clearly there are many kinds of paintball. And there are many kinds of players, to a degree created by the entrepreneurs of paintball. There is the professional model, the one that emulates successful professional sports marketing schemes. One example is the ProBall paintball advertisement profiling Dave Youngblood: "Profession: Paintball Player," "Quote: 'Having the best equipment is not enough to win at paintball anymore. Winning requires nothing less than total dedication. Play with the best, play your best, play it straight!'"[60]

There is also the rogue model of paintball, one that I only marginally explored.[61] There is, more often than not, the mass participation model as well. This model invites many people into participation; indeed, the rogue model and the mass participation model seem antithetical to each other: the former is exclusionary, and its ideology betrays an elitism; the latter, by definition and for its financial survival, welcomes all and avows a pluralistic egalitarianism.

It is this uncertainty, this "multitude of voices" sneaking up one against another,[62] that makes a new sport such as paintball interesting to study, and makes the emerging power relationships between paintball's promoters, purveyors, and professional and amateur and recreational and occasional players so basic and profound. The dynamics between emergent, residual, and dominant practices and the practitioners of those sport forms is a "velvet noose," a "soft [and often not-so-soft] struggle"[63] in which participants, "interpellated as equals in their capacity as consumers," are "impelled to reject the real inequalities which continue to exist."[64] The play is real, the struggle is real, and within a postmodern sport form such as paintball, the rejection of inequalities continues to be played out in daily enactments of individual and group dynamics.

But, still, the ideology of such inequalities is insistent, the hyperbole manly, the myth substantial:

> He was tall and terrible there in the road, looming up gigantic in the mystic half-light. He was the man I saw that first day, a stranger, dark and forbidding, forging his lone way out of an unknown past in the utter loneliness of his own immovable and instinctive defiance. He was the symbol of all the dim, formless imaginings of danger and terror in the untested realm of human potentialities beyond my understanding. The impact of the menace that marked him was like a physical blow.[65]

Robert McPherson Starrett (the narrator) would grow up and not have to take the same road that Shane had, for Shane had told him, "Go home to your mother and father. Grow strong and straight and take care of them."[66] Some of the inequalities were balanced out by Shane, if only just for a moment in time, but the symbolic (and real) struggles would continue to play upon the western psyche.

Or at least a part of the western psyche, the folk wisdom, idiomatic, "tacit knowledge,"[67] "practical consciousness"[68] portion, would continue to play, the portion that admits to certain knowledge yet is not the total context of a given situation. The cultural knowledge and emotional attachments that most people have—especially concerning popular cultural events and performances such as sport—have, for the most part, become naturalized. They have entered into folklore status, just as Shane has entered into folklore status. They are, like sweet onions, in need of deconstruction, of deep readings that not only can see the surfaces, the onion's layers, but also can peel back each successive equivalent core to reach the myriad layers within.[69]

SEVEN | Sport as Constructed Audience
A Case Study of ESPN's *The eXtreme Games*

Spectacularism: A fascination with extreme situations.

—Douglas Coupland, *Generation X: Tales for an Accelerated Culture*

Ethnography, popular culture, critical studies, and cultural studies work have all examined the media's logic of spectatorship and audience formations. Cultural studies in particular has interrogated the ways in which the media contribute a certain logic of sense-making, yet examination of the sport media's contribution to this logic is largely lacking.[1] An overriding goal of this chapter is to deconstruct, ethnomethodologically, some of the electronic media's logic of sports production. The "scientific project of ethnomethodology," as defined by Alain Coulon, is an attempt "to analyze the methods, or the procedures, that people use for conducting the different affairs that they accomplish in their daily lives."[2] Thus, in this chapter I will co-opt ethnomethodology and turn it to an examination of one of ESPN's 1995 sport programming ventures, *The eXtreme Games*.[3]

More specifically, I seek to discover how ESPN has framed production of *The eXtreme Games* so that it will gain acceptance and power in the larger culture and yet promote a sense of diversity, appearing to remain true to the internal logics of the individual athletes, audience, and practitioners.[4] What are the overriding themes that ESPN uses to draw in audience for this spectacle? Additionally, how does ESPN create verisimilitude—a "you are there" feel and a sense of participation—for the viewer?

According to ESPN announcers Suzy Kolber and Chris Fowler, *The eXtreme Games,* a made-for-cable-TV sports event, includes nine sports, with thirty different events, played by four hundred athletes from six continents, representing twenty-five countries. With so many different sports, and varied events within each sport, the micro-logics of shooting the sports obviously must vary. But, as with programming for the Olympics (with its multitude of sports), the electronic media have learned consistent ways (macro-logics) to "tell the stories" so that viewers can understand the logics of the sports as they are presented for viewer consumption.

Dominant Metanarratives

A quick overview: *The eXtreme Games* is a postmodern, self-consciously constructed, result-driven form of sport endeavor. The viewer has learned a common television sports language from other sport productions, so that, when watching, she anticipates a short introduction to each game or sport.[5] She also expects to see one or more of the key athletes profiled, with a story that emphasizes the athlete's individual uniqueness but also contextualizes the athlete within the larger logics of the sport and within the collectivity of fellow sportspersons. This individual/collective dynamic, in which individuals' agency and belongingness are both privileged, is termed "universal singularity."[6]

The viewer, moreover, expects to see multinational corporate advertisements, specifically designed for and intertextually linked to this *eXtreme Games.* Thus, she easily consumes advertisements for Taco Bell and the movie *Congo,* Chevy trucks, and Mountain Dew, with catchy, smarmy, self-effacing Madison Avenue–driven tones and sound bites evocative of the constructed, made-for-television nature of *The eXtreme Games.* In many cases, the most memorable portion of televised sport for the television viewing audience is the commercials—especially around Super Bowl and Olympics time.

For example, the following advertisement for Mountain Dew aired during the run of *The eXtreme Games.* It depicts four mountain bikers, and begins with a voice-over (sports) announcer, in super-hype mode, proclaiming various progressively difficult, progressively absurd mountain-biking tricks:

> Announcer: "Extreme mountain biking . . . forty-five miles an hour."
> Biker #1: "Did it."
> Announcer: " . . . sixty-five miles an hour."
> Biker #2: "Done it."
> Announcer: " . . . blindfolded."
> Biker #3: "Been there."

Announcer: " . . . then, a four-thousand-foot vertical drop."
Biker #4: "Tried that."
Announcer: "All while slamming a Dew."
All bikers: "Whoa."
Announcer: "Nothing's more intense than slamming Mountain Dew. Oh,
   yeah—while watching *The eXtreme Games* on ESPN."
Biker #3: "Decent."[7]

At the same time ESPN has constructed a sport-familiar terrain for viewers, the producers of *The eXtreme Games* have promoted the theme that this is unusual, cool, exceptional, *extreme* sport. And the advertisers have learned that intertextuality—simply put, the combining of formerly disparate cultural signifiers—sells. Thus, using " . . . while watching *The eXtreme Games* on ESPN" seems appropriate in a Mountain Dew commercial, and easily elides into another commercial or the show itself.

The viewer, although she may not know it, thus expects to be told certain logics of the sporting show. She fully expects to be informed, at some level, how to "read" this televised text. Thus, the idea of themes, or metanarratives,[8] enters into the logic of sports programming which is on the modernist/postmodernist cusp. Sports programmers, using what has formerly worked while still attempting what *might* work, continue with a largely modernist strategy, a comfortable logic that is, for the most part, sequentially (or temporally) "logical." At various times, innovations that might seduce sponsors are attempted, even though readers (television sports viewers) seem content with most familiar methods of presentation. Thus, the viewer learns to expect some kind of theme(s) to the show. The dominant themes, or mythoi, of these *Games* include (1) the normalcy of the athletes, (2) the paradoxical uniqueness of the players, (3) the inextricable link between all players of all sports, (4) the historical link among all sports, and (5) the basic fact that ESPN's *The eXtreme Games* is sport.

One of the themes/mythoi of ESPN's *The eXtreme Games* is the ideological paradox of this sporting event being done by normal people who perform extraordinary feats:

> These are Marines, bankers, engineers, even a window cleaner. Teams of regular folks from all over the world attempting something very irregular: hiking, peddling, and paddling, from ancient Indian hunting grounds in the isolated wilderness of Maine, all the way here to Fort Adams on a course that they have to help chart themselves.[9]

The paradox is that anyone can do it, despite the fact that the viewer is reminded that these are professionals who have spent years perfecting their athletic skills.

A second dominant theme of *The eXtreme Games* is the uniqueness of its players: the audience is informed that many of the athletes and spectators, even the two announcers, are members of Generation X. This marker of generational individuality at once creates a space for and defines a target market for ESPN. As co-anchor Chris Fowler says, emptily, it "helps to explain why, when it comes to sports, Gen X is Gen eXtreme."[10] In line with an advanced capitalistic logic "in which the relationship to consumption seems to have at least slightly displaced the relationship to production,"[11] the *eXtreme Games* television programming encourages consumption (indeed, that is a fundamental and perhaps ultimate purpose of any television programming). It does so through an ideological logic of the "American values" of rugged individualism, perseverance, egalitarianism, cooperation,[12] fairness, and deservedness. The viewer is told that "Fort Adams represents New Age sports values,"[13] yet the same modernist consumer values, hypertrophied, are presented to the audience.

As with most ideology, there is some basis for the claims—and for counterclaims. Certainly the generation of people born in the sixties and seventies, with their training and facility with computers, computer simulations, digitizing for biomechanical analysis, and use of electronic/cybernetic software, has leapt forward into an arena of sports innovation and technological construction which may rival that of the mid- to late 1800s.[14] As in-line skater Arlo Eisenberg says, "It's really exciting to be a part of something and to know that you're the first ones to do it, that you're pioneering it, that you're the ones that are in control."[15] He might see himself as a sort of avant-garde artist. But then Alf Imperato, a windsurfer, says, "Everyone wants their own identity. And specific tasks and specific identities sometimes make a lot of money. And that's what a lot of the people are looking for."[16] A statement of kitsch.

Tied in with the uniqueness of its players is the third theme of *The eXtreme Games*: that the players are inextricably linked to other players in other times. ESPN airs interviews that generally reinforce this idea. Thus Chris Fowler, speaking of the former outlaw status of many of the sports that have first been shown on television as part of *The eXtreme Games*, says of barefoot water skiing, "This is a great moment for guys in the sport. This is a sport searching for a sponsor, without a pro tour: these guys are used to just jumping for fun and the cheers of the crowd."[17]

As with the growth of professional beach volleyball (and the status of its athletes), many of the "eXtreme" sports and some of the athletes involved in *The eXtreme Games* are seeking sponsorship, big-money tournaments, recognition, and power. They are modeling themselves after other professional sports: "You know, athletes in alternative sports have been craving a stage where they can prove, just like football and basketball players, they are serious competitors who leave as much sweat on the playing field as anyone."[18] It is a tenuous balance, working between the allure of the professional sports model and the idealized purity of the amateur sports model.

Another example links athletic generations. In case the viewer is not clear on the historical and thematic ties between the Olympics and *The eXtreme Games* (and the athletes of each), Suzy Kolber makes it explicit:

> There's more history to many of these sports than you might think. Quite a bit of evolution along with the revolution. . . . Yes, we will concede that the Olympics carry unmatched prestige, but they've been around since 1896. We must say, though, in our first go-round, we're not lacking in international flavor.[19]

Postmodern technological advances, while seen as innovative, are also a link to the previous modernist technological advances in the ongoing process that is sport. As Chris Fowler says,

> Technology here is another story. You're gonna see some high-tech coverage never used on any sport before. Our cameras and mikes are going to be everywhere: on helmets and handlebars, an inch off the street at sixty miles an hour, and free falling from thirteen thousand feet.[20]

Thus the technological theme becomes a subtheme; it serves to connect athletes with their predecessors. For example, in order to properly judge the performance of a sky-surfing combination, the judges look at a video shot by the sky surfer's partner. Via a "Sony Jumbotron™ and microwave hookups," the television viewer is told, the audience on the ground can see the generated performance as it occurs. Thus the cameraperson and the sky surfer combine to generate the performance, which is then conveyed, via videotape, to the judges. The performance is judged on the technique and artistic merit of both the surfer and the cameraperson. Simultaneous use of cutting-edge technology (e.g., helmet cams), technological jargon and name-dropping (e.g., Sony-Jumbotron™), and a subtle link to familiar scoring methods (technical and artistic merit) provides the viewer with an acceptable stretch to his sporting imagination.

The fourth dominant theme of *The eXtreme Games* is its historical linkage to other sports. Appreciation of a significant historical sporting past—and *The eXtreme Games'* justifiable place in that past—becomes a constant, overriding theme. The event itself is packaged to represent, in hyperbolic ESPN language (with announcers hawking loudly, reminiscent of WWF announcers' work), a "sports revolution" in that athletes are only part of the "story"; technology and technological advances in equipment and communications have combined to create specific ways of documenting the performances, and in some cases have become integral to the generation of new sport forms.

Sport as Constructed Audience

It is useful to contrast and compare the ultilization of this specific historical myth for *The eXtreme Games* (e.g., the Eco Challenge, which traces a course along "ancient Indian hunting grounds") with the televised construction of other celebrated, massified sport. In the 1993 Ironman Triathlon, the opening framing theme advanced by NBC Sports is one of a stereotypic Polynesian native (who, incidentally, looks like Hulk Hogan) picking his way across the lava fields of the Big Island. This visual is accompanied by text that sets up the viewer's understanding of the Ironman Triathlon as an epic struggle between the human spirit and the harsh Hawaiian elements. In hushed, solemn, reverent, and evenly cadenced tones (until the final sentence, which is an echo of the "Let the games begin!" of *The American Gladiators,* or the "Play ball!" of major league baseball after the National Anthem), the announcer introduces this abiding theme:

> Ancient Hawaiian religion tells us of the unbreakable chain: how Man, along with sky, land, and sea, are inextricably One, forever united and interdependent. The early Hawaiian sought to mesh with the forces of nature, not fight them. He'd be a fool to upset the threads that bind him together with nature and the gods. In Hawaiian culture, spirit and matter are one in themselves, but, like the gods, matter is truly just as powerful, fully capable of thinking . . . and willing. It is, indeed, alive, conscious, and receptive to human communication. The modern triathlete talks to it, exists with it, not against it. This big island is all-powerful, imposing, and treacherous. But the successful athlete will never challenge it, knowing the race with nature is never won. It is only carried on.
>
> Today, the world's greatest athletes perpetuate the everlasting bond. . . . The rules of the island were cast thousands of years ago, and the teachings of ancient Hawaii still tell us today that the chain shall never be broken. Welcome to the Gatorade Ironman Triathlon World Championships.[21]

The shift from the secularism of playing the sport ("Play ball!" or "Let the games begin!") to celebration of a multinational corporate sponsorship ("Gatorade") is, I think, significant. The historical connection is tenuous at best, with the nostalgic purity of a bygone era linked with a plug for Gatorade. Similarly, NCAA college football bowl games, whose corporate sponsors unashamedly have incorporated their names into the very titles of the bowls, hawk those sponsors' products every time the event itself is announced.

However, in the links with historical discourse, there is an attempt to establish and reify cultural myths, societal tropes that inform and establish standards by which members of societies (a televisual sports audience society) can enact their lives. By reaching out to multiple audiences with such culturally significant tropes, ESPN's producers have keyed in on multivocal representations, none of which is necessarily privileged over the other.[22]

In generating the themes and mythos of *The eXtreme Games,* the ESPN producers and writers have (re)constructed a sport-familiar metalanguage for viewers, which consciously promotes and assumes dominant, oppositional, and consensual readings. These readings are not discrete, but rather fluid, with the readers moving in and out of the positions as they and the producers co-produce the event. In this way, a kind of reader identification—and a television viewing audience—is created.

The use of modernist strategies (such as establishing certain themes and stories that the viewer can see reach a satisfactory closure) is, of course, not excluded by a postmodern sensibility. If, in fact, we "live in an age of transition" between modernism and postmodernism,[23] both logics may coexist.[24]

Thus, the athletes are said to be "not daredevils, . . . not weekend warriors, they're hard-core professionals," yet they are also common people, "regular folks." The "culturally literate" audience may identify with the athletes along a continuum rather than in a bipolar fashion. The "sports-savvy" viewer sees not a continuous event, shown in real time from start to finish, but one constructed in MTV style, with quick cuts, increasingly familiar logos of *The eXtreme Games,* and thematically seamless advertising. The difference might be compared to viewing a Greek tragedy, in which characters deliver long, uninterrupted speeches, versus watching almost any (post)modern drama on film, in which characters interrupt, make assumptions, speak to each other and the situation, and demonstrate indexicality.[25]

Given the modernist use of cultural myth, it is important to remember that one of the key elements of televised sports (indeed, of television) is its major emphasis on selling products. Quick viewer recognition and identification (generally on a sensory level) is one of the keys to successful product marketing. Identification—and simulated participation—of the audience helps accomplish this goal.

The opening sequence of *The eXtreme Games* shows a spinning eXtreme Games symbol, which, over the course of ten days, two cable stations (ESPN–2 and ESPN), and thirty-plus hours of coverage, will become easily and quickly identifiable. In many cases, of course, with pre-publicity on ESPN and ESPN–2, the symbol has already become a signifier of *The eXtreme Games.* Its red "X," crossed dramatically like two skis, is logoed onto everything—and in fact incorporated into the very name of the event itself.

Similarly identifiable to the viewer is the MTV-style, quick-cut, split-screen visual "bites" that accompany the Games' identifier. Included in the "in-your-face" visuals (that is, helmet-cam visuals in which the footage is shot from the close-up point of view of a co-participant or of someone who is in peril of collision from a participant) are rapid shots of a bungee jumper cascading toward the camera, a sky surfer wheeling in midair, an in-line skater pulling a

360, a barefoot water skier spinning on his back, a mountain biker somersault-ing, a street luger pulling a hard corner, a rafter digging in for control in frothing whitewater. These hyperactive clips all serve to entertain—and to educate the viewer about just what these *eXtreme Games* might be. Addition-ally, there is a global symbol, a sort of elongated line drawing of longitudinal and latitudinal frames, which subtly serves to remind the viewer that this is an international competition. This is a fact that will be reinforced to the viewer over time. A key subtheme of *The eXtreme Games* that is foreshadowed in the opening frames is that these games rely on cutting-edge technology: thus we hear the creak of metal on metal, and we see computer-generated graphics of fragmented, generic wheels and gears coexisting with humans propelling them-selves through space.

The symbol of *The eXtreme Games,* the red elongated "X," becomes quickly recognizable—much like the five Olympic rings, the Olympic flame, or the colors of Olympism.[26] If *The eXtreme Games* are eventually successful, of course, a whole historical ethos will develop around and surround them. Much as with the thirty-year-old Super Bowl, "traditions" will be invented and, eventually, reified.[27] But in order for this "alternative" sport extravaganza to succeed, the sports themselves must gain credibility. Thus, the most dominant, overriding theme, which often coexists simultaneous with and recursively informs the other themes—that athletes are normal people, that the players of *The eXtreme Games* are unique, that the players are linked to all sports players, and that *The eXtreme Games* links historically with other sports—emerges: *The eXtreme Games* is real sport. According to Suzy Kolber, though, it is a new form of sport (with obvious historical links):

> This is an attitude toward life; passion that comes from the soul. From its beginnings, Rhode Island has been distinguished by its support for freedom, its rebellious, authority-defying nature. Fort Adams, built to defend, looms large this week as a new generation makes its stand. It's an opportunity to redefine the way we look at sports.[28]

The next section will examine how these five themes are specifically enacted, and how the enactments serve to construct audience(s) for ESPN and its sponsors.

Logics of *The eXtreme Games*

The two news anchors—they call themselves "hosts"—of the event have been placed in a set overlooking Fort Adams in Newport, Rhode Island. Clearly, ESPN's producers have overtly replicated much of the successful for-mulae of the Summer and Winter Olympic Games. But they have also imitated on another level: they have doled out story segments, framed in certain ways familiar to culturally literate viewers. The segments can be analyzed by the ways they work on viewers.

The producers and directors provide the audience a simplified entry into each new sport form, via explanation and/or demonstration; they personalize the players through the use of biographical sketches or profiles, and foster viewer identification with those athletes; they create suspenseful drama by cutting, mid-event, to other events; they ground the event in a constant returning to the sports anchors for reiterative commentary and summation of what just happened; and they preview what is to come.

Throughout, though the narrative is not cloying, the viewers receive reinforcement and confirmation that what they are seeing is real sport—in fact, "EXTREME" sport (the announcers emphasize the word "extreme" nearly every chance they get; interviewees do the same).[29] Not just anyone can do these sports, and yet most of the athletes are proclaimed as true amateurs.

For most of *The eXtreme Games'* sports, the first type of segment, explanation/demonstration, is fairly straightforward. Prior to each event, there is a "What It Is" segment, with a rough explanation of the goals and scoring. But, as with *The American Gladiators,* the examples that ESPN's programming uses link these events to other sports—or segments of sports—that the viewer already knows. With in-line skating (vert), for example, the television audience is informed that "each skater will attack the wall for two forty-five second rips, while Your Honor grades on a 100 point scale."[30]

As well, the audience is told that the subjective scoring ("judging") for sky surfing is based on "a hundred total points on a fifty-second performance. Half goes toward the technical, half toward the artistic portion of the performers' routine."[31] Chris Fowler explains sky surfing: "These are two-man teams, both judged on their artistry, one with a board, the other with a helmet cam, while falling at a hundred twenty miles per hour." Suzy Kolber adds that sky surfing "is a timed event, but there isn't much importance put on the time, much like figure skating or gymnastics. You don't really think about how much time they're out there, just what they do with that time."[32] The links to mainstream, and in this case "legitimate," sport are obvious.

The second type of segment is the personalization of athletes. Both in the show previewing *The eXtreme Games* and in the actual *eXtreme Games* itself, ESPN has taken great pains to familiarize viewers with individual sport practitioners. There is a segment that profiles Bob Pereyra, who, the viewer is told, "is street luge."[33] The story is that Pereyra is generous of spirit, a street luger whose greatest concern is for the sport. However, in setting up for ESPN (in a trial run) for *The eXtreme Games,* the first ever major event for a formerly "outlaw" sport, Pereyra cracked a bone in his left heel. Can he compete with a broken bone? The cameras roll as *The eXtreme Games'* orthopedic surgeon (a graphic supplies his name and title) suggests that competing would be a major risk for Pereyra. Nevertheless, at the eleventh hour, Pereyra is allowed to compete in the duals, but not in the mass event. Now, how will he do? A sense of tension, identification with Bob Pereyra and his troubles, and hope for a judicious result creates viewer involvement, which leads to a larger viewership.

There are similar profiles of potential champions in every event. As in the televised broadcasts of the Olympics, the Hawaiian Ironman Triathlon, and countless other events, human interest stories frame the events so that viewer identification with the athletes—thus a doubly reflective participation, by both audience and athlete—is assured. Bob Pereyra represents Integrity: a hard-working blue-collar type who might attract an audience grounded in the "American values" of rugged individualism, hardy perseverance, and reliance on the rightness of rules (much like Shane).

Chris Edwards, a young in-line skater, is called "'The Air Man,' because he believes in big tricks. [He is] the ultimate pioneer of aggressive in-line."[34] He is also, by his own statements, a "psycho skater," attempting innovative moves that have never even been thought of before; a dedicated and loyal father and husband (the audience sees him holding his infant son); and a youth pastor for the local ministry whose goal is to become a minister. He, like Pereyra, has great integrity, but he represents a more clean-cut, youthful image. With two different profiles, ESPN has managed to target at least two segments (and undoubtedly more) of its demographic market.[35]

The third way ESPN's directors and producers have utilized production techniques is in their segmentation and fragmentation of the actual sporting events. As with the presentation of professional football on television, the choice is up to the directors.[36] Only intermittently does the television audience see an event from start to finish. Instead, viewers are given a taste of the Eco Challenge, then switched to sky surfing, on to sport climbing (bouldering), and so on. The frustration level may mount, but the director's ability to complete events intermittently generally gives the viewer enough purchase to feel almost satisfied.

Choosing to put already taped results in a following segment of ESPN's broadcast of *The eXtreme Games* similarly accomplishes the goal of creating suspense. Viewers are previewed with expectations—teasers—of upcoming events, and this works to increase tension and anticipation, and to heighten the sense of drama for especially undramatic events. Linked with stories of years-long rivalries (such as the barefoot water-skiing rivalry tracing back to the 1970s between Ron "The Raging Bull" Scarpa and Mike Seipel, the first man to invert a barefoot jump), the technique is to find symbolic difference between contestants wherever possible.

And if the "rivalries" do not pan out, it matters little: segments have been completed, the continuing story that is *The eXtreme Games* has been furthered, sponsors have reached an audience. Furthermore, the stories stand alone: to always follow the winner would make the production seem canned. The fact that ESPN has not gotten every winner only adds to the seeming "uncertain outcome"—the apparent verisimilitude—for attentive viewers of the events, and further legitimates *The eXtreme Games* as real sport.

A fourth technique that is used to enhance story segments is the centralized set. By using a set overlooking Fort Adams in Rhode Island, ESPN has sited *The eXtreme Games* in place—but also in history. Canned pieces that "educate" the viewer about the cultural and historical placings of Newport, Fort Adams, and *The eXtreme Games* provide a justifiable linkage with "legitimate" televised sport.

After this justification has taken place (it is continual), the audience touches base with the hosts at the central set. This serves several purposes: it allows for review of events "just" completed, it lends ultimate authority to Suzy Kolber and Chris Fowler, it makes for summative commentary, it provides a stabilizing force, it creates smooth transitions to and from commercials, and it aids in self-promotion of *The eXtreme Games*.

Finally, the fifth technique that producers utilize for segments is the preview. Before each commercial "break," visual "bites," accompanied by supporting narrative, inform viewers about what to expect. Producers seem to think that expectations—and partial to complete fulfillment—are what drive viewer loyalty. This "preview" logic also carries over from show to show, as in the Olympics. Thus the audience is told to tune in for the later show if they expect to see the finals of a specific event.

Constructing the Audience

In both the use of a historical mythos and the use of celebrated, massified sport, the hoped-for outcome by ESPN is a legitimation of the new sport itself; the electronic medium is, not unlike any other medium, an arena replete with power struggles. Grounding sport in something that someone has already done justifies someone's doing it again. Imitation—with only slight homage to innovation—is the dominant model in television. The hoped-for result of the hoped-for outcome, of course, is further massification, which in turn will most likely lead to increased sponsorship and receipts.

Has this imitative strategy been successful for ESPN's *The eXtreme Games*? According to Joan Wilson, ESPN's director of marketing for affiliate sales, *The eXtreme Games*' ability to promote local ad sales has meant that they have slightly exceeded the number of affiliates that the NFL carries on ESPN. They have followed the Olympic and World Cup terminology: "ESPN signed Advil as its 'official pain reliever' and sold six 'gold-level sponsors.'"[37] Those sponsors, whose one or two spots specifically designed for *The eXtreme Games'* coverage continually bombard the viewer, are "Miller Lite Ice, Taco Bell, Mountain Dew, Nike's ACG brand, AT&T, and General Motors."[38]

But even this co-opting by corporations appears paradoxical: in *The eXtreme Games,* the television audience is told that until recently, many of the games were "outlaw" sports. An "outlaw" sport, of course, is one most decidedly *not* sanctioned by a governing body or given sanctions by the established corporate world. Now, with ESPN promoting and selling the sports in a packaged form, the "cutting-edge," "outlaw" nature of the sports themselves becomes problematized.

Thus audiences see a BMX dirt bike rider sneering into the camera before his event, only to state during the post-ride interview, "I thank HYPER for sponsoring me." Another athlete thanks Schwinn Bikes. We discover that yet another athlete, a street luger who is celebrated by his fellows as being a nonconformist, is "president of RAIL, a sanctioning organization for [street] luge." Co-opting by conformity standards is everywhere. It is not unlike the co-opting that has occurred in the art world, of the so-called "cutting edge" artists whose work is seen as avant-garde, yet whose commercialization far exceeds their artistic output.[39]

Of course, introductions to sports events always work on several levels. The audience is made to understand the (produced) theme of the event. The audience is directed to the key points of the "story" to come, told how and what to watch. But the audience is also given access to identity-making with the athletes, with a potential for hero(ine) worship. The producers' ultimate object is not just to tell a good story, but also to create a broad-based market that is receptive to the commodities being sold.

To that end, they produce segments that amplify the audiences' individuality while creating links to a larger collective. This is done intertextually, so that the target audiences identify with four mountain bikers sucking down Mountain Dew, so that viewers listen patiently to an explanation of what makes them unique and what their generation—Generation X—may have to offer.

The target audiences, therefore, are not really unlike any market created by businesspeople, except in kind: they must buy into the vertiginous aspects of these "new" kinds of sports, as offered by ESPN, yet they must remain true to their own lived experiences.[40]

For some—for example, in-line skaters or skateboarders—the experience is similar, but not identical, to that portrayed by ESPN. Thus, subscribers to *InLine: The Skate Magazine* were informed that *The eXtreme Games* has promoted "'aggressive skating more in the public eye. I don't know if that's good or bad. It has created a whole professional class of rock-star-like people.'"[41] There are possibly some good outcomes from increased exposure, this magazine for in-line aficionados seems to say, but with growth comes a certain loss of innocence. The skateboarders' reaction to *The eXtreme Games* (as evidenced in a less mainstream magazine, *Thrasher*) was less ambivalent. The title says it all: "For Love or Money? Extreme Showcase Predictably Network."[42] But many other viewers' lived experiences are simply not even close to duplicates of *The eXtreme Games'* athletes' experience. So their ideal lived experiences are reconstructed, reconstituted seamlessly for their visual consumption.

Throughout the ESPN-produced *eXtreme Games,* the use of intermittent "teases," drawing from a kind of folk behavioralism,[43] creates a reward system of flashing lights and color, jolting sound, and satisfying recognition of the intersections of popular culture for the attentive viewer. This "MTV look" shapes some viewers' loyalty just as the action at Las Vegas might shape the fixated gambler. It serves to create a divide between people by demonstrating difference—for example, generational difference—at the same time that it protests their similarity. There is diversity, but there is also power, agency, and strength in being part of a group.

The "MTV look" is a strategy that segments the audience, parcels them out into neat demographic units, while insisting on their community. The object, of course, is to create a larger audience, reaching parts of each potential viewer. And the rhetoric of the show—that is, the narrative of the anchors and reporters, the visuals of what is portrayed—reinforces this seeming paradox: witness Chris Fowler, who says of the sport events to be shown, "We're not going to treat them like music videos." But that is exactly what ESPN has done, and in so doing, they have created a new, mutated sport form, a televisual, simulated sport form that is just as highly fragmented and segmented as many music videos. The non-linearity of the sports, the use of techniques that tell stories but tell them in chunky segments, assumes reader involvement. Thus these techniques ensure audience co-opting and participation.

EIGHT | **Sport as Postmodern Tourism**

Warp Speed in Barcelona (Olympism, Ideology, and Experience)

> In the world culture of the past there is much more irony, a form of reduced laughter, than our ear can catch.
>
> —Mikhail Bakhtin, *Rabelais and His World*

The Olympic Games have evolved into more than sport.[1] The Games themselves are a wonderful example of Umberto Eco's hyperreality, of an instance in which racial macro-values are demoniacally skewed, one in which the permutations upon a common theme exceed the original intent of the theme itself. Discourse surrounding the Olympics may be scholarly, popular, or private, and discourse in each of these areas may collude with itself to produce textual permutations working upon the (concrete) permutations within the Games. To catch and demystify any experience of the Olympics, then, it is not always sufficient to unravel the threads of scholarly, popular, and private discourse;[2] rather, one must notice the twistings and interrelationships between such discourses and view experience in its context and totality. That, then, is the first purpose of this chapter: to examine assumptions and constructions of and in sport, in this case the 1992 Summer Olympics in Barcelona, Spain. Adjunct aims are to propose that "sport tourism" falls within the "tours of desire" rubric suggested by Edward Bruner;[3] to examine evidence of the concept of "kitschman" as tourist,[4] a collector of experience, souvenirs, photographs, and as a growth industry at the Olympics; to locate and examine the sport tourist/tour operator/host country/sport discourse with the Olympic experience; and to demonstrate attempts at a Bakhtinian upheaval and reversal in some Olympic spectators' experience.

Since I am examining my singular experience prior to, at, and after the Olympics as a location for travel discourse, I intend to move in and out of those scholarly, private, and public discourses at will (sometimes abruptly), and to let the reader's interaction with my text become a part of its making. This text, then, is a self-conscious construction, not the original experience but a simulacrum of that experience: therefore, to successfully enwrap the reader in an approximation of my experience, I must create verisimilitude at several levels. One is a sensory level (Does it *feel* real?); another is an experiential level (*Could* this have happened?); yet another is a so-called objective level (Is this what really happened?). Since I am merely one of many "firsthand" experiencers of the 1992 Barcelona Olympics, my experience, while it "really happened," could, of course, never be replicated. So it may serve metonymically, as a work of fiction does, its particularity perhaps leading to more understanding and insight than might any generalizations.

I spent much of the summer of 1992 in Alaska, trying to make money at a salmon cannery, sleeping in a tent pitched on ground made uneven by pillaging gold miners, reminding myself of the scene in *Paint Your Wagon* in which rain is falling in sheets and the men—they were all men, it seemed—are singing a mournful "They Call the Wind Mariah," looking distracted and lonely. The reds never ran full tilt while I was in Alaska, but I did manage to read *The Written Suburb* and Dean MacCannell's *The Tourist*. The two or three times we worked, I enjoyed slinging huge frozen decapitated salmon into plastic bags bound for Japan, or binding fifty-pound boxes of them with an automatic strapper. It was hard work, but a certain dazed rhythm took over the one day we worked for nine hours.

My two children and then-wife, expecting money from me to last through the summer (as any migrant worker's family wishes), never saw any money. In fact, I earned only about seventy-five dollars over five weeks, and I knew I would not be able to sustain my family, much less live comfortably in Barcelona at the Olympics. The breathtaking views of snowcapped mountain ranges, the steam issuing from Mount Redoubt, the moose traipsing across someone's front lawn, the eagles as plentiful as seagulls on Homer Spit—it all began to look bleak to me.

I hitched to soup kitchens in Kenai and Soldotna, Alaska, and gratefully ate with hundreds of other stranded college students. I began to understand—in my gut as well as my brain—a distinction between the terms "slumming it" and "being homeless." As Barbara Kirshenblatt-Gimblett writes, "Slumming, like tourism more generally, takes the spectator to the site, and . . . whole territories become extended ethnographic theme parks."[5] There is the element of "at play" involved, but there is more to it. Slumming is privilege, it is recourse, it requires both the hope and the memory of a better time, and the assurance that one, while playing at being the "other," may safely reinstall oneself into a former position of privilege at any time. It is choice. Being homeless, on the other hand, is dependency, it is powerlessness, it requires both despair (depending upon, perhaps, the dissonance between a former state and one's current life) and a nihilistic existentialism, and the assurance that one's life is worthless, static, and predetermined. It is circumstance.[6]

In some ways, this distinction between slumming and being homeless is, ironically, parallel to the classical ethnographic distinction between tourists and natives. Yet this pat set of bipolarities probably does not exist, if only because homeless people (read "natives") have learned adaptations and coping mechanisms that accord them some privilege. Though their positioning is weak, and they lack a full set of dominantly hegemonic options from which to operate, they are not totally powerless. As bell hooks puts it,

> Understanding marginality as position and place of resistance is crucial for oppressed, exploited, colonized people. If we only view the margin as sign marking the despair, a deep nihilism penetrates in a destructive way the very ground of our being. It is there in that space of collective despair that one's creativity, one's imagination is at risk, there that one's mind is fully colonized, there that the freedom one longs for is lost. . . . I want to say that these margins have been both sites of repression and sites of resistance.[7]

Thus, natives, as well as the homeless, are, like hooks, of the margins and yet aware of the center. And the very fact of their positionings creates spaces for resistance—without their positionings, there would be no need (or desire) for resistance. Contrarily, tourists and those who are slumming it may be less aware of, or unaffected by, the margins—they have only a temporary taste of the need for resistance.

Fortunately for me, my credit cards allowed me to fly home, to manage flights to and from Spain, to generate some cash, which I needed for housing and food in Europe. I had eaten Top Ramen and pork and beans in the pot I purchased for three dollars at the secondhand store in Kenai, Alaska; scrounged paper coffee cups, extra toilet paper and paper towels, and plastic spoons and forks from Carr's Supermarket; lifted wooden pallets for a tent base, and pocketed free condiments whenever possible; earned five dollars witnessing a marriage between two strangers, Chip and Lisa, cannery workers from Minneapolis; hitchhiked everywhere, usually walking between three and ten miles a day in my calf-high rubber cannery worker's boots; filled up on a ninety-nine-cent loaf of French wheat bread, which usually lasted three days before I finished it or mold set in; waxed the seams of my tent with a candle to prevent it from leaking during the night; swatted mosquitoes or bathed myself in the fire's wood smoke to deter them; and slept in a sleeping bag on an Alaskan

Airlines mini-pillow. In my whole time—five weeks—in Alaska, I paid three dollars each of three times to get a hot, soapy shower, with a bath towel supplied. Returning to Champaign, I felt lucky.

Going on to Europe (the flight already paid for, but with little cash), I was apprehensive, but up to the task, whatever it might be. I found myself somewhere between "homeless" and "slumming," located somewhere between ethnographer and package tourist. Since I was going to the Olympics—which some say is the penultimate sporting event in the world—I might more nearly approach what Mayor Frank Fasi of Honolulu termed a "peasant in Paradise."[8]

I was a participant-observer, I told myself, and these were my circumstances: my flights to and from Paris were paid for; my Olympic venue tickets, from Olson Travelworld, were in hand; I would have to arrange my train from Paris to Barcelona and, after the Olympics, back; I had spoken to two fellows from Chicago about housing in Barcelona, and would meet them there, giving them five hundred dollars for six nights of lodging in central Barcelona.

Food? Money? Ability to speak French, Spanish, or Catalan? I managed to get an advance on my over-the-limit credit card for the lodging and some extra cash. It was not going to be a luxury vacation, but I would be able to "be there" and take in my brand of the tastes and sights and smells and sounds of the Olympic experience, whatever that became. And certainly, most Olympic tourists were just that, tourists. It would be an international setting, and everyone would be speaking different languages. (In fact, announcements at the Olympic venues were in Spanish, Catalan, French, and English.) The Spanish themselves, I gathered from an Olympic preview article in *Sports Illustrated*,[9] were going to be tourists in Catalonia. I wondered if part of a Texas swim team family's preparation for the Olympics was learning to speak Catalan. I doubted it. I had grown up in California, taken a little Spanish in elementary school, and recently listened to a language tape of Spanish. I would manage, as any tourist might. And in an event of such "sheer enormity,"[10] I, the participant-observer as co-actor, would cause scarcely a ripple in the fabric of the 1992 Barcelona Olympics.[11]

Besides, for the purposes of this text, I wasn't any more or less interested in the Spanish or Catalonian culture than a sport tourist would be. According to Bruner, many types of tourism are "tours of desire and tell us more about our society than about the society to be visited."[12] Though he lists many recent types of tour, he fails to mention the sport tour as a "tour of desire," though it might, in fact, be more buried in the "deepest recesses of the Western imagination" than so-called sex tours, for example.[13]

As a sport tourist participant-observer, I was concerned with the experience of and for the loosely aligned "package" tourist[14]—not a tourist who might be considered, in Crick's terms, to "exhibit a vast range of motivations" (since viewing sport was the primary goal for most Olympic travelers[15]—at least during the two weeks of the Olympics), but rather a tourist whose motivations were nebulously focused on the Olympics, yet "clearly fuzzy or overlapping."[16] However, my interest in the Olympic Games as sport was subservient only to my interest in the overall experience as a study, with Spain and sport serving to contextualize this experience. I went to the Olympics with as much of a critical attitude toward it as I could muster. Though Barbara Babcock wrote of the Southwest, her words could as easily be applied to the Olympics: "I wonder why we have not looked more critically than we have at the economics, the technologies, and the politics of inventing this region. Perhaps it is because we are all, scholars and shopkeepers alike, *caught up in it, seduced, co-opted* into selling the Southwest or, in some cases, into being sold."[17]

While I am certain that Catalonia and Barcelona, as region and city respectively, were variously (re)invented for the Olympics by,[18] among others, the media, I am more concerned with the invention, or "selection," of the "region" of the Olympics per se. The sense of "authenticity" that Barcelona, the IOC, and all the Olympic players create is a part of a performance, not terribly unlike the performances of Balinese dancers for tourists,[19] the performances of sex workers for varying audiences,[20] or the "house music" performances of queer nationals for themselves and others.[21] Audience matters. And the audience's views of the "authenticity" of things sporting unalterably change how such sport is presented. But, of course, the pretense that we, as audience, are unseen or unheard, with little impact, is a necessary pretense so that sport "tourists" can feel that what they are seeing is truly "authentic."

I contend that, much as our re-invented tangible spaces or movements are keyed into geographic locales (e.g., Barbara Babcock's Southwest, and the Scottish Highlands and Wales),[22] we ("scholars and shopkeepers alike") passively participate in a selection and, to the extent that it is tacitly accepted, invention of a non-critical Olympic (and, more generally, sport) movement.

Probably because of an interweaving of this Olympic and self-"seduction," I was made to feel that this was a "one of a kind" experience: Olson Travelworld previewing the experience for me in its slick litho brochures; VISA's advertisements, including a "U.S. Olympic Commemorative Book" at a "special pre-publication price of $34.95 (reg. price $49.50)," in which I was urged to "reserve [my] Olympic memories now" and to "collect the memories of Olympic swimming, boxing, volleyball and more";[23] the local electronic and written news media whetting my interest with human interest and profile pieces of possible Olympians, places to stay, things to do; in May of 1992, WILL-TV, Urbana's local PBS affiliate, running a show entitled *Travels* dealing with Barcelona; NBC's Triplecast "infomercials," standard fare on Saturdays during the spring; the Olympic Trials, in various sports, dominating sports "news" coverage as well as prime sporting chunks on television (for example, the women's and men's gymnastics, swimming, and track and field); in Alaska, the scores and antics of the "Dream Team," playing in the Tournament of Americas; weekly and monthly popular magazines' "timely" articles and advertising; a profile piece on Frank Krasnowski of Urbana, Illinois, a self-styled Olympic Games pin collector with more than fifteen hundred Olympic pins.[24]

Seemingly everywhere, this Olympic rhetoric, through the sheer enormity of its omnipresence, engulfs the senses. Then, in a fitting parody of itself, the rhetoric turns back to simplicity, to ideology. The lead article in the San Francisco *Chronicle*'s "Sporting Green" for July 23, 1992, was titled "Olympics: A Small World":

> The 1992 Summer Games will be my fifth Olympics, and there are two things I've noticed about them: They are smaller than you might think, and people cry there.[25]

Or, as one syndicated writer summed it up, admitting to the rhetoric yet also admitting to a sense of hope,

> You can see pieces of the new world, changing before your eyes, this fort-night, in Barcelona and on NBC. . . . The Olympics are the medium. . . . There you have it: global trade, market economics, democracy, pluralism, technology, competitiveness. It is not a bad recipe for peace and prosperity, which may be just around the corner.[26]

Additionally, Randy Travis and Natalie Cole, in a Coca-Cola commercial on NBC, intone,

> Randy Travis: Because while we all have different cultures and traditions, underneath it all—
> Natalie Cole: —you know, we're all pretty much the same: we all celebrate the Olympic spirit.[27]

Such unchallenged "Olympic ideology," elided into "melting pot" theories, reintegration of the individual, and the modern myth that through hard work (where better shown in microcosm than in sport?) one can achieve anything: these glosses of possible positive aspects of the Olympic spirit or movement do not account for the conflictual and oppositional forces that are also at work. Well documented is the gross use of the Olympics for political advancement.[28] But less grand attempts can be made. There are two pages of "advertisement" in *Time* magazine: the first page contains a black dot (marked "Barcelona") within a solid yellow field, surrounded by a maplike longitude and latitude border, with "IN WHICH COUNTRY WOULD YOU PLACE THIS POINT?" at the bottom of the page. Turn the page: "IN CATALONIA, OF COURSE." The text and advertisement, purported to be sponsored by "Generalitat de Catalunya/

Autonomous Government of Catalonia," begins, "This is where Barcelona is, in Catalonia, a country in Spain with its own culture, language and identity."[29] *A country in Spain.*

All of this—all of my sports and cultural, personal and public, knowledge and feelings and emotions and experiences—shaped my attitudes toward the 1992 Games. And when I removed myself to the confines of Alaska, my family and friends who knew I was going to the Olympics reminded me of, for example, the "Dream Team's" prodigiousness, or of this being Magic Johnson's last time in uniform (a foreshadowed nostalgia which has become, in an interesting bit of hypernostalgia, no longer an issue), or of the fact that Reebok's "much publicized $25 million advertising campaign" surrounding the drama between Dave Johnson and Dan O'Brien had collapsed when O'Brien failed to qualify for the U.S. Olympic decathlon team.[30] In that sense, I found myself anticipating, as any eager tourist might, retelling my story.

That the experience was, to a degree, pre-packaged for my consumption did not matter much to the sport tourist in me. For my unique story of having gone to the 1992 Barcelona Olympics may be my only resistance to the vulgar sameness that Nelson Graburn, following Lévi-Strauss, says permeates contemporary society. It could be my personal demand for "sources of observable difference" between myself and others, between here and there. And, like many who went to the Olympics (and the Super Bowl; and youngsters and some adults who attend the live performances of *The American Gladiators* and the World Wrestling Federation, and the players of paintball and *The eXtreme Games* who travel to exoticized locales to participate and watch), I have, with much media prompting, constructed and "demand[ed] that [the site] be significantly different from the homeland, for without any differences why would one bother to travel."[31]

Though a self-conscious criticality delineates me from many of the sport tourists at the Olympics,[32] tourists may indeed be critical thinkers. As Bruner has stated, "Tourists are not dupes, and they realize that the native performances on their tour itinerary are constructions for a foreign audience."[33] But the tour of which Bruner speaks is of East Africa, and explicitly (and, some would say, blatantly) a construction; those same tourists might readily accept constructions of sport at home and abroad as "authentic." Such sport tourists are less likely to see sport as constructed, less likely to critically examine such a quotidian event as sport.[34] Sport has become naturalized to them. Thus it is important to notice the constructed nature of international (and national) sporting milieus, if only because through knowledge power may evolve.

How this construction occurs, of course, is a major question. It is both insidious and blatant, but certainly constant, beginning before you get to Barcelona, ongoing while you are there, and echoing after the Olympics is over.

And it is assumed as a natural state: "The Olympics have always been a part of my life." Much like a good short story, my life, in terms of the Olympics, began *in media res*. This genealogy, however, of the coincidence of a life and the life of the Olympics becomes more obvious when the 1992 Barcelona Olympics is taken as a case study of a particular moment for a particular individual.

▼ ▼ ▼ ▼

With the memory of Alaska still fresh in my mind, I board Amtrak's *City of New Orleans* for Chicago. It is 4:30 a.m. Kenai time, and the rhythmicity of the train lulls me to sleep. I become disjointed, unsure of where to go from Union Station to O'Hare Airport. I wonder, "How can I find my way around in Paris or Barcelona when I can't even get to O'Hare—and it's in English?" I finally ask (my then-wife says that I, like "all men," refuse to ask directions when I'm lost) at the Amtrak information booth, and board the West/Northwest subway/el. Again, another rougher kind of clickety-clack. We remain underground for miles, then emerge to elevated status. There is graffiti everywhere on this overcast, foggy day: "RLM" in plain white letters on a black background; "Woozy" spelled out in balloon-shaped letters. And below, at street level, a multicolored mural of some kids following an important leader decorates the underpass. Institutionalized or not, the impulse to make a mark, or to decorate or embellish surroundings, is present.

I march to the British Airways terminal. I wait for six hours (a wonderful foreshadowing—so-called "economic" travel requires waiting around, unlike more expensive travel, in which timetables ensure an approximation of Americans' propensity for time),[35] then board my flight. What a contrast in the view: from the graffiti-ed Chicago Transit Authority train, with no one looking you directly in the eye, with admonitions delivered coarsely from the conductor to "step back from the exit doors" and signs warning of imprisonment if anyone "assaults" anyone else on the train—to the British Empire's national airline.

As we board, American accents direct our movements. In the tunnel to the plane, several Asians and Easterners profess their innocence—about what? About taking out more than $10,000 American. U.S. Customs agents pull them aside. But on board the bulbous 747, everything changes. We hear a cultured Britspeak. As we sit delayed at the gate waiting for, as our British Airways captain tells us, "one errant passenger who we're scouring the airport to find," we are served "complimentary" orange juice and handed printed menus for the evening meal: for the main course, "Grilled salmon in basil and lemon sauce/Accompanied by mange tout, and new parsley potatoes." Salmon! Silverware, and warm fragrant cloths to exorcise any errant droplets or residual stickiness of the orange juice. So civilized, and so comforting. Chuckling over the irony of salmon, I listen to Richard Strauss's *Don Juan* performed by the

Vienna Philharmonic and Brahms's *Symphony No. 2 in D* by the London Phil-harmonic, and read in British Airways' "in-flight" magazine, *Highlife,* articles about the value and tradition of Olympic medals; about the limitations of the sports in the Olympics; about sports stars' clothing; about sailing, with references to Barcelona; about sports films starting with Leni Riefenstahl's *Olympia 36.*

I even peruse advertisements that allude to Spain, Expo '92, or the Olym-pics. Rank Xerox™ runs an ad pertaining to Expo '92 in Sevilla, as does Fuji Film; there is an article on Spain's wines; there are the nearly subliminal "Official Sponsor" ads: Budget Rent-a-Car sponsors the "1992 British Olympic Team"; Panasonic is a "Worldwide sponsor 1992 Olympic Games"; there is even an advertisement for "Heathrow BMW" (p. 73) which states, "Paris, Rome, Munich, Barcelona. Where were you when your car was last serviced?" Of course, these are cities in Europe; but they are also former Olympic host cities—ending with the current travel destination for the Olympic tourist. The tie-ins to the Olympics often would be hard to notice, would seem natural, if not for the advertisements' "British-ness" and, for me at least, the slight skew of "otherness."

Somehow, embarrassed in France at my inability to communicate and halt-ingly consulting my *Fodor's 92* guide to Paris for its infantile French vocabulary, I get on the correct Metro to Paris, where I overhear "The 'Dream Team' is just for national pride. They'll win it, show the rest of the world, and it'll go back to being a college team." They are young and American, probably college kids, speaking too loudly while three "Metro musicians" (a guitarist, female vocalist, and tambourine/percussionist) sing Normanized Beatles tunes, and I remain silent.

When the Other looks identical to the self, but with only slightly skewed features (such as language), the disorientation is twofold: first as a figurational altered mirror image that distorts the sense of self; second as the realization sinks in that this other person thinks, speaks, and acts (and has thought, spoken, and acted) independent of the self. Some choose to react to this disjuncture by reinforcing the surety of the self (e.g., talk louder, speak more slowly); others (like me, usually) become more shy, and call it "observing." (Of course, these young Americans are Others to me as well. In fact, the very idea of an other is redundant: self is singular, and while we may identify with others of like sensibilities, they are still others.)

I sit on the tile floor at the Gare d'Austerlitz. It is a Friday, a bustling afternoon, and I wait for the possibility of getting a second-class reservation filled at 9:30 P.M. At the ticket counter I said, "Par-lay vouz ahng-glay?" meeting with mixed shrugs, a little help. I felt a fool, asking them to speak *my* language in their country. It is as if I am learning to ski, and four- and five year-olds constantly, expertly, spray snow on me as I struggle to get up after another fall on the bunny hill. I've been homeless (Alaska), unemployed (Alaska, home, here), and illiterate (France, and probably Spain, too). Travel can be so humbling. (I hear Victor Turner's whisper in my ear, *The humbling, my boy, is just the beginning. You expect change, growth, understanding? First, the liminal period. Shake 'em up.* Of course, Victor Turner is with me only in my thoughts, to bolster my sense of self mired in insecurities. *Communitas, communitas, to insure you experience communitas,* he chants.)[36]

There also exists, I suppose, a certain amount of age-ism when one is traveling as I am. College kids from America and England are here in great profusion, obviously having "linked up" (I regard Michener's *Caravans*) with one another in a foreign land. "The group" has practical advantages. If one wants to go buy *au pain* or *café au lait,* one can leave a backpack with the group. If one is reticent to discover or explore, the group pulls him or her along. This I found in Alaska, but there my link to the group was my twenty-four-year-old brother-in-law. Since I am forty-one, my status (college student, but older, older but not financially able to kick up into a higher socio-economic level) is paradoxical.

I am sure I look nonplussed as I watch the people shuttle around. I finally get up, huge backpack strapped on, and hike ("stroll" is not the word) up the Seine toward Notre Dame. It is the Left Bank, and there are couples who are not ashamed to fulfill my traveler's (voyeur's) fantasy. Bodies interlocked, they are all over one another; I see a couple disappear into a parked double-decker bus that is closed for business, but normally serves as a tourist diner. They emerge on the second level of the bus, and immediately their silhouettes become horizontal upon a table. I march on.

I finally get on the train, track 22, bound for Barcelona at 1925. A guy associated with a French international aid mission helps me to occupy two seats on a non-smoking, air-conditioned car with reclining seats. He takes over two seats across the aisle. It is dark outside, and I am tired. But I cannot sleep, because there is a young French couple in the seats behind me, making love all night.

We switch trains at the Spanish border. I am disappointed that customs agents at Heathrow and Charles de Gaulle airports, and now in Spain, have not stamped my passport. I realize it is a marker of authenticity, of "having been there," no less than a photograph or souvenir. It has a "Heathrow" stamp from 1986, "Australia," "New Zealand," and "Fiji," but no France or Spain.

Saturday night, July 25. The opening ceremonies. I feel like Dan Rose, writing notes after having three beers. The Aussie support group invited me (actually two guys I've been hanging out with invited me) to watch the opening ceremonies with them on the "telly" at their base. (I'm also staying here one night—$30 U.S.—since I cannot get sleep in my co-rented apartment in Barcelona yet.) It's a former hospital, high up in the hills north of Barcelona. One guy said, "If they want to watch in person, the athletes have to pay as well. Otherwise, athletes would fill up the stands," and I thought, "Why not?"

At first I felt bad, not getting tickets to the prestigious opening ceremonies; Olson Travelworld said they were sold out. I called Olson, in Santa Monica, and spoke to a woman who told me that I could probably get scalped tickets for "oh, maybe fifteen hundred or so." Much like the Super Bowl, much of the Olympics is intended for conspicuous consumption—for visiting dignitaries, other entertainers including (rich) athletes, and corporations (generally as perks or incentives to employees). I later saw several luxury cruise liners, with impressive security, docked just off the Moll Bosch i Alsina.

I decide to watch the opening ceremonies on television. I can imagine myself wandering around Barcelona, getting lost, missing even the televised equivalent of the experience, and having nothing. Besides, I rationalize, the majority of people in the world are doing as I am doing—but not with a group of drunken (mostly older and affluent) Australians. My brother Jim is watching on KRON-TV in the San Francisco area, taping the show for me.

I occasionally feel defensive, as if this experience is not authentic enough, yet quickly realize that the issue of authenticity is absurd: of course watching television and drinking Spanish, American, and Australian beer with a group of Australians[37] in a renovated hospital in northern Barcelona is authentic, just as watching the opening ceremonies on a wide-screen monitor in Estadi Olimpic while the opening ceremonies unfold is authentic. What we do is authentic to our experience; it is the recollection of it (to ourselves or others) that impoverishes or sustains the experience.[38] It is the *meanings* we give to gifts that make them memorable; so too with experience.[39]

But an exchange between Bob Costas and Dick Enberg during the "fashion show" segment of the opening ceremonies (which is specific to this moment but also serves to represent all of the texture surrounding large commercialized and commodified sporting events)[40] reinforces and molds our perceptions of what we see:

> Costas: We are told, Dick, that the costumes do not necessarily signify anything. But they sure look good. . . .
> Enberg: Well, they're not related to any Olympic tradition or custom. This is just simply a fashion show to showcase, uh, Barcelona's top fashion designers.

Of course, Olympic fashion shows may become an invented (or, more to the point, selected) tradition for future Olympic opening ceremonies.[41] However, "signification," "tradition," and "custom," all important nouns used by Costas and Enberg, are juxtaposed with the implied negations and diminutive modifiers "But they sure look good" and "This is just simply."

I resist saying, as everyone stills to begin actually concentrating on the TV during the operatic singing, that it appears that Jaume Aragall, Plácido Domingo, Teresa Berganza, Montserrat Caballe, Joan Pons, and José Carreras are lip-synching. Their gestures are grand, theatrical, staged, and operatic. They wear no microphones, and there is little pretense—except good approximations of lip-synching—that what they are singing is authentic or genuine, in the sense of "live."[42] Spanish TV has fewer commercials, the connotation of things is not apparent to a non-Spanish speaking viewer, and still, the emotion is best conveyed by the art form of music. Twenty-odd people in our little basement room cheer, and genuinely seem to enjoy the moment ("That Olympic flag's a full kilometer long!" said one, exaggerating by only a little).

Sunday, July 26. Swimming at Piscines Bernat Picornell. Hot, hot, hot. Brazilians singing and playing drums and trumpets, M & M sponsorship, Coca Cola, souvenirs everywhere. Jenny Thompson breaks the Olympic record in the 100 free, then loses to a Chinese swimmer in the finals. On the ride down into Barcelona on the national train,[43] I find out that Sydney is trying to get the 2000 Games, but the Aussies say that Beijing is a shoe-in: "Ah, they've a lock on it, mate. They don't get it for the Commonwealth Games, they threaten to pull out. They've got so many people, it works." But I notice that the "Sydney 2000" campaign has taken out a full-color two page advertisement, with their logo prominent, in the "Official Souvenir Program: Games of the XXV Olympiad." My soon-to-be roommate, Cole, says the same thing: in fact, at Seville they were "talking it up at their booth." Politicking and bidding for an Olympics occurs at least eight years ahead of the actual event.

There is a lot of dead time, even between the preliminary heats. There is a lot of ceremony, as the officials march in and out of each venue with the Olympic theme blaring over the loudspeakers; the athletes are paraded in by Spanish hosts and hostesses, who are dressed in bright green or blue; Nelson Mandela is announced as being at the swimming prelims, and he stands and waves as the crowd politely applauds.

A guy sitting next to me, an American, complains about the seats we have at swimming (almost to the top, in the back section, but with a cross-view of the fifty-meter pool), seeing as they are in the "middle price range." He says, "I think the only way you can get tickets to the Finals is if you take the complete tour package from Olson Travel. They even wrote, 'Chances are 90% you can get any seat you want.' The tour package and travel agent shouldn't go through the same company."

Back at the apartment, I finally meet Cole and Matt, the two men from Chicago who advertised on an electronic billboard for a third roommate for the first week of the Olympics. Back in March I called Cole, and learned that he had gone to the Seoul Olympics in 1988. He said, "I just wrote away to the Korean yogwans—they wanted five hundred dollars a night for the Hilton in Seoul—and we got a room for twenty-one dollars a night. I think it was a whorehouse." So over the telephone, I agreed to spend five hundred dollars for the week in Barcelona. Now I give the money to Cole, who states that I am "really not supposed to be here."

That afternoon we watch on Spanish television as the "Dream Team" (that and the players' names are all we can understand) beats Angola. As we watch the U.S. team play on Canal Olimpic on a color TV in an apartment in Barcelona, Spain, while the actual game is going on less than fifteen miles away, Cole says, "I mean, I want to see this, too. It's something to say you've seen. It's the Dream Team." Later he states, "I'll get my picture taken at the Eiffel Tower, the Arc de Triomphe, so I can show that I've been to Paris. That way I can show that my trip has been successful. I don't even need to go inside, just get my picture taken outside." (Many do this, for example, at Gaudi's Sagrada Familia in Barcelona—refusing to pay the entrance fee to see "an inside that is empty.")

Cole, who rarely lacks an opinion, disagrees with the man from Texas about the coincidence between the tour package and good seats: "I went to Seoul and here—I got everything I wanted and haven't taken the tour yet. You just have to order at the earliest possible time."

A striking feature of contemporary sporting venues seems to be their commercial aspect, as their officials seek to authenticate them as purely sport. Closely tied in to this is the selling of mass products for sport tourists' consumption (and, of course, the souvenir). The Olympics, long considered a bastion of amateurism and purity in sport (and therefore, the ideology goes, a "purer" form of sport than is found anywhere else), are not immune to many of the same marketing schemes used by the World Wrestling Federation, *The American Gladiators,* ESPN, and the National Football League. Olympic memories quickly sold for mass consumption at prominent yellow booths set up inside any of the venues include consumables: Coca-Cola, Mars, Frigo, Campofria, Damm, and Danone. The take-home souvenirs are complete with a 3" x 5" "Certificado," the authenticating certificate, which states in three languages, "This Certifies that this Item was Purchased at the 1992 Barcelona Olympic Games" and has a Joan Miró–like Barcelona '92 drawing and a caricature of Cobi, the Barcelona Olympics symbol. These certificates accompany such items as Cobi-stamped T-shirts, visors, postcards, stickers, balls, lighters, ashtrays, keyrings, pins, mugs, spoons, waistpacks, sets of six glasses, various stuffed Cobis, sweatshirts, plastic and metal watches, polo shirts, backpacks, sports bags, traveling bags, and sunglasses (Ray-Ban, with a free kite emblazoned with the words "Ray-Ban™" and the Olympic rings included with each purchase). I saw no action-figure dolls or shot glasses, but there were glow-in-the-dark tubes sold.

Monday, July 27. Boxing at Pavelló Club Joventut Badalona. The "staging" of this event is more cynical than the staging of the World Wrestling Federation: one main camera at ringside, with three of the four sides of the ring totally taken over by the press—photo, electronic, and print media. In front of the camera, much like a Hollywood talk-show set, eight rows of white seats rise, half of which (fewer than four hundred seats) are unoccupied, apparently reserved for some sort of Olympic-aligned dignitaries.

The seats are mostly vacant, so I wander over to the edge of the press area. There is another American sitting four rows above me, who tells me, "I rode my bike down here to the venues. I'm stationed in Frankfurt. I lucked out and got a flat in the Gothic section of Barcelona as soon as I got here for twenty-seven bucks a night. It's wild." He rubs his eyes. "The Ramblas is going till three, four in the morning. Crazy. But I wouldn't miss this. This and weightlifting. That's it for me."

The boxing—another in a series of preliminaries—is between people I have very little interest in, but the crowd is very partisan. Two men in front of me, from Nigeria, exult or recoil with each punch thrown, and get me cheering for their fighter. They are loud, oblivious to the fact that their support seems in a vacuum. In fact, many of the other spectators look at the three of us as if we are inappropriately intense. After all, these are merely qualifying rounds, and the match-ups lack the drama that should come in later fights. For interest, even among the fight fans, there is a pecking order.

I am fascinated by the "Dream Team" phenomenon. Marketing-driven, it is western sport at its most fascinating—no dramatic metaphor, yet a morbid fascination with the process and outcome of each game, even in (especially in) Spain. But no one questions whether it is "sport." And yet just about everyone agrees that the outcome is a foregone conclusion. I hear one man telling another (whenever English is spoken, I feel an unjustified kinship), "The Angolans were asking Magic and Michael Jordan for their autographs *during* the game!"

This night, I drink three expensive—and powerful—Spanish beers, watching swimming finals at an outdoor "mall" on a giant-screen television. It is at the base of Montjuïc, where all the track and swimming events are held. I bought eight event tickets and have received two more from Cole and Matt, who I think feel guilty for fleecing me on the cost of the apartment. Ten events is a lot more than some people here have, yet I find myself watching television a great deal of the time.

Later, I wander to Font de Montjuïc, below Palau Nacional, where the *Chariots of Fire* theme screams over a loudspeaker system as huge (at least fifty feet high) cascades of water dance, lit by yellow, salmon, orange, red, green, and blue lights. One elderly lady, seeing that I am enraptured, says, "Hove ami fiesta." She is sitting with a man and a woman while the martial music (Stravinsky, *Barcelona*) blares. The frail old man makes kissing gestures to say that it moves him deeply, and I smile back, agreeing. There are literally thousands of people sitting and milling around. It is 11:30 P.M.

The privileged aspect of this extravaganza is continually driven home to me. There is a knife and fork symbol outside a pavilion, the door to which reads "Acreditats Acreditados Accrédités Accreditation Holders" only. The milling throngs are parted by "Cuerpo Nacional de Policia" for specially marked ("Olympic Car Barcelona") white cars to get through to the Palau Nacional.[44]

Music comes from the Estadi Olimpic up the hill, so groups of people run to the gates and stand watching the gigantic-screen stadium "TV" of people practicing in the empty stadium! Literally hundreds stand outside a barred gate, some even videotaping the practice, under the glow of the Olympic flame, while national anthems play, "The Star-Spangled Banner" among them. Obviously at 2330 a rehearsal for something upcoming, but the people are transfixed. Everyone gasps, or takes pictures of the Olympic flame.

At the Speedo Shop above the Palau Nacional, I meet an American bumming through Europe who has just landed this job. "It's okay, you get to meet a lot of people. I was lucky, really, to just get this job today. They needed someone who spoke English," he says, handing me a dozen Speedo stickers. "I miss English, in a way."

Riding back on the Metro, I meet a pair of Canadian high school girls, sisters, their faces painted in bold crimson and white maple leafs in support of their country. Everywhere I look, sport tourists have engraved their national identity on their person somehow: on their faces, in the designer or painted or embossed or silk-screened clothing they wear. For example, the quick identifiers of U.S. tourists are their "USA" baseball caps with "AT&T and Olson Travelworld, Ltd." inscribed on the back, or their reference to the "Traveler's Companion" supplied by Olson Travelworld.

Tuesday, July 28. It is amazingly hot and stuffy at the Piscina de Montjuïc, the pools designed for some of the water polo and all of the diving events. I sit, working on my tan, at least seventy-five meters away from the diving events. During warm-ups, I wandered over next to the diving well and filmed the layout, some of the divers, the vast empty seats that are fitted for the world press.

I trek back to my seat, and find that the area is filled with a block of Americans. The woman seated next to me, a policewoman from the Chicago area in her late twenties, says, "We figured if we wanted to *see*, we would've stayed at home in front of the tube. Here, you get the atmosphere." She informs me that she and a friend are staying in a youth hostel off the Ramblas and near the Columbus statue—a pretty good location, since the Metro is extremely efficient—for twenty-five dollars a night. I do not tell her how much I am paying for the week.

A guy seated below us, a history teacher from San Diego, answers, "I heard seats at swimming finals were going for a hundred and fifty, and any of the Dream Team for three thousand! This isn't so bad." He has two dozen flags of different countries in a canvas bag at his feet. Every time a diver is announced (this is men's three-meter springboard preliminary round), this man pulls out the flag of the diver's country and waves it. "I might get on television!" he laughs. We all cheer for everyone as well, hoping to have our faces projected to an Italian, German, Russian, British, or Gambian audience at home. At this distance, being a spectator is getting to know other people, but the catch is that, for most of us (the ones I get to "know"), that means we all must speak English and share some semblance of cultural heritage.

The policewoman and I walk out of the diving together, to meet her friend and get stamps and a cash advance on her VISA card. The three of us run into Rob, an Aussie who says he designs and builds houses, and whom they know from the youth hostel. He has an opinion on the men's basketball: "Last night made it all worth it. I saw your 'Dream Team,' but to be right about it, the one between Spain and Brazil made the whole trip. 101-100, Spain won, with only a few seconds left on the clock. The wave went 'round the building several times, and the Spaniards kept yelling and pointing to another section so they'd imitate 'em. It was crackers! Much more exciting—though watching Michael and Magic play was good in its own way—than the earlier game." Rob has saved up enough, he says, to travel through Europe and Asia before going home from his "'round-the-world."

Tonight Cole and Matt offer me a ticket for the women's team gymnastics finals. It is worth about seventy dollars. They could sell it easily, but I imagine they feel a certain guilt about the price of the room, especially since I still have not received a key. I can afford only a loaf of bread, one meal a day, and copious amounts of bottled water. I have finally found two public water fountains, so that when I am locked out and thirsty, I do not get too dehydrated.

It seems the security is heightened for this finals. Perhaps the security people believe that, since this is a premium event, any terrorists might pick this one for greater exposure. We get double-checked, gone over with a electronic wand, and people's bags, camera cases, and personal effects are opened and examined.

We have great seats for the gymnastics finals, and watch the first four teams (Spain, Bulgaria, Hungary, and Austria) perform before there is an intermission. We see Scottie Pippen, who refuses to give autographs to anyone. (As a spectator, I "collect" Scottie Pippen's image, with the women's gymnastics apparatus in the background, on my video camera.) There is speculation around us: people muse, "He doesn't want to take away from the gymnasts. It's their night, after all"; "He just wants to relax"; "He's a pro. He gets tired of this all the time. Just let him be an Olympian for now."

The next four teams are the Unified team, the United States, Romania, and China. The athletes are ritually marched, to the Olympic theme, upon entering the performance area; they are then, with a "hostess" holding a team sign in front, ritually marched between apparatuses. In the previous venues I have attended, there has been a great deal of "dead" time. In this event, someone from each team is performing on each of four apparatuses (vault, uneven bars, balance beam, free exercise) at any given time. There is a three-minute warm-up between apparatuses. The first competitor from each team is generally the fourth-best, so that the last performer on each piece of equipment is usually the best from each team. This, of course, serves to increase any drama already inherent in the event itself.

As in all the other venues, there is a large-screen television to which most of the spectators refer after the initial performance. This is a very knowledgeable crowd, cheering for an outstanding move on one apparatus, for example, while I am looking at an ordinary move on another apparatus. So the replay serves a purpose when there are multiple performances occurring.

Wednesday, July 29. At the morning swimming preliminary event, I realize how relatively unimportant sport has become for the attendees.[45] In fact, Cole told me last night that while he was in Seoul, he "blew off a couple of events here and there. I'd seen it. I was too tired, so I stayed in bed instead." At the swimming meet, we all watch the heats, but communicate in different ways while we watch. As Deborah Tannen has shown, "Boys and men sit at angles to each other . . . and never look directly into each other's faces. . . . The girls and women anchor their gaze on each other's faces. . . . "[46]

While the meet goes on, I sit away from Cole and Matt, whom I met only this week, who have given me the ticket. I want to meet and talk with new people, as if their new stories will be more "real." Cole's stories—of Seoul, of his knowledge of gymnastics, of his son who is marrying a Japanese in Hawaii in the fall, of his Japanese class—are becoming repetitive for me. Though key elements seem the same, he refines them a little each time to suit the situation or privilege himself as an expert.

The pomp of the swimming and the athletes' efforts are impressive. For example, Mike Barrowman sets an Olympic record in the 200-meter breast-stroke, and in the finals tonight, a world record. I have coached swimming (including eight All-Americans and one United States high school record holder), so I know what it takes to compete at this level. But I must confess that I find it fairly uninteresting, since I have not directly worked with the athletes. I do not know their "stories." To be ensnared in the myth of contemporary "sport" requires my active participation in the athletes' stories, whether by reading the sports page, envying their abilities (as compared to mine, if I participate in the same sport), or chatting with friends. This may or may not, of course, be a strictly male phenomenon in American culture, or it may be unique to me, but I rather doubt the latter.

After the swimming, I take the Metro to the Sagrada Familia. I think how Mark Twain might have walked the Carrer de Valencia, and how tourists themselves are reproductions of other tourists, from other times, cross-informed by popular and scholarly accounts. I first read Twain's *Innocents Abroad* before going to England in 1985, but I was reminded of it by Malcolm Crick's introductory remarks.[47]

After the Sagrada Familia (I did not go inside), I Metro to the Ramblas (where everyone strolls, or "rambles," in groups at dusk along a pedestrian roadway between two traffic lanes—and on into the wee hours of the morning). I walk to the Coca-Cola Pin Trading Center with a 1984 Los Angeles Olympics "badge" of "Sam the Eagle" doing the horse in gymnastics; to me, it is really a cheap throwaway badge. Authenticity? It's so relative. A man from somewhere in the former Soviet Union gestures at my pin and to his pin-thick cloth to say, "Choose any one of mine for that one?" So I pick one with a red Olympic flame and the word "Moskva 1980" on it. It all happens so fast, and I am happy to get a Moscow pin in my first pin trade.

Such an experience—actually speaking with another human being, who is owner, not maker, of the product for which you are bartering—may lend to an object greater value. I certainly felt exultant after picking up the "Moskva" pin, much more so than when I purchased a Cobi pin for a souvenir for my friend back at home. There was an element of uncertainty in the pin trade, only an element of commerce in the buying of the souvenir. But there were exceptions:

"Sit down here, now. You've been so nice, talking to me, and asking me these questions," he says. He is old, neat as a pin in his dress, and folds his arthritic legs under a metal table, in the shade. His eyes are rheumy, clouded. "Rest yourself here for a while. I'll tell you something. Jesse Owens was my master. At the 1948 Olympics, I was speed-training for Sri Lanka, and I missed making the team by one. I live in Hawaii, and this pin collection is just a part of my collection. Ever since 1948," he says, running his right hand from his left hand up to his heart, "the Olympics has been in my blood. I have a collection of over forty thousand pieces."

From underneath the table he pulls three thick photo books, filled with photos of plates, pins, scarves, framed Olympic Committee letters, medallions—a record of his collection of Olympic memorabilia. (The books have become collections in and of themselves. "There are," he says, his eyes gleaming, "one hundred and twenty books, all like these.")

Thursday, July 30. Canal Olimpic—TV 3—and Eurosports have twenty-four-hour coverage, which the three of us watch until 2:00 A.M. We are on the fifth floor, yet we can hear partying and yelling from the street all night long. We open the window screens to let any slight air in, but in the mornings my bed linens are soaked with sweat. Of course, each morning I have to shove my repacked backpack in with Cole's baggage, to make it look as if there are only two people living here. I don't care much—my bargain is with Cole, and I know now that I could find housing quite easily if I need to.

I have weightlifting this morning, at Pavelló L'Espanya Industrial, near the Sants Estació, which is the central train station where I came in from Paris. The weightlifting is much like a rodeo (bareback bronco riding): a bell starts the attempt, the athlete hangs on, and a bell tells (him) when to drop it. The weightlifters have friends or family for support, but some athletes are adopted by the crowd. One British weightlifter makes broad, theatrical gestures as he cleans the bar, then jerks it. He grunts exultantly—and any show of emotion brings cheers from the crowd. They (we) love the constructed drama, the playing to the crowd, by the athletes, because "This is the Olympics!"

Midway through the weightlifting, I go over to the women's basketball venue, all the way across Barcelona to Badalona, at the Palau d'Esports (China v. Spain). This is the only overlap of events I received from Olson Travelworld. I sit down, expensive beer in hand (yesterday I ate a loaf of hard French bread and drank a bottle of coarse red wine by myself).

Two older women, physical educators from a college in Ohio, sit next to me. They are wonderful, full of stories about their exploits with the various types of toilets throughout Europe. They are also sure to let me know that one of them is married. In almost any other social setting, two older women traveling together would not make them defensive. But the conversation does not turn toward homophobia in athletics.

Instead they tell me about a men's basketball game they attended. "They start the wave, and then the Brazilians would wave the flag in front of us, so we left. We couldn't see. But that's what's fun about going to games—seeing all the people."

It is so loud inside the arena, and in the international game, that officials' verbal calls wouldn't be understood anyway—but there is an international language of gestures (e.g., rolling the hands one over the other for traveling) that is clear and easily understood, and has become theatrical (much like the baseball umpire's calls behind the plate, weightlifters' efforts, the WWF wrestlers, the American Gladiators, the celebrations of touchdown-scoring football players). Three other women, all physical education teachers at a private school in New York, arrive to submit that "it's all just acting." After I tell them my tales of woe (I guess), they buy me a beer and invite me to a supposedly nude beach in Sitges on Saturday. I cannot go, of course, so I suggest tomorrow. They cannot go tomorrow. But, my interest piqued, I look Sitges Beach up in *The Real Guide: Barcelona:* "Beyond the hotel, following the railway line, you eventually reach the more notorious nudist beaches, the so-called 'Playas del Muerto,' a couple of which are exclusively gay."[48]

Of course, it would have been tourists gazing at tourists, for the most part, which, after the train ride from Paris to Barcelona, would have probably exceeded my expectations. But there is something more to this. The transient nature of being away from home seems to embolden people to assume seemingly attractive parts of the "traveled-to" culture,[49] even if (or especially since) those might be taboo at home.

Friday, July 31. Athletics is a sports smorgasbord, similar to gymnastics, where you have a choice among events, similar to the combinations in *The American Gladiators,* with dead time filled with "other observations." As the shot put awards begin—Mark Hodler (Member Committee Executive IOC) presenting—I realize that the pomp of presenting begins to seem more important than the glory of the medal winners: Michael Stulce (gold, USA), James Dehring (USA), Viacheslav Lykho (EUN) ("Representing Russia," the announcer calls).

I move from the English-speaking section, since it is underneath the scoreboard and I cannot tell what or who is going on, to a Catalan section. I am seated, crowded in tightly, in a section across from the Royal Box, where King Juan Carlos has watched most of the proceedings.

The awards ceremony, especially "The Star-Spangled Banner," moves me much more than it does those around me, but they are polite and respectful, and seem to enjoy seeing me get choked up. Right afterward, the announcer says that the awards for the 20K walk (won by a Spaniard) will be held tomorrow evening. The whole Estadi Olimpic explodes, whistling and waving white handkerchiefs, yelling "fueda" all through the second heat of the 10,000-meter run for men (five to ten minutes), strong. (The people around me explain, quietly, that "fueda" means "exit," or "bye." I find out later that it means something approximating "fuck off.") The crowd cheers for the 10,000-meter runners, an impromptu "wave," as they run around the track, but every time the announcer attempts to talk in a language other than Catalan, they shout him down. One man even stands up and gestures toward the announcer (and in the direction of the Royal Box), grabbing his elbow and forcefully driving his forearm up ten or fifteen times. People laugh and jeer, and shout for the announcer "to leave." Someone says he thinks the reason for the delay—and the upset of decorum—is that King Juan Carlos has already left. The crowd respectfully allows the announcement to be made in Catalan (everything is announced in Catalan, Spanish, French, and English), but then everyone begins jeering and whistling at the onset of Spanish. In other words, "You have power over us, but we don't have to listen to you."

To me, this is the first large rent in the orderly fabric that is the 1992 Barcelona Olympics. It is a reversal of order—not necessarily a condoned, sanctioned reversal, or an appeasement; it is on the order of "folk humor," about which Bakhtin states:

> [It] existed and developed outside the official sphere of high ideology and literature, but precisely because of its unofficial existence, it was marked by exceptional radicalism, freedom, and ruthlessness. Having on the one hand forbidden laughter in every official sphere of life and ideology, the Middle Ages on the other hand bestowed exceptional privileges of license and lawlessness outside these spheres.[50]

In this age of the so-called "death of the subject," the arena of sport may be one of the few places where seemingly uninhibited resistance to order may occur. If it is seen as false consciousness, it is so only because individual, particular stories are not taken into account by such a generalizing theory as Marxism. Again, as Bruner has written, "tourists are not dupes."[51] They form small, seemingly insignificant resistances which, taken as a whole, may become empowering: "It's not only easy to change culture, but we do it all the time."[52] Players of sport, demonstrating their own agency, enact forms of symbolic resistance, which encompass "a middle area[53] between outright, open rebellion and underground, passive resistance, and it involves the socially-accepted practices of symbolically 'killing' one's enemy and regaining one's land while being monitored by the world according to the rules of sport."[54] It may be that the dynamic between Spain and Catalonia serves as a catalyst, providing the sacred element, which in turn serves as a counter to the secular. That is to say, sport is not sacred to the Catalans, but their (perceived and real) heritage and history vis-à-vis Spain is. The secular Olympics may become a socially acceptable arena in which Rabelaisian counters to hegemony are encouraged.

In terms of the sport tourist's arriving *in medias res* at the Barcelona Olympics, it is entirely possible that s/he is a willing participant in self-delusion, a reveler, a venturer into a safe, pseudo-Bahktinian carnival replete with the opportunity for reversed order (or observed instances of reversed order), and that this sense of irony and self-referentiality (to a degree already missing in the

1930s, when Bakhtin wrote the epitaph that introduces this chapter) may in fact be a tenet that delineates the postmodern from the modern. The circle may have completed itself,[55] and rather than the prophesied nihilism as the end of (post)modernity, the end has become a return to this sense of laughter wedded with grief.

Ironically, it is the sport forum—seen by many scholars as insignificant, but by aficionados as dense with "meaning that resists the insinuations of the mythological process and the postmodern reduction to surface effect"[56]—that provides a critical contemporary setting for an examination of Bakhtinian (and Rabelaisian) resurgence.

On a more everyday level than the expression of anger and abandon I witnessed at the athletics competition, the Brazilian fans bring their own creation of a carnival atmosphere. They fill the Metro cars, chanting and singing, laughing and dancing into the night while the train runs. One six-foot-four-inch woman jokingly banters at the Coca-Cola Pin Trading Center with a pin trader about having the AIDS virus; otherwise she would gladly have sex with him. During the first day's swimming prelims, a large group of uniformed Brazilians (wearing bright yellow shirts with "Brasilia" imprinted on the back in green) play music, sing, and cheer for their (and some other Latin American) competitors. At the spectacle, they are themselves a spectacle. In a sense, they provide role reversal: swimmers, unused to anything but applause and an occasional plastic horn, look up to find a seven-piece orchestra playing merengue music during the most important meet of their lives. The Brazilians seem to take over whole areas; they have no qualms about bringing a Mardi Gras atmosphere to the Olympics.

Saturday, August 1. At the Piscines Bernat Picornell, I see Donna, the former diving coach from Pomona-Pitzer (she and her husband are spectators), and Mike Sutton, coach at Claremont, who is the United States water polo team's "team manager." It is the first round, and the U.S. is favored for the gold. Mike says, "They're really serious about this one." Having coached against Claremont (and been soundly thrashed—always) in water polo, I wonder when an Olympic water polo team hasn't been "really serious." I know Terry Schroeder, the two-meter man, and realize that this is his third consecutive Olympics, so I agree that there is a certain urgency to this tournament.[57]

"The Czech and Slovak Federative Republic" is how the announcer puts it. They play the Unified team. The sets are somewhat sloppy; the game drags on and on. There are Americans—mostly young women who are aligned with the team members—decked out in Stars and Stripes shirts and hats, anticipating the upcoming match against Australia, which the United States easily dominates.

As I wander back to the Ramblas, I think of "The Sport Tourist as Kitsch-

(Wo)Man": at the beginning of the Olympics, you could almost be certain of a spectator's nationality by caps, T-shirts (designs), badges, and other paraphernalia, but by the end of this first week, that superficial difference between the subject and the Other has collapsed or disappeared. On the Metro, I see a man wearing a cap inscribed "CANADA" over a red maple leaf. He holds the hand of a little boy. Expecting to hear English (and perhaps strike up a conversation), I am jolted when he speaks Hungarian to his son. You cannot be absolutely sure where someone is from until you actually verbally exchange histories. Such is trading among sport tourists—the gathering around the self of tangible, meaningful objects which may or may not supply remembrance of things past.[58]

I visit with my acquaintance from Sri Lanka again, and he tells me, "Get the Dream Team pin. Not the one with ten players, the one with all twelve names printed right there on the back. That will be valuable." Though he has told me that he has more than forty thousand Olympic-related items in his collection, though he says that he spends his days contacting people for memorabilia, I do not ask him if he has sold his collection. Value, to this man (and to many of the pin traders), is not measured monetarily; rather, value seems to be flexible, "what the market will bear," a sense of tradability in an object.

One pin collector, a chain-smoking woman with a raspy whisper of a voice, tells me that she won't trade for enameled pins: "There're too damn many of 'em. Coke makes 'em, Nuprin makes 'em, Bausch and Lomb, you name it." The ones with the recessed features, she explains, are more one-of-a-kind, therefore valuable.

I head to the train station, where I have stored my backpack. I have had my train ticket from Barcelona to Paris in hand for three days. But the train leaves two hours late, and I am worried that I will miss my connection at the French border. The system functions, but time glitches may throw everything off, and upset an otherwise comfortably planned trip. I don't see how having a travel agent plan the trip months ahead would rectify this, either.

Ways around it may be to buy a total-care package, or a hermetically sealed coach, or to rent a car—like the two college professors I met at the women's basketball. The package tourist and the pre-organized tourist, unlike me on both counts, probably get to more places in a shorter amount of time. But the minimal-cost tourist generally has a great deal of time. Rob, the Australian, is a good example. He purports to "live as the natives do," imagines that he would have to pay out money to live in Australia as well, and takes his time. He also feels, with time to see people in depth, that he has a "more genuine" experience than those who travel through quickly. Of course, Baudrillard's *America* contends that in an era of exponentially proliferating simulacra, it is entirely appropriate to apprehend such sights as they are sensed:

> Speed creates pure objects. It is itself a pure object, since it cancels out the
> ground and territorial reference-points, since it runs ahead of time to annul
> time itself. . . . It is not the discovery of local customs that counts, but dis-
> covering the immorality of the space you have to travel through, and this is
> on a quite different plane.[59]

Perhaps knowing a culture is a lifetime's work. That, paradoxically, is one
reason why the study of sport is disparaged: "everyone knows about sport."

Wednesday, August 4. British Airways, their agents all French, will not
change my ticket.

Since Sunday, I've been at Charles de Gaulle Airport. There are built-in
snack tables on the lower level of the airport, where I slept one night, surrounded by twenty sleeping Chinese and one guy who teaches at an Indian
reservation in Arizona. He is returning from Thailand.

"My wife and kid are there," he says. "She can't handle the reservation for
more than a year at a time—too much shooting, suicide—so she goes home to
Thailand for six months every other year."

We talk. He's been stuck at the airport two days, and is due out tomorrow.
His voice rises as he tells me about almost getting shot on the reservation. We
hear a voice say, "'Scuse me, could you be a littler more quiet? We sleep?"

The teacher from Arizona shouts, "You wanta fuck with me? Shut the hell
up, you Chink mother! I'll talk as goddamned loud as I want!" He must see my
face, because he adds in a whisper, "Don't ever let the Orientals push you
around. They push and push, and if you give in, they'll take more. Don't let 'em
fuckin' push you."

Later he asks me, "Have you ever had sex with a Thai girl?" I wonder if
anonymity makes him speak this way. "My wife will do anything for me: she's
always asking if I'm unhappy with her, offering to find me another woman.
When I left this time, I went up to northern Thailand. I'm wandering around
the street, and this guy asks me if I want a woman. So I follow."

His hands shake as he cups his cigarette. "They were the most beautiful
women you'd ever see. Sixty dollars for the night! I tell you, it was incredible."
He smiles to himself, and closes his eyes to sleep. It is a memory, a sex memory,
he has collected.

While taking up my daily seat to watch the Olympics on a wide-screen
television (Eurosports Channel), I speak with a German guy apparently back
from a sex tour in Madagascar. In rapid order, he makes loud fun of women's
sports ("they should yust be in the kitchen, ja?"), synchronized swimming, and
equestrian.

"Golf," he says. "Golf and tennis. Those are the sports I like." He proceeds to
instruct me (loudly) on Madagascar as a travel destination: "Cheap—um, a

dollar and ten cents American for a five-course meal? Five to six dollars for a hotel. Each day. And the women are friendly. They love Europeans. The money, you know."

Here, the Barcelona Olympics is diversionary at best. I talk with some Americans (two canoeists, quickly jetting back to the United States after competing in the Olympics; a woman with two children from San Francisco, who gives me a peach; a few college students), some male Aussies (who agree with the German about women athletes and those "non-sports"), and, at separate times, two seventeen-year-old Irish nannies rushing home from disastrous summers working for French families.

Another American, who lives in Adelaide, Australia, says, "I don't like badminton. And table tennis is a real spectator sport, too. How about that one where the girls twirl ribbons and balls? There's a real sport, eh?"

▼ ▼ ▼ ▼

Though of course I have arbitrarily assigned the beginning and ending—and blocked it apart from most of my authorial intrusions—of my Olympic experience as, respectively, the Amtrak ride from Champaign and sitting in the Charles de Gaulle Airport in Paris, the "experience" is never so easily apprehended. I intended it to be ironic that in discussing the Olympics, with its connotations of pure, "high,"[60] and penultimate sport, the final quote should question whether rhythmic gymnastics is a "real sport."

Writing itself is a seduction of the reader; writing about seductive process, then, becomes a doubly seductive move, almost akin to actual experience.[61] The actual experience of movement is a secret borne only by the athletes who perform; secondary (and vicarious) experience branches out several ways: through on-site spectating, apprehending and recording the process with electronic media, apprehending and recording the process in some other way; third-level witnessing involves watching or reading that which has been selected out by someone else. At each level, the danger of sensory involvement is reduced. At each level, what Barbara Babcock calls "seduction" is deepened; at each level, rhetorical (by this I mean not just writing, but all communicative modes of experience) devices are often employed to approximate the sensory nature of the original experience. Such "suspension of disbelief" occurs with willing readers of texts.

Witness how I authenticated my "being there" with proper names of the venues, environs, and customs: Estadi Olímpic, Piscina de Montjuïc, Piscines Bernat Picornell, Sagrada Familia, Badalona, Bitllet Olímpic; notice how I used the present tense throughout to lend urgency to the experience; recall how there came to be an emphasis on the vicarious experience of things sexual that paralleled things in sport. Similarly, the reading (and enjoyment) of ethnographic texts tends toward a form of voyeurism. Such is the form seductions may take: as readers, we become willing producers and constructors of our own seduction, of our own travels.

▼ ▼ ▼ ▼

The structure of this text might imply a linear seduction, an undermining of the postmodernist project. Its sense-making might, in effect, challenge the ideas advanced in chapter 2. Of course, on one level this is absolutely accurate: read as a modernist document, with a beginning, middle, and end, this Olympics chapter (re)enforces the drama metaphor.

However, postmodernism borrows willingly from modernism. Scholars live in a postmodern world of pastiche, irony, and flow, and yet, especially in sport studies, there is a security to remembering clear and unchallenged ways of research, to discussions bathed in binaries.

Further, an undermining of the authorial voice, of authorial privilege as an exceptional, omniscient seer, cannot be a bad thing. If I have only slightly succeeded in my vision for this work, I have invited the reader to disagree, to challenge, to explore his or her own experience relative to mine. What is it to experience sport in the late twentieth century? How have nineteenth-century rituals and myths of authenticity become interwoven into the fabric of (postmodern American) sporting life? How have we all become players involved in contemporary postmodern sport forms?

These are the questions I ask, and keep coming back to in this work. And these are, ultimately, the questions that we all must answer for ourselves.

I close with two forms of ideological seduction. They are both worthy of critical response, and both contain elements of verisimilitude. Though they are not advertisements in the strict sense, they are commercial: they serve to sell the Olympics. They tie in to the Olympics, and tie in to the "sport" experience. The first is the postmodern origination myth (with biblical overtones) of Cobi, the example, *in toto,* drawn from the Anchorage *Daily News.* As background, it must be realized that Cobi was omnipresent in Barcelona, but even before the spectators got to Barcelona, the venue tickets informed them of his (Cobi is male) importance: a holographed Cobi, Olympic rings above his head, arms outstretched in greeting, big goofy grin intact, is imprinted on each ticket. The second example is drawn from an essay by John Updike, from the *Official Souvenir Program of the Olympics.*

First, "Cobi the pooch—not your average Olympic mascot":

> Barcelona, Spain — First, he considered a shrimp. But a shrimp looked stupid on a bicycle.

Then he tried a sheep dog as the Olympic mascot. But the hairy creature was dropped when it began resembling an ape.

And on the third attempt, Javier Mariscal created Cobi—the cubist cartoon dog who seems to be everywhere these days.

Visitors to Barcelona need only travel a few hundred feet from the airport to be bombarded by Cobi billboards—Cobi drinking a Coke, Cobi wearing Ray-Ban sunglasses, Cobi pecking at a Brother typewriter, Cobi sipping a Damm beer.

But the cockeyed pooch with the sly grin is not just a start for sponsors. He is on T-shirts and coffee mugs and watches; he stars in a TV cartoon series; he is available as a cuddly bedtime doll or a two-story-high balloon.

There are statues of Cobi performing each of the 28 Olympic sports. There are pins of Cobi as a journalist, professor, bellboy and doctor. There is even Cobi bath gel.

Yet Cobi, whose name derives from the Barcelona Olympic Organizing Committee (COOB), is not your average mascot. Just like his creator, Mariscal, he is far from ordinary.

"Cobi is the first Olympic mascot to be sad, to be crying, to be depressed. They're usually concealed with a smile, but this guy has a sly grin," Mariscal says.

"He's like a chameleon—he can be a baby, a poor little boy, a druggie, a guy who is cleaning your car windows, an athlete, an idealist carrying the Olympic flag, or a disillusioned youth."

Mariscal, a social critic and first-class cynic, proudly points out Cobi "is not like a super athlete" or a bouncing bundle of joy such as Sam the Eagle (1984 Los Angeles Olympic mascot) or bears Hidy and Howdy (1988 Calgary Winter Games).

"He has a big stomach, like a baby. This is happiness," Mariscal says. "And he's small, with a thick neck, like people here in the Mediterranean."

Cobi is simple enough for a child to draw. It takes Mariscal about 4 seconds to doodle a Cobi, and he delights in showing how basic the cartoon is by encouraging a guest to draw one.

He brags that "I was very stoned" when he first drew Cobi, but refuses to say which drugs inspired the character.

"I can't tell you, because then everybody would smoke the same dope and everybody could make Cobis, and I wouldn't make any money," he explains, tongue firmly planted in cheek.

While Cobi wears suits and hawks Coke, Mariscal is a 42-year-old hippie. He's a self-proclaimed "rebel with a cause"—sex, drugs and rock 'n' roll.

His influences were musicians Frank Zappa and Jimi Hendrix, as well as painters Pablo Picasso and Joan Miro. And he was greatly impressed by Pop Art and the American culture of the 1950s and 1960s.

Mariscal, who began his art career as an underground cartoonist during the repressive Franco era, was a successful designer and artist long before Cobi.[62]

This piece has the proper feel for an Olympics piece. It is light and irreverent, and confirms what most people already feel they know: artists go against the grain and don't care about money (hence the demurral: "'and I wouldn't make any money,' he explains, tongue firmly planted in cheek"). Also, while there have been problems, the Olympics is just one huge happy family, including in its embrace sad and happy, "super athlete[s]" and people with "big stomach[s]"—in short, the Olympic movement is inclusive, even of druggies and artists who must get "very stoned" to work.

Next, selections from John Updike's paean to the unshakability of the Olympics, and of the individual triumphing over the collective, of the purity of movement defeating the construction of drama:

> With the old communist-capitalist dualism no longer present to lend drama, what use will the world have for the Olympic Games? They will serve, I suggest, as a quadrennial source for televised images of humanity at its most physically exalted.
>
> . . . it is essential that these performances appear to be, like those of the poet and the prophet, purely gratuitous, undertaken to gain glory but not lucre, in a state of selfless exertion.
>
> . . . Thanks to the electronic handmaiden who carries them to us, the Games ever more closely approach the condition of the Dionysian dance—an abstract rapture of our physical species, in its plurality of color and sex, as it angelically defies gravity. Political allegiance falls away, the ideal human form remains, vital and precise, at the center of this age-old celebration.[63]

These are ideological constructions, seductive in their own ways, meant to be swallowed whole, seamless and unchallenged and unproblematic. They are a series of "Been There, Did That" T-shirts, masterfully woven into the fabric of contemporary life. They are "how it is," simply because the very act of capturing experience paradoxically may pin it down, and classify experience as stable rather than processual. It is perhaps the greatest challenge, however, to resist that which we cannot see—but to carry on with what we feel.

NOTES

FOREWORD

1. Lee Shappell, "Today's Athlete: Athletes at Center of Change Sweeping Sports Society," *The Arizona Republic*, 19 January 1997, p. C1.

2. John Bale, "Cricket," in *The Theater of Sport*, ed. Karl B. Raitz (Baltimore: Johns Hopkins University Press, 1995), p. 85.

3. In fact, a recent scholarly book plays off this dominant sports metaphor. See note 2 for information on *The Theater of Sport*.

4 Michael Holquist, ed., *The Dialogic Imagination: Four Essays by M. M. Bakhtin*, trans. Caryl Emerson and Michael Holquist (Austin: University of Texas Press, 1981), p. 410.

5. See Jean Baudrillard, *America*, trans. Chris Turner (London: Verso, 1988), for an evocative, evanescent portrayal of the American "authentic."

6. Advertisement from *USA Today*, 26 January 1996, p. 4D.

7. Steve Woodward, "Olympic Wannabes May Be Left Out in the Cold," *USA Today*, 6–8 November 1992, p. 1A.

8. Walter Berry, "Dallas Makes Hottest Ticket Even Hotter," *The Windsor Star*, 22 January 1996, p. D4.

9. Jack Carey, "Want Men's Final Four Ticket? Good Luck!" *USA Today*, 27 March 1996, p. 1C.

10. "Fans Eagerly Await Call to 'Play Ball!'" *USA Today*, 26 March 1996, p. 1C.

11. Gene Sloan, "Baseball Tours Catch On Again," *USA Today*, 29 March 1996, p. 9D.

I. SPORT AS PERFORMANCE

1. This is reminiscent of a *Saturday Night Live* sketch in which a group of young men, blustering about their conquests, sit around a table discussing current Hollywood female stars. "Drew Barrymore?" one queries. "Did her," they all answer, one by one. It becomes absurdist, which, of course, serves to make a wonder-

ful point about the emptiness possible in contemporary life. To me, this is an exemplar of a paucity in relationships in an age of "objectification," "interfacing," and "networking," in an age in which bureaucracies have served to blend the private and public sectors. Similarly, the capturing of experiences in tourism—and in the cases documented in this text of sport tourism—may include collecting and preserving the experience (idealistic, realistic), enjoying the experience in the here and now (existential), or seeing the experience as furthering some other goal (pragmatic). (The philosophical keys are rough estimates and are not meant to define the quality or depth of experience.)

2. See chapter 6.

3. This, of course, is a questionable assertion—was sport ever truly innocent, or have contemporary culturists re-created its innocence in yet another nostalgic trope?

4. For a clear explanation of biography's insertion into the text at the level of lived experience, see Norman K. Denzin, *Interpretive Biography* (Newbury Park, Calif.: Sage Publications, 1989); for selected examples of much of the popular pseudo-critical or adulatory work in sports biography, see, for example, Paul Hoch, *Rip Off the Big Game: The Exploitation of Sports by the Power Elite* (New York: Anchor Books, 1972); Jerry Kramer, ed., *Lombardi: Winning Is the Only Thing* (New York: World Publishing Co., 1970); Dave Meggyesy, *Out of Their League* (Berkeley: Ramparts Press, 1970); Gary Shaw, *Meat on the Hoof: The Hidden World of Texas Football* (New York: St. Martin's Press, 1972); and Jack Tatum, *They Call Me Assassin* (New York: Everest House, 1980); for an example of recent critical work discussing commoditization and sport, see Karl B. Raitz, ed., *The Theater of Sport* (Baltimore: Johns Hopkins University Press, 1995); for a cultural studies approach to lived experience and critical sport studies, see Charles Fruehling Springwood, *Cooperstown to Dyersville: A Geography of Baseball Nostalgia* (Boulder, Colo.: Westview Press, 1996).

5. Benjamin Lowe, *The Beauty of Sport: A Cross-Disciplinary Inquiry* (Englewood Cliffs, N.J.: Prentice-Hall, 1977).

6. See work portraying the postmodern moment by Adorno, Barthes, Baudrillard, Bourdieu, Brantlinger, Bruner, Calinescu, Denzin, Derrida, Eco, Foucault, Giddens, Habermas, Harvey, Huyssen, Jameson, Lyotard, Rosenau, and Sayre, among others.

7. But one must be careful here: the term "extend" implies a sense of linear time, which, as Octavio Paz says, is a "trap." See note 24 in this chapter.

8. Cited in Henry M. Sayre, *The Object of Performance: The American Avant-Garde since 1970* (Chicago: University of Chicago Press, 1989), pp. 90–92.

9. Sayre, *The Object of Performance.*

10. Steven Durland, "When the Personal Gets Political," *Utne Reader* 49 (1992): 16.

11. Ibid., p. 18.

12. John Blades, "Performance Prose: Not All Chicago Poets Think Poetry Slams Are Grand," *Chicago Tribune,* 3 February 1992, sec. 2, p. 3.

13. C. Carr, "C. Carr on the Poets' Slam," *Artforum* 29 (1991): 20.

14. Leslie Shepherd, "Soviet Profit Motive Causing the Death of an Art Form," *Chicago Tribune,* 22 January 1993, sec. 2, p. 3.

15. Taylor Buckley, "Chess Foes Put WWF to Shame," *USA Today,* 6 November 1992, p. 3C.

16. Martha T. Moore, "Reebok Ad Almost Thrown for a Loop," *USA Today,* 6 August 1992, p. 1B.

17. Jeff Z. Klein, Paul Park, Stan Fischler, Gian Trotta, Michael Tomasky, and Andrew Hsiao, "Jockbeat: Sacrificial Byrd," *The Village Voice,* 15 December 1992, p. 158.

18. Martha T. Moore, "Advertisers Try Different Game Plans," *USA Today,* 29 January 1993, p. 1B.

19. "Legitimate" sport is an arena in which the financial rewards seem to justify the hearty defense of the label "legitimate." See Mark Neuzil, "Report: NFL a $1.4 Billion Business—Financial Statements Show League Made $850 Million from TV, Radio," *Anchorage Daily News,* 7 July 1992, p. C5.

20. Mikhail Bakhtin, *Rabelais and His World,* trans. Hélène Iswolsky (Bloomington: Indiana University Press, 1984 [1936]), p. 53.

21. "We," that is to say, is a descriptor of a vague imperialist westernness, which has touched most, if not all, parts of the world and continues, through multinational corporations' efforts to homogenize the world, to remain one of the strongest cultural imperialist forces yet known to humankind.

22. Bakhtin,*Rabelais,* p. 135.

23. In 1991, at their annual meeting, the North American Society for the Sociology of Sport (Milwaukee, Wisc.) included a session (chaired by Alan Ingham) on the Americanization/globalization of sport. See also Todd Gitlin, "Postmodernism: Roots and Politics," in *Cultural Politics in Contemporary America,* ed. Ian Angus and Sut Jhally (New York: Routledge, 1989), pp. 347–360; debate over these terms—and their meaning—proliferated in the first half of the nineties: see Joe Maguire, "More Than a Sporting Touchdown: The Making of American Football in England, 1982–1990," *Sociology of Sport Journal* 7 (1990): 213–237; Eric Wagner, "Sport in Asia and Africa: Americanization or Mundialization?" *Sociology of Sport Journal* 7 (1990): 399–402; Bruce Kidd, "How Do We Find Our Own Voices in the 'New World Order'? A Commentary on Americanization," *Sociology of Sport Journal* 8 (1991): 178–184; Allen Guttmann, "Sports Diffusion: A Response to Maguire and the Americanization Commentaries," *Sociology of Sport Journal* 8 (1991): 185–190; Jean Harvey and François Houle, "Sport, World Economy, Global Culture, and New Social Movements," *Sociology of Sport Journal* 11 (1994): 337–355; Barrie Houlihan, "Homogenization, Americanization, and Creolization of Sport: Varieties of Globalization," *Sociology of Sport Journal* 11 (1994): 356–375; John Williams, "The Local and the Global in English Soccer and the Rise of Satellite Television," *Sociology of Sport Journal* 11 (1994): 376–397; Joseph Maguire, "Sport, Identity Politics, and Globalization: Diminishing Contrasts and Increasing Varieties," *Sociology of Sport Journal* 11 (1994): 398–427; and Steven J. Jackson, "Gretzky, Crisis, and Canadian Identity in 1988: Rearticulating the Americanization of Culture Debate," *Sociology of Sport Journal* 11 (1994): 428–446.

24. As Octavio Paz said in a recent interview, "To call the present condition 'postmodern' is still to refer to modernity; it is to fall into the trap of linear time, the narrative from which we have departed altogether." I am not so sure that the sport world (those enmeshed within it, those who study it, and those who dance

between the two worlds) has departed from "the trap of linear time." See Nathan Gardels, "West Turns East at the End of History," interview with Octavio Paz, *New Perspective Quarterly* 9 (1992): 5.

25. Bakhtin, *Rabelais,* p. 90.

26. This group is not, certainly, confined to sport scholars; sport marketers "study" sport: they study demographics of audiences and trend analyses.

27. For a fascinating parallel discussion of this very point, see Raitz, *The Theater of Sport.*

28. To all intents and purposes, this was the showdown match between the top two teams in the Big Ten, and occurred on November 27, 1992. The "bigger-than-life" aspects of this introductory ritual presumably might result in better crowd support, intimidation of the Penn State players, and a "home court" advantage. While sport studies have demonstrated ambivalent results in the benefits of playing at home or away, popular wisdom still believes in the advantages of playing at home.

29. In fact, the Super Bowl is awarded to a neutral (but not indifferent) site, one that generally has little affiliation with either team.

30. Kevin Maney, "Computerized Puck Keeps Check of Action," *USA Today,* 19 January 1996, p. 5B.

31. C. Wright Mills, *The Sociological Imagination* (London: Oxford University Press, 1959), p. 114.

32. Ibid., p. 167.

33. Walter Benjamin, "The Work of Art in the Age of Mechanical Reproduction," in *Illuminations* (New York: Schocken, 1969 [1936]), p. 867.

34. It is those unheard-from voices that beckon many researchers toward collaborative efforts which couple the researchers' expertise with the expertise of the researched: see, for example, Karen McCarthy Brown, *Mama Lola: A Voodou Priestess in Brooklyn* (Berkeley: University of California Press, 1991).

35. Clifford Geertz, "Blurred Genres: The Refiguration of Social Thought," in *Local Knowledge: Further Essays in Interpretive Anthropology* (New York: Basic Books, 1983), p. 34.

36. This quote is from a book review of Lawrence W. Levine, *Highbrow/Lowbrow: The Emergence of Cultural Hierarchy in America* (Cambridge, Mass.: Harvard University Press, 1988), in George Lipsitz, "High Culture and Hierarchy," *American Quarterly* 43 (1991): 520.

37. This phenomenon is not confined to such seemingly mundane matters: while sitting around a table at a local restaurant, I found myself explaining the forms of my writing in this work. One of my friends said, "But, Bob, your writing's filled with footnotes and references. You're not just telling a story; you're falling into the same scholarly trap." I responded, "Isn't it interesting that fiction writers feel comfortable, and 'scholarly' writers feel comfortable, but those who try to cross over and blend the two genres are under attack from both of those camps?" (And that there *are* such "camps"?) Power is based upon perspective and point of view. But unexamined use of power, even if morally justified (a point of view itself), is reprehensible.

This problem is touched upon in a profile of Ariel Dorfman, who says, "'There may be major contradictions between the world of the artisan and the industrially produced world of mass media, but I'm looking for a way these two can nurture each other.'" Quoted in Debra E. Blum, "Giving Voice to the Tragedy of Oppression," *The Chronicle of Higher Education,* 8 April 1992, p. A5.

38. The founders of the Gay Olympics discovered that the International Olympic Committee would not allow the word "Olympics" to be attached to their event. Thus the sporting event was renamed the Gay Games.

39. This is a significant omission: see Mary McDonald, "Rethinking Resistance: Olympic Games and Alternative Models," paper presented at the annual meeting of the North American Society for Sport Sociology, Toledo, Ohio, 4–7 November 1993, referring to the Gay Olympic Movement and the dearth of media coverage.

40. Lowe, *The Beauty of Sport,* p. 29.

41. "Group Touts Official Sport for Maryland," *Champaign-Urbana News-Gazette,* 28 October 1991, p. A–10.

42. "Taking Stock," *Champaign-Urbana News-Gazette,* 25 October 1991, p. 23

43. Julie Deardorff, "They're Hardly Run-of-the-Mill Sports: Some Schools Offer Titles Off the Beaten Track," *Chicago Tribune,* 3 May 1992, sec. 3, p. 2.

44. George Sage, *Power and Ideology in American Sport: A Critical Perspective* (Champaign, Ill: Human Kinetics Books, 1990).

45. Levine, *Highbrow/Lowbrow,* p. 230.

46. Ibid., p. 231.

47. Thorstein Veblen, *The Theory of the Leisure Class* (New York: Penguin Books, 1979 [1899]), chap. IV, passim.

48. Ben Brown, "Organizers Set to Launch Ticket Plans," *USA Today,* 28 April 1995, pp. 1C, 2C.

49. Christopher Drew, "Hitting Some Bumps on the Road to Atlanta: Sticker Shock for an Olympics Vacation," *New York Times,* 21 January 1996, p. F9.

50. Levine, *Highbrow/Lowbrow,* p. 231.

51. Lowe, *The Beauty of Sport,* p. 29.

52. A dualistic "us versus them" mindset, tied to a modernist framework, has influenced athletics in colleges and high schools for the past one hundred years, so that athletic departments are perpetually in a quandary about "major/minor," "revenue-producing/non-revenue-producing," and "men's/women's" distinctions in their sports.

53. Dorothy Ross, "Against Canons: Liberating the Social Sciences," *Society* 29 (1991): 10.

54. Ibid.

55. The use of a non-narrative/narrative distinction in art forms is, I feel, quite similar to my concept of avant-garde and drama as metaphors in the study of sport. See chapter 2 for further explanation of this topic. From Barrett Watten, "Nonnarrative and the Construction of History," lecture sponsored by the Unit for Criticism and Interpretive Theory and the Department of English, University of Illinois, Urbana-Champaign, 26 October 1992.

56. Possible reasons for this lack of reflexivity in sport studies may include resistance to cross-pollination from other fields, a sense of the importance of carving out a niche in which scholars who study sport can operate, or a clinging to the ideology that in sport, if nowhere else, things are clear. In regard to the last option, I was once told by the sports editor of a newspaper (who was interviewing me

about my largely unsuccessful water polo team), "There is winning and losing. You can't tell me that those kids feel good when they only lose by four." When I protested that losing by four to a nationally ranked water polo team was no mean feat, and that the team was extremely happy because we had played well against a superior group, he answered, "Bottom line, you lost. That's all anybody cares about." A similar bipolar attitude may exist in those who study sport as well.

57. Style of writing, of course, disguises the "personal bias" of the writer. For example, scholarly writing in the sciences, though not deity-inspired, is generally written in the passive voice (as if by Someone whose Truth is immutable), with few if any references to authorial intention or existence. Like many interactionists (but not all: see Norman K. Denzin, *Symbolic Interactionism and Cultural Studies: The Politics of Interpretation* [Oxford, UK: Blackwell, 1992], esp. chap. 2), I prefer to write my "biases" up front, and allow/encourage the reader the latitude of disagreement.

58. Jim Thomas, *Doing Critical Ethnography* (Newbury Park, Calif.: Sage Publications, 1993), p. 4.

59. Denzin, *Symbolic Interactionism and Cultural Studies,* p. 22.

60. This discussion owes to Denzin, ibid., pp. 22–28.

61. I am grateful to Susan L. Greendorfer for this image.

62. See Geertz, "Blurred Genres," pp. 19–35; see also his more recent *After the Fact: Two Countries, Four Decades, One Anthropologist* (Cambridge, Mass.: Harvard University Press, 1995).

63. Geertz, *Local Knowledge,* p. 16.

64. Norman K. Denzin, "Representing Lived Experiences in Ethnographic Texts," *Studies in Symbolic Interaction* 12 (1991): 62.

65. For just one example, see Jerome Bruner, *Acts of Meaning* (Cambridge, Mass.: Harvard University Press, 1990). "Chaos theory" has, in a sense, evolved from this basic premise.

66. Film study, as proposed by Denzin particularly, is yet another viable arena for studying cultural performance, but the process of filmmaking is highly scripted and mediated, while there still resides some degree of spontaneity within sport. Because of this, it appears that sport (in its macro manifestation) may be a more fruitful realm than film studies for the study of Denzin's concept of the epiphanic moment. See, e.g., Norman K. Denzin, *Images of Postmodern Society: Social Theory and Contemporary Cinema* (London: Sage Publications, 1991); Denzin, *Hollywood Shot by Shot: Alcoholism in American Cinema* (New York: Aldine De Gruyter, 1991); Denzin, "White Men Can't Dunk? Race, Gender and the Postmodern Emotional Self," In *Social Perspectives on Emotion,* vol. 3, Special Issue on "Interdisciplinary Approaches to the Study of Emotional Experience," ed. Carolyn Ellis and Michael Flaherty (Greenwich, Conn.: JAI Press, 1995), pp. 33–54.

67. See Denzin, *Symbolic Interactionism and Cultural Studies,* chap. 4.

68. The Bud Bowl, an advertising campaign for Budweiser Beer, is annually anticipated during the Super Bowl broadcast.

69. See, for example, Madeline Blais, *In These Girls, Hope Is a Muscle* (New York: Atlantic Monthly Press, 1995); Pamela J. Creedon, ed., *Women, Media and Sport: Challenging Gender Values* (Thousand Oaks, Calif.: Sage Publications, 1994); Todd

W. Crosset, *Outsiders in the Clubhouse: The World of Women's Professional Golf* (Albany: State University of New York Press, 1995); Ron Rapoport, ed., *A Kind of Grace: A Treasury of Sportswriting by Women* (Berkeley, Calif.: Zenobia Press, 1994).

70. Though this is well-known legislation, writers recently have seen fit to discuss the ramifications of Title IX twenty to twenty-five years after its installment. See, for example, Ed Sherman, "Title IX: The Landmark Decision," *The Beaver County Times* (Pennsylvania), 21 February 1993, p. B4.

71. Such bipolar terms as "feminine" and "masculine" work within a modernist framework as well, and tend to reduce complexity of issue to a "sound bite," "bumper sticker" mentality.

This nostalgic remembrance is not specifically oriented to baseball or any other sport, or to the so-called "high" or "low" ends of the "sport canon." The remembrance itself is a result of the commodification process, wherein consumers' needs are created, then fulfilled. See Grant McCracken, *Culture and Consumption: New Approaches to the Symbolic Character of Consumer Goods and Activities* (Bloomington: Indiana University Press, 1990).

For an excellent treatment of the voluminous array of contemporary artifacts that celebrate our love of (mostly masculine) sport, see Synthia S. Slowikowski, "Subterranean Tradition: Ancient Greek Motifs in Contemporary Physical Culture" (unpublished manuscript).

72. Joseph Tybor, "Sports in the Future: Average Fan Could Be Victim of Shutout," *Chicago Tribune*, 19 January 1992, sec. 3, p. 11.

73. See Jean Baudrillard, *Simulations* (New York: Semiotext(e), 1983); Jean Baudrillard, *America* (London: Verso, 1988); Umberto Eco, *Travels in Hyperreality*, trans. William Weaver (London: Pan Books, 1987).

74. See Benjamin R. Barber, *Jihad vs. McWorld: How Globalism and Tribalism Are Reshaping the World* (New York: Ballantine Books, 1995), especially pp. 59–72.

75. See Henry M. Sayre, "Pursuing Authenticity: The Vernacular Moment in Contemporary American Art," *South Atlantic Quarterly* 91 (1992): 139–160.

76. Donald Hall, *Fathers Playing Catch with Sons: Essays on Sport [Mostly Baseball]* (San Francisco: North Point Press, 1985), pp. 52–53.

77. The advent of such technologies as the parabolic dish, which directs natural sounds to the television viewing audience, has furthered at-home spectatorial inclusion (audience participation) in contemporary sport. See chapter 2 for further discussion of such technologies; William Oscar Johnson, "Sports in the Year 2001," *Sports Illustrated*, 22 July 1991, pp. 40–48; and Ron Fimrite, "What If They Held a Sporting Event and Nobody Came?" *Sports Illustrated*, 22 July 1991, pp. 49–50, 52.

78. "Does tolerance allow for intolerance?" is another way of putting it.

79. See Suzi Gablik, *Has Modernism Failed?* (New York: Thames and Hudson, 1984); Paul Mann, *The Theory-Death of the Avant Garde* (Bloomington and Indianapolis: Indiana University Press, 1991).

80. Denzin, "Representing Lived Experiences," p. 65.

81. Cited in John Carman, "The Whole World Is Watching: NBC Tries to Put Best Foot Forward as the Olympics Open," *San Francisco Chronicle*, 19 July 1996, pp. D1 and D7.

82. Michael Hirsley, "Success, Failure Equally Riveting on Games Telecast," *Chicago Tribune*, 22 July 1996, sec. 3, p. 10.

83. Correspondence with Andrea Fontana, ed., *Symbolic Interaction*, 1 February 1993.

84. For non-narrative art, see Watten, "Nonnarrative." "Mindscreen cinema" is a "subjective, personal cinema [which] is often non-linear, reflexive, filled with after-images, and faces which merge with one another" (Denzin, "Representing Lived Experiences," p. 66).

2. DROPPING HIERARCHIES

1. This chapter is informed throughout by Matei Calinescu, *Five Faces of Modernity: Modernism, Avant-Garde, Decadence, Kitsch, Postmodernism* (Durham, N.C.: Duke University Press, 1987). The term "avant-garde," as delineated by Calinescu, includes a "sharp sense of militancy, praise of nonconformism, courageous precursory exploration, and . . . confidence in the final victory of time" (p. 95).

2. Richard Gruneau, "Making Spectacle: A Case Study in Television Sports Production," in *Media, Sports, and Society,* ed. Lawrence A. Wenner (Newbury Park, Calif.: Sage Publications, 1989), pp. 134–154.

3. Rowland Lorimer and Jean McNulty, *Mass Communication in Canada*, 2nd ed. (Toronto: McClelland and Stewart, 1991), pp. 148–149.

4. Nicole L. Muller, "As the [Sports] World Turns: An Analysis of the Montana–49er Social Drama," *Journal of Sport and Social Issues* 19, no. 2 (1995): 157.

5. Ibid, p. 158.

6. Janet C. Harris and Laura A. Hills, "Telling the Story: Narrative in Newspaper Accounts of a Men's Collegiate Basketball Tournament," *Research Quarterly for Exercise and Sport* (1993): 108.

7. Other metaphors, of course, have been utilized in social science (see Clifford Geertz, *Local Knowledge: Further Esssays in Interpretive Anthropology* [New York: Basic Books, 1983]), as well as in sport studies: among them are "sport as a reflection of society," in which sport merely mirrors the larger society; and "sport as war" (game) (deriving from Erving Goffman's work), which, I feel, is conflated with the "sport as drama" metaphor.

8. This is a difficult task, since I hope to charge sport scholars with the task of examining sport through a postmodern refracted lens, and yet persist in utilizing many modernist conventions. It is my view that this apparent inconsistency may be forgiven when one realizes that one of the tentative tenets of postmodernism is its ability to use effective tools for the task. To speak to readers in a disjointed, non-linear fashion pushes the borders of research to a select few: but that is not my object here.

9. The concept of the avant-garde is not merely a modernist concept, though many critics conflate the avant-garde with modernism itself: see Marjorie Perloff, *The Futurist Moment: Avant-Garde, Avant Guerre, and the Language of Rupture* (Chicago: University of Chicago Press, 1986); Perloff, "Avant-Garde and Difference," *New American Writing* 7 (1991): 81–96; Perloff, *Radical Artifice: Writing Poetry in the Age of Media* (Chicago: University of Chicago Press, 1991); Henry M. Sayre, *The*

Object of Performance: The American Avant-Garde since 1970 (Chicago: University of Chicago Press, 1989).

10. Though, of course, the discussion of metaphor by some scholars takes a reflective turn: see, for example, Sue Curry Jansen and Don Sabo, "The Sport/War Metaphor: Hegemonic Masculinity, the Persian Gulf War, and the New World Order," *Sociology of Sport Journal* 11 (1994): 1–17.

11. In producing the text, I seek to employ methods that reinforce my points— a sort of form/function, subject/object, creator/audience relationship akin to that of the modernist avant-garde—and draw the reader of the "text" into the process and experience.

12. Note, for example, the guerrilla tactics employed by revolutionaries in the U.S. Revolutionary War, or the advent of Blitzkrieg tactics by the Nazis prior to World War II. In fact, the etymology of the word "avant-garde" arises from a now-archaic term ("aduant garde") meaning "the foremost part of an army" (*Oxford English Dictionary*, 1989, p. 813.)

In this military formation, a vanguard (or, literally from the French, "fore-guard") of an army, generally a highly prepared and innovative corps, waged initial combat with its enemy. This action served to soften up—indeed, occasionally morally paralyze—the enemy for what, presumably, would follow.

Appropriated by the modern art movement, the term "avant-garde" soon came to connote an innovative, non-bureaucratic, original art movement. Of course, the very term "movement" in avant-garde begins to show signs of bureaucratic wear as soon as it is stamped: thus the avant-garde cannot be static, cannot be classified in any ordinary or typical sense. It was the "fore-guard" of organic change in art, and foretold a constantly rearranging art universe. "The avant-garde not only negates the category of individual production but also that of individual *reception*" (Peter Bürger, *Theory of the Avant-Garde* [Minneapolis: University of Minnesota Press, 1984], p. 53). The collapse of individual/group binaries is at work here, but Perloff writes, "What the case of the Russian avant-garde suggests is that autonomy and individualism don't necessarily go hand in hand" ("Avant-Garde and Difference," p. 93). She goes on to say that the Russian avant-garde sought to "destroy . . . the ring of personality" (ibid.). Clearly there are many avant-gardes, with various projects vis-à-vis their complex cultures.

13. R. S. Perinbanayagam, "Drama in Everyday Life," in *Studies in Symbolic Interaction*, vol. 8, ed. Norman K. Denzin (Greenwich, Conn.: JAI Press, 1987), pp. 121–141.

14. John Fiske, drawing from de Certeau's work (Michel de Certeau, *The Practice of Everyday Life* [Berkeley: University of California Press, 1984]), underscores the distinction between Euro-American literacy and African-American orality. See Fiske, *Power Plays, Power Works* (London: Verso, 1993), pp. 212–213, for this discussion. Certainly there exists a cultural "literacy" which is visual in nature, which aligns much more closely with the tradition of orality than with literacy, and which has found its zenith in late-twentieth-century American televisual culture.

15. There are at least two senses of drama to which I refer (and they parallel the modernist and postmodernist avant-garde): (1) traditional, linear, binary opposi-tions, which are reminiscent of Lévi-Strauss's French Structuralist schema, and (2)

drama as tension, which exists in both modernist and postmodernist world-views. Tension may or may not be linear, may or may not be bi- or polyvocal, and so forth.

16. See Benjamin Lowe, *The Beauty of Sport: A Cross-Disciplinary Inquiry* (Englewood Cliffs, N.J.: Prentice-Hall, 1977). But while the concept of "avant-garde" derives largely from the modernist art movement, there is, as well, a flourishing postmodernist avant-garde. The debate concerning, among other issues, the commodification and appropriation (and thus reification, which would deny the very spirit of an organic and dynamic process such as "avant-garde") of such a movement continues to rage. See, for example, Bürger, *Theory of the Avant-Garde*; Sayre, *The Object of Performance*; Paul Mann, *The Theory-Death of the Avant-Garde* (Bloomington and Indianapolis: Indiana University Press, 1991).

17. Peter Donnelly, "Resistance through Sports: Sport and Cultural Hegemony," in *Sports et Sociétés Contemporaines* (Paris: Société Française de Sociologie du Sport, 1983), pp. 397–406.

18. From Barrett Watten, "Nonnarrative and the Construction of History," lecture sponsored by the Unit for Criticism and Interpretive Theory and the Department of English, University of Illinois, Urbana-Champaign, 26 October 1992.

19. Joey Reaves, "9th-Inning Rally Drops Pirates." *Chicago Tribune,* 15 October 1992, sec. 4, p. 1.

20. Joseph Kupfer, "Waiting for DiMaggio: Sport as Drama," in *Rethinking College Athletics,* ed. J. Andre and D. N. James (Philadelphia: Temple University Press, 1991), p. 109.

21. John Fiske, *Television Culture* (London: Routledge, 1987), p. 79.

22. Home Box Office, Inc. (HBO), "Play by Play: A History of Sports Television (Part 2)," 1991.

23. Norman K. Denzin, *Images of Postmodern Society* (London: Sage Publications, 1991).

24. NFL teams "made $850 million, or nearly two-thirds of their income [$1.4 billion], from radio and television. . . . Network television accounted for the vast bulk of that amount, nearly $783 million," as reported by Mark Neuzil, "Report: NFL a $1.4 Billion Business—Financial Statements Show League Made $850 million from TV, Radio," *Anchorage Daily News,* 7 July 1992, p. C5.

25. Phil Patton, *Razzle-Dazzle: The Curious Marriage of Television and Professional Football* (Garden City, N.Y.: Dial Press, 1984), p. 51.

26. Randy Roberts and James S. Olsen, *Winning Is the Only Thing: Sports in America since 1945* (Baltimore: Johns Hopkins University Press, 1989, p. 149.

27. Note that the names are of males; female sport figures—including Bonnie Blair, Jackie Joyner-Kersee, Nancy Kerrigan, even Picabo Street—certainly have received advertising contracts, but they have been given relatively short shrift compared to males. Ironically, it may be in part this lack of media hype that simultaneously undercuts the public's perception of women as sports figures and maintains women athletes' "pure" status as non-professionals who largely "participate for the love of the game."

28. Based on a "1991 study by Marketing Evaluations TVQ," Michael Jordan was

rated number three of all celebrities in "popularity, likability, appeal, and image." Cited from a sidebar ("TV Watchers Like Mike") to Greg Boeck's article "Talent Takes Stars Only So Far: Public Acceptance a Must," *USA Today,* 8 October 1991, p. 7C.

29. See chapter 4 for more on this aspect of sports marketing and self-marketing.

30. Suzi Gablik, *Has Modernism Failed?* (New York: Thames and Hudson, 1984, p. 15.

31. See Jacques Barzun, *The Use and Abuse of Art* (Princeton: Princeton University Press, 1974), p. 21: "while we tend to venerate art as one great and good thing, its various uses are most often antagonistic: art can dignify and exalt the civilization that gives it birth and also weaken and destroy it."

32. Commercial value is something else: scarcity of copies increases commercial value, while mass production decreases individual value. But it is all culturally driven. For a superb discussion of this topic—which I see as quite applicable to the technology of sports television programming—see Rosalind E. Krauss, "The Originality of the Avant-Garde," in Rosalind E. Krauss, *The Originality of the Avant-Garde and Other Modernist Myths* (Cambridge, Mass.: MIT Press, 1986).

33. Walter Benjamin, "The Work of Art in the Age of Mechanical Reproduction," in *Illuminations* (New York: Schocken, 1969 [1936]), p. 227.

34. Robert Rinehart, "Sport as Kitsch: A Case Study of *The American Gladiators,*" *Journal of Popular Culture* 28 (1994): 25–35.

35. See, for example, Becky Beal, "Disqualifying the Official: An Exploration of Social Resistance through the Subculture of Skateboarding," *Sociology of Sport Journal* 12, no. 3 (1995): 252–267; Nancy Midol and Gérard Broyer, "Toward an Anthropological Analysis of New Sport Cultures: The Case of Whiz Sports in France," *Sociology of Sport Journal* 12, no. 2 (1995): 204–212.

36. See, for example, Sal Ruibal, "Crowds Catching On to Combination Events," *USA Today,* 1 August 1997, p. 9C.

37. The sport of sky surfing reached a mass audience for the first time in the summer of 1995, when ESPN broadcast *The eXtreme Games.* See Robert F. Rinehart, "Cyber-Sports: Power and Diversity in ESPN's *The eXtreme Games,*" paper presented at the annual meeting of the North American Society for Sport Sociology, Sacramento, California, November 1995.

38. Though, of course, this seeming "passivity" is superficial only when contrasted to sport aficionados' more physical, observable involvement and participation. And, of course, there exists avant-garde, participatory theatre, whose impulse coincides with the themes that I am suggesting work for sport.

39. The ideology that sport is pure, that sport remains aloof from its fanatics, that "sport" is somehow separate from "spectacle," is a long-standing (and attractive) perspective. From popular culture (newspaper) op-ed pages, see Donald Kaul, "Is This What Sports Has Come To?" *Champaign-Urbana News Gazette,* 10 August 1992, p. A–4, and Ben Wattenberg, "Olympics Highlight Good Things," *Champaign-Urbana News Gazette,* 2 August 1992, p. B–2.

40. "Pamwatch," *Playboy,* November 1994, pp. 82–84. Whether such a story is true or apocryphal seems irrelevant if it has found its way into the popular idiom.

41. Joe Chidley, "The Most Famous Canadian on the Planet?" *Maclean's*, 27 November 1995, p. 49.

42. Certainly there exists a precept of an avant-garde that "begins in a kind of originary purity. . . [marking] its absolute purposelessness." Krauss, "The Originality of the Avant-Garde," p. 158.

But "the key point is that such a text, such a work of art, is no longer self-referential. . . . As Barthes points out, all these quotations, traces of previous texts, are focused in one place—in the reader, or the spectator." Sayre, *The Object of Performance*, p. 125. If there is a key point in avant-garde, it surely is slippery: Krauss sees some as proposing "purposelessness" as art's object; Sayre (and Barthes) sees instillment of the audience as an important facet.

43. Norman K. Denzin, *Symbolic Interactionism and Cultural Studies* (Oxford, UK: Blackwell, 1992), p. 32.

44. See ibid., pp. 33–34. In this Oedipal logic, it is argued, privilege and power always stem from male sanctions—that is likely one reason why Mariah Burton Nelson, among many others, terms sport a "male domain."

45. Norman K. Denzin, *Interpretive Interactionism* (Newbury Park, Calif.: Sage Publications, 1989).

46. HBO, "Play by Play," Part 2.

47. Ibid.

48. Ibid. In part, competition drove this technology surge: while ABC had the slo-motion replay, CBS counted it a coup to broadcast the first instant replay. The first slo-motion replay was utilized in 1961 in a football game broadcast by ABC between Boston College and Syracuse University, while the first instant replay occurred in 1963 in the Army-Navy game: there was a technological "race" going on between networks for technological advantage.

49. Ibid.

50. The concepts of hyperreality and the simulacra are examined—indeed, to some degree suggested—in Jean Baudrillard, *Simulations* (New York: Semiotext(e), 1983), and Baudrillard, *America* (London: Verso, 1988).

51. Rudy Martzke, "Enberg 'Stunned' by NBC Golf Job," *USA Today*, 14 October 1994, p. 3C.

52. Benjamin G. Rader, *American Sports: From the Age of Folk Games to the Age of Televised Sports* (Englewood Cliffs, N.J.: Prentice-Hall, 1990), p. 197.

53. Todd W. Crosset, *Outsiders in the Clubhouse: The World of Women's Professional Golf* (Albany, N.Y.: State University of New York Press, 1995), pp. 215–216.

54. Ibid, p. 207.

55. In sport studies, many of these stories may be self-congratulatory, success-oriented, and simplistic—often reflecting a structural-functional orientation, often reflecting, as Sage calls it, a "pluralistic" orientation, in which the concept of cultural hegemony is replaced with a concept of egalitarianism.

56. Dave Anderson, "The Father of the Pride of the Braves Reminisces," *New York Times*, 22 October 1991, p. B10.

57. Jack Curry, "A Tearful Cone Exits the Stage as Gooden Re-enters," *New York Times*, 4 October 1997, p. B15.

58. Denzin, *Images of Postmodern Society*, pp. 17–18.

59. Victor Turner, *Dramas, Fields, and Metaphors* (Ithaca, N.Y.: Cornell University Press, 1974, p. 28.

60. George Sage, *Power and Ideology in American Sport: A Critical Perspective* (Champaign, Ill: Human Kinetics Books, 1990), pp. 126–127.

61. See, for example, Herbert J. Gans, *Popular Culture and High Culture: An Analysis and Evaluation of Taste* (New York: Basic Books, 1974), and Lawrence W. Levine, *Highbrow/Lowbrow: The Emergence of Cultural Hierarchy in America* (Cambridge, Mass.: Harvard University Press, 1988). See also Joan Shelley Rubin, *The Making of Middlebrow Culture* (Chapel Hill: University of North Carolina Press, 1992), for an important adjunct to this issue.

62. Janet C. Harris and Roberta J. Park, "Introduction to the Sociological Study of Play, Games, and Sports," in *Play, Games and Sports in Cultural Contexts*, ed. Janet C. Harris and Roberta J. Park (Champaign, Ill: Human Kinetics Publishers, 1983), p. 15.

63. See Gruneau, "Making Spectacle"; John A. Walsh, "Sports: Media Created Images vs. Reality," *National Forum* 62 (1982): 3–4.

64. See, for example, a discussion of fight fixing and the collusion of the media in Jeffrey T. Sammons, *Beyond the Ring: The Role of Boxing in American Society* (Urbana: University of Illinois Press, 1990), pp. 66–72.

65. The list is seemingly endless: the 1919 Black Sox scandal; Art Schlichter's gambling; Pete Rose's gambling. And so on.

66. Sharon Mazer, "The Doggie Doggie World of Professional Wrestling," *Drama Review* 34 (1990): 96–121.

67. Indeed, even sport scholars who study so-called "trash" sports instead of "real" sports may be stigmatized (and themselves marginalized) by more traditional colleagues. When I told colleagues that I was studying the WWF and *The American Gladiators*, I was met by amused, deprecatory looks—until I hastily added that I was also looking at the Super Bowl and at the Barcelona Olympics. (In passing, it might be noted that only recently have mass-communication scholars begun exploring televised sport in any depth. Sport is seen as aligned with play, which is most emphatically devalued as "not work.")

68. David Best, "The Aesthetic in Sport," *British Journal of Aesthetics* 14 (1974). 197–213; Best, "Sport Is Not Art," *Journal of the Philosophy of Sport* 12 (1985): 25–40; Spencer K. Wertz, "Are Sports Art Forms?" *Journal of Aesthetic Education* 13 (1979): 107–109; Wertz, "Representation and Expression in Sport and Art," *Journal of the Philosophy of Sport* 12 (1985): 8–24.

69. Christopher Cordner, "Differences between Sport and Art," *Journal of the Philosophy of Sport* 15 (1988): 31–47; Seymour Kleinman, "The Athlete as Performing Artist: The Embodiment of Sport Literature and Philosophy," in *Coroebus Triumphs: The Alliance of Sport and the Arts*, ed. Susan J. Bandy (San Diego: San Diego State University Press, 1988), pp. 47–56.

70. Not the least of which problems include extending the metaphor to absurd lengths; narrowing the foci of the two comparatives, which in turn may limit pragmatic use of the metaphor to inform and enlighten; and overreliance on the world of metaphoric simulacra.

71. Which Victor Turner, and those who follow him (e.g., MacAloon), see as a

master narrative for cultural practices, rehearsals for some great final spectacle (drama) in which no diversions will be broached. Thus, little spontaneity—or genuine upsetting of the social order—exists in such cultural rehearsals.

72. See John J. MacAloon, "Olympic Games and the Theory of Spectacle in Modern Societies," in *Rite, Drama, Festival, Spectacle: Rehearsals toward a Theory of Cultural Performance,* ed. John J. MacAloon (Philadelphia: Institute for the Study of Human Issues, 1984), pp. 241–280.

73. Philip Auslander, "Going with the Flow: Performance Art and Mass Culture," *Drama Review* 33 (1989): 123.

74. István Deák, "Standing in the Tempest: Painters of the Hungarian Avant-Garde, 1908–1930," Exhibition Notes, 7 (Santa Barbara, Calif.: Santa Barbara Museum of Art, 1991).

75. Auslander, "Going with the Flow," p. 132.

76. Bürger, *Theory of the Avant-Garde,* p. 53.

77. See n. 11.

78. One has only to look to the recombinant histrionic formations of the professional wrestler Gorgeous George (circa 1950s), the boxer Muhammad Ali (1960s–1970s), and the professional wrestler Hulk Hogan (1980s–1990s) for examples of this sport pastiche.

79. Barry D. McPherson, James E. Curtis, and John W. Loy, *The Social Significance of Sport: An Introduction to the Sociology of Sport* (Champaign, Ill: Human Kinetics Books, 1989, p. 15.

80. Mazer, "Doggie Doggie World."

81. The privileging of any metaphor over another is antithetical to my purpose here: I seek to open up the study of sport forms, so that, for example, sport as drama, sport as avant-garde, sport as war, sport as mirror, and so forth coexist, overlap, and become utilitarian tools to better explain contemporary sport.

82. David Sansone, *Greek Athletics and the Genesis of Sport* (Berkeley: University of California Press, 1988), p. 37.

83. Ibid., p. 11.

84. See, for example, the listing in *USA Today* (23 October 1991, p. 13C) of the 114 "Most Popular Sports" in America, "according to a survey by the Sports Marketing Group of Dallas," which includes "30. Pro wrestling; 31. Tractor pulling; 32. Rodeo . . . 35. Bodybuilding . . . 58. Roller derby." Other sports listed, possibly outside some "sport canons" for one definitional flaw or another, include beach volleyball, arena football, motocross, daredevil acts, arm wrestling, dog racing, frisbee, cliff diving, mountain bike Velodrome bicycling, and the television show *The American Gladiators* (no. 102).

85. Harry F. Waters, "'Rough, Tough and Rotten': Two New 'Sports' Shows, So Outrageous They Hurt," *Newsweek,* 14 August 1989, p. 64.

86. Edward M. Bruner, "Ethnography as Narrative," in *The Anthropology of Experience,* ed. Victor Turner and Edward M. Bruner (Urbana: University of Illinois Press, 1986), pp. 139–155.

87. Gablik, *Has Modernism Failed?* p. 62.

88. See Sayre, *The Object of Performance.* The debate regarding even the very existence of a postmodernist avant-garde continues; the reader is directed to the body of art theory literature previously cited in this chapter and chapter 4. As well,

for an interesting, mostly modernist view of the component parts of the debate, I direct the reader particularly to Matei Calinescu, *Five Faces of Modernity*.

89. Norman K. Denzin, *The Cinematic Society: The Voyeur's Gaze* (London: Sage Publications, 1995), p. 37.

90. Denzin, *Images of Postmodern Society*.

91. Linda Hutcheon, *A Theory of Parody: The Teachings of Twentieth-Century Art Forms* (New York: Methuen, 1985).

92. David Kolb, *Postmodern Sophistications* (Chicago: University of Chicago Press, 1990).

3. SPORT AS KITSCH

1. There exists a large body of literature surrounding the interplay between children's socialization and television. However, I direct the reader (as a start) to some of Neil Postman's work, including *Amusing Ourselves to Death: Public Discourse in the Age of Show Business* (New York: Penguin Books, 1985) and *The Disappearance of Childhood* (New York: Delacorte Press, 1982).

2. Susan Birrell and John W. Loy, Jr., "Media Sport: Hot and Cool," in *Sport, Culture, and Society: A Reader on the Sociology of Sport,* 2nd ed., ed. John W. Loy, Gerald S. Kenyon, and Barry D. McPherson (Philadelphia: Lea and Febiger, 1981), p. 303.

3. The Los Angeles Coliseum was not used for WrestleMania VII because of "the gulf war [and] the attendant fear of terrorism and the necessity of a complex (and expensive) security system to guarantee everyone's safety outdoors." See William Oscar Johnson, "Wrestling with Success," *Sports Illustrated,* 25 March 1991, pp. 42–54.

4. Ibid., p. 51.

5. Kevin Maney, "Computerized Puck Keeps Check of Action," *USA Today,* 19 January 1996, p. 5B.

6. For an interesting discussion of the -ization of art, see Suzi Gablik, *Has Modernism Failed?* (New York: Thames and Hudson, 1984); of sport, see Allen Guttmann, *From Ritual To Record: The Nature of Modern Sports* (New York: Columbia University Press, 1978), esp. chaps. 2 and 3, "From Ritual to Record" and "Capitalism, Protestantism, and Modern Sport." This work, of course, derives from what Guttmann calls Max Weber's "view of social organization" (p. 80).

7. There are, of course, exceptions to this standard definition—the ice skater who skates for aesthetic reasons is but one example—but the problem is one of measurement: How does one measure what determines an individual's choice to participate in sport? And do those motivations change from moment to moment?

8. Benjamin Lowe, *The Beauty of Sport: A Cross-Disciplinary Inquiry* (Englewood Cliffs, N.J.: Prentice-Hall, 1977), p. 29.

9. The phenomenon of ready-made television is somewhat reminiscent of *The Monkees,* a television situation comedy in which four actors learned to sing and play instruments to satisfy the demands of the show. The Monkees' success as a pop group became emblematic of life imitating art.

10. John Fiske, *Television Culture* (London: Routledge, 1988), p. 267 and chap. 14, "Quizzical Pleasures."

11. Shows similar to *The American Gladiators* have come and gone, but TAG seems to have found its way into popular culture, with a savvy blend of striking costumes, flashy games/contests, campy style, aggressive promotion, and appreciation of physical skill.

12. E. Ann Kaplan, "Introduction," in *Postmodernism and Its Discontents,* ed. E. Ann Kaplan (London: Verso, 1988), pp. 1–9.

13. Of course, the avant-garde and kitsch elements now are somewhat blended and certainly co-dependent: it would do just as well to ascertain avant-garde, or innovative, elements within sport as kitschian elements. See Clement Greenberg, "Avant-Garde and Kitsch," *Partisan Review* 6 (1939): 35. See also the next chapter for a case study of the avant-garde elements of the World Wrestling Federation.

14. I have chosen to use the term "mainstream," as the term "traditional" sport is an inaccurate appropriation of such sport forms that still exist from so-called traditional cultures. For further discussion of this distinction, see Victoria Paraschak, "Variations in Race Relations: Sporting Events for Native Peoples in Canada," *Sociology of Sport Journal* 14 (1997): 1–21; Jørn Møller, "The Symbolic Significance of Traditional Sports and Games: Pre- or Postmodernism? A Cross-Cultural Perspective," in *Fragmenter af et Kalenderår* (Idrætsforsk, 1995).

15. This, of course, leads to the question of whether an industrialized, highly media-influenced contemporary society such as the United States has retained any "traditional" sport at all—or if, in fact, a concept such as "traditional sport" is any longer valid in westernized, commodified culture. But see Møller, "The Symbolic Significance of Traditional Sports and Games"; he makes a good case that pockets of traditional sport still exist in highly industrialized societies. One example is pelota, in Basque Spain.

16. Clifford Geertz, "Deep Play: Notes on the Balinese Cockfight," *Daedalus* 101 (1972): 1–37; Jon Donlon, "Fighting Cocks, Feathered Warriors, and Little Heroes," *Play and Culture* 3 (1990): 273–285.

17. Richard D. Mandell, *Sport: A Cultural History* (New York: Columbia University Press, 1984).

18. Fiske, *Television Culture,* chap. 13.

19. See Michael Holquist, "Introduction," in *The Dialogic Imagination: Four Essays by M. M. Bakhtin,* ed. Michael Holquist (Austin: University of Texas Press, 1981), p. xx. I am thinking particularly here of the local candlepin bowling tournaments that I viewed on local networks in the Portland, Maine, region, and of the paintball broadcasts from Danville, Illinois. How do these "esoteric" sports get enough local sponsorship to broadcast?

20. According to Holquist, "Heteroglossia is Bakhtin's way of referring, in any utterance of any kind, to the peculiar interaction between the two fundamentals in all communication. . . . A mode of transcription must . . . be a more or less fixed system. But these repeatable features . . . are in the power of the particular context in which the utterance is made." Holquist, "Introduction," pp. xix–xx.

21. George Sage, *Power and Ideology in American Sport: A Critical Perspective* (Champaign, Ill: Human Kinetics Books, 1990), pp. 126–127.

22. ABC-TV, 10 November 1990; my emphasis.

23. After he had failed to complete fifty-five pushups and had been disqualified

from any further attempts, one frustrated man muttered, "Let me do the real events. I show them big boys something."

24. See chap. 5, in which I discuss some of the religious and secular trappings of the 1992 Super Bowl.

25. See Hal Foster, "Postmodernism: A Preface," in *The Anti-Aesthetic: Essays on Postmodern Culture,* ed. Hal Foster (Seattle: Bay Press, 1983), pp. ix–xvi; Mike Featherstone, "In Pursuit of the Postmodern: An Introduction," *Theory, Culture, and Society* 5 (1988): 192–215; and Kaplan, "Introduction." I would also include in this company, for his prescient thoughts regarding a societal disassembling of bi-polarities into "tensions in American society" (most notably, work/play and mascu-line/feminine), Gregory Stone's work "American Sports: Play and Dis-play," *Chicago Review* 9 (1955): 83–100.

26. Kaplan, "Introduction," p. 4.

27. Lowe, *The Beauty of Sport,* p. 29.

28. Mandell, *Sport: A Cultural History,* p. 153. See also Thorstein Veblen, *The Theory of the Leisure Class* (New York: Penguin Books, 1979 [1899]), particularly chaps. IV ("Conspicuous Consumption") and VI ("Pecuniary Canons of Taste"), for an exploration of the leisure pursuits—and "conspicuous consumption"—of persons of privilege at the beginning of the twentieth century.

29. See Anne Sheppard, *Aesthetics: An Introduction to the Philosophy of Art* (Oxford: Oxford University Press, 1987), who poses a compelling argument against long-held traditional aesthetic theories (i.e., imitation, expression, and form) that gives way to interpretation and evaluation, and finally to a morality of art. In fact, the nature of contemporary works of art has compelled aestheticians to rethink aesthetic theory in order to encompass such postmodern work.

30. Lowe, *The Beauty of Sport,* pp. 27–56, 91–105. But, of course, this art-sport relationship is not without historical precedent: for example, see Neville Cardus, *Cricket* (London: Longman, 1930), as cited in John Bale, "Cricket," in *The Theater of Sport,* ed. Karl B. Raitz (Baltimore: Johns Hopkins University Press, 1995), p. 78.

31. Attempts to bridge the gulf have occurred, however stultifyingly: see Michael J. Parsons, *How We Understand Art: A Cognitive Developmental Account of Aesthetic Experience* (Cambridge: Cambridge University Press, 1987).

32. Jean Baudrillard, *America* (London: Verso, 1988).

33. Matei Calinescu, *Five Faces of Modernity: Modernism, Avant-Garde, Decadence, Kitsch, Postmodernism* (Durham, N.C.: Duke University Press, 1987), p. 234.

34. Greeenberg, "Avant-Garde and Kitsch," p. 35.

35. The "success" of the avant-garde (or of individual avant-garde works—see Wendy Steiner, *The Scandal of Pleasure: Art in an Age of Fundamentalism* [Chicago: University of Chicago Press, 1995]) is, admittedly, a point of contention, yet that fine point does not detract from the links between sport and artistic concepts.

36. Baudrillard, *America,* p. 101.

37. Of course, the modernist avant-garde, it is said, appropriated such an oppositional tone to demonstrate disregard for the then–art establishment and to include works in which the artist and the viewer contributed to the production of the work. For a problematic approach to this dilemma, see Rosalind E. Krauss, "The Originality of the Avant-Garde," in *The Originality of the Avant-Garde and*

Other Modernist Myths, ed. Rosalind E. Krauss (Cambridge, Mass.: MIT Press, 1986), pp. 151–170.

See also Quentin Bell, *Bad Art* (Chicago: University of Chicago Press, 1989), pp. 6–7: The "taste of the establishment . . . was challenged by what we now call the *avant garde,* expressing a view of art which, although it varied, was invariably hostile to the establishment. The establishment, on the other hand, considered that the artists of the *avant garde* were either negligible or despicable. In the eyes of the vast majority, theirs was bad art."

38. Involvement in the "stories" of athletes, thus, has become a marketing strategy: similar to immersion into the culture of soap opera, sport enthusiasts' knowing the background and context of the "characters" becomes a critical factor. But the very kitschiness of the stories is comfortable, and the "characters" then reduce to types.

39. Calinescu, *Five Faces,* p. 249.

40. Ibid., p. 229.

41. Greenberg, "Avant-Garde and Kitsch," p. 40.

42. W. J. J. Gordon, "On Being Explicit about Creative Process," *Journal of Creative Behavior* 6 (1972): 296.

43. See, for example, the videotapes that have "captured" highlights of Michael Jordan's career, his outstanding moves (which resonate with the culturally literate viewer in the context of the actual game, game situation, and so on). The very "capturing" of transitory experience becomes problematic, however; there are positive relationships between first creations and avant-garde, and derivations of first creations and kitsch.

44. See, as another example (though certainly less kitschy) of a westernized view of sumo, Andy Adams and Clyde Newton, *Sumo* (New York: Gallery Books, 1989).

45. Pamela Brown, "Bottoms Up in Latest Bar Crazes," *USA Weekend,* 12–14 March 1993 ("What's Next: Tips, Trends, Teasers"), p. 18.

46. See Mike Snider, "Faux Sumo Wrestling Is Bellying Up to Bars," *USA Today,* 4 October 1993, p. 1D. Bar scenes seem to be sites of invented—and faddish—sport as well: "Biosphere Bowling" is reported to have become a bar fad. See "They're on a Roll!" *People,* 12 April 1993, p. 89; Brown, "Bottoms Up in Latest Bar Crazes," p. 18.

47. Calinescu, *Five Faces,* p. 249.

48. See *USA Today's* weekly "Inside TV" section.

49. Laura Mulvey, "Visual Pleasure and Narrative Cinema," *Screen* 16 (1975): 10–11.

50. Marketers believe that creating a voyeuristic feel works: speaking of the use of sumo wrestlers as spokesmen, Martha T. Moore ("Sumo Wrestlers Latest Ad Heavyweights," *USA Today,* 2 August 1993, p. 4B) writes, "Sumo wrestlers are instantly recognizable, quintessentially Japanese and a bit mind-boggling. Mike Gallagher, who wrote the Sprint ad for agency J. Walter Thompson, says, 'I equate it to a car crash. It's kind of weird, bizarre, but you kind of have to look at it anyway.'"

51. Louis Golding, *The Bare-Knuckle Breed* (New York: A. S. Barnes and Co., 1954).

52. ABC-TV, *The American Gladiators,* 10 November 1990.

53. Margaret Morse, "Sport on Television: Replay and Display," in *Regarding Television: Critical Approaches—An Anthology,* ed. E. Ann Kaplan (Frederick, Md.: University Publications of America, 1983), pp. 44–66.

54. Barry Brummett and Margaret Carlisle Duncan, "Theorizing without Totalizing: Specularity and Televised Sports," *Quarterly Journal of Speech* 76 (1990): 227–246.

55. A customary gambit of the professional wrestling circuit is to pit ethnic groups against one another. See Thomas Hendricks, "Professional Wrestling as Moral Order," *Sociological Inquiry* 44 (1974): 177–188; Brendan Maguire and John F. Wozniak, "Racial and Ethnic Stereotypes in Professional Wrestling," *Social Science Journal* 24 (1987): 261–273; Jeffrey J. Mondak, "The Politics of Professional Wrestling," *Journal of Popular Culture* (Fall 1989): 139–149.

56. Curtis F. Brown, *Star-Spangled Kitsch* (New York: Universe Books, 1975).

57. Ibid., p. 171.

58. Margaret Carlisle Duncan and Cynthia A. Hasbrook, "Denial of Power in Televised Women's Sports," *Sociology of Sport Journal* 5 (1988): 1–21. Interestingly, of the women I have spoken to regarding the show (two dozen or more), all but one have considered *The American Gladiators* a positive force for female athleticism and empowerment.

59. Margaret Carlisle Duncan, "A Great Athlete . . . and a Cute, Sexy Flirt, Too!" *Extra!,* January/February 1992, pp. 20–21.

60. Janice C. Simpson, "Real-Life Davids vs. Goliaths," *Time,* 21 October 1991, pp. 102–103.

61. *USA Today,* 18 June 1991, p. 3D.

62. Margaret Carlisle Duncan and Barry Brummett, "Types and Sources of Spectating Pleasure in Televised Sports," *Sociology of Sport Journal* 6 (1989): 205.

63. Csonka's condescending bit of consolation to Margaret McCargo echoes NBC's blatant attempt (at the 1996 Atlanta Olympics) to dramatize the human interest stories of selected athletes: it was believed that humanizing stories would build a larger (read, more female) audience.

64. This was particularly true when *The American Gladiators* first was broadcast: since 1991 (when this particular segment of textual analysis was done), the format has clearly been laden with higher "Hollywood" (and NBA, NFL, and MLB) production standards (e.g., more cameras shooting from more angles).

65. Jean-Claude Suares, "A Designer's Guide to Schlock, Camp and Kitsch—And the Taste of Things to Come," *Print* 29 (1975): 25–35.

66. There exist elements of a sport avant-garde as well: so-called "innovators" in sport might as easily be termed such creative geniuses. See chapter 4.

67. Lowe, *The Beauty of Sport,* pp. 92–103.

4. SPORT AS AVANT-GARDE

1. See John Long, *How To Rock Climb!* 2nd ed. (Evergreen, Colo.: Chockstone Press, 1993); and issues of *Climbing* and *Rock and Ice.*

2. See chapter 7 of this book for further discussion of ESPN's coverage of *The eXtreme Games.*

3. Not just athletes, but coaches, managers, and even owners are commodified:

witness the proliferation of coaches–turned–color commentators (e.g., John Madden, Bill Walsh) or discussants (e.g., Joe Gibbs, Mike Ditka); the now-famous Ultra Slim-Fast hucksters (e.g., Tommy Lasorda, Buddy Ryan); and hype surrounding owners that threatens to overshadow the exploits of the players (e.g., the saga of George Steinbrenner and the Yankees; the signing of "Rocket" Ismail to the Canadian Football League's Toronto Argonauts by, among other owners, Wayne Gretzky). The commodification and intertextuality between "players" and the entertainment industry is not accidental.

4. For a fascinating discussion of the false nostalgia for previous times, as well as a discussion of commodification and the sign, see Mike Featherstone, *Consumer Culture and Postmodernism* (London: Sage Publications, 1991), esp. chap. 4.

5. HBO, "Play by Play," Part 2.

6. Richard Gruneau, "Making Spectacle: A Case Study in Television Sports Production," in Lawrence A. Wenner, ed., *Media, Sports, and Society* (Newbury Park, Calif.: Sage Publications, 1989), pp. 134–154. See also chapter 1 of this volume.

7. A third possibility is often cited: advertisers representing media moguls create a public appetite, create a market and a need. While this is an interesting and vital avenue of query, the former two—pure athletics and public clamor—suffice for the purposes of this chapter.

8. I see this moment, for individuals, as an interweaving between postmodernism and modernism: though distinctions are made in academe and within scholarly discourse, for the individual, the whole of the contemporary experience is conflated with the gestalt of postmodernism and modernism as lived experience. Thus, while it is useful to study these historical moments as distinctive, I caution the reader to imagine the distinctions as not being quite so obvious. There is overlap, there is slippage, between modernism and postmodernism—there is borrowing from and sharing with one another: but, of course, this slippage itself could be categorized as a characteristic of the postmodern moment. See Chris Rojek, *Decentring Leisure: Rethinking Leisure Theory* (London: Sage Publications, 1995).

9. See, for example, work by Andrew Benjamin, Matei Calinescu, Linda Hutcheon, Andreas Huyssen, Paul Mann, Marjorie Perloff, and many others, discussing the points of departure between and among modernism, postmodernism, kitsch, avant-garde, the historical avante-garde, and other elements of contemporary society.

10. For an excellent discussion of this point, see Lawrence W. Levine, *Highbrow/Lowbrow: The Emergence of Cultural Hierarchy in America* (Cambridge, Mass.: Harvard University Press, 1988).

11. Kenneth Clark, *Moments of Vision* (London: John Murray, 1981), p. 66.

12. See, for example, Suzi Gablik, *Has Modernism Failed?* (New York: Thames and Hudson, 1984), or Paul Mann, *The Theory-Death of the Avant Garde* (Bloomington and Indianapolis: Indiana University Press, 1991). See also Jerome Bruner, *Acts of Meaning* (Cambridge, Mass.: Harvard University Press, 1990), pp. 36–43, for a discussion of the use of folk psychology by scholars to understand what is really happening as opposed to what theory might tell us.

13. See Gablik, *Has Modernism Failed?* p. 16.

14. Mike Featherstone, "In Pursuit of the Postmodern: An Introduction," *Theory, Culture, and Society* 5 (1988): 195–215.

15. This might be a partial explanation for fads' recurrence and for the success of such games (and spinoffs of games) as Trivial Pursuit. See Jeff Holubitsky, "Fads: Crazes Rely on Time to Put Mark on History," *Windsor Star,* 8 February 1996, p. B4.

16. Andrew Benjamin, *Art, Mimesis, and the Avant-Garde* (London: Routledge, 1991), p. 138.

17. Marjorie Perloff, *The Futurist Moment: Avant-Garde, Avant Guerre, and the Language of Rupture* (Chicago: University of Chicago Press, 1986).

18. Marjorie Perloff, *Radical Artifice: Writing Poetry in the Age of Media* (Chicago: University of Chicago Press, 1991).

19. Benjamin, *Art, Mimesis,* p. 140.

20. See, for example, John Naisbitt, *Megatrends: Ten New Directions Transforming Our Lives* (New York: Warner Books, 1982), pp. 249–252, or John W. Loy, "Social Psychological Characteristics of Innovators," *American Sociological Review* 34 (1969): 73–82.

21. Holubitsky, "Fads," p. B4.

22. Andreas Huyssen, *After the Great Divide: Modernism, Mass Culture, Postmodernism* (Bloomington: Indiana University Press, 1986), p. 193.

23. John Fiske, *Television Culture* (London: Routledge, 1988).

24. Jack McCallum and Dostya Kennedy, eds., "Scorecard: Knight Errant," *Sports Illustrated,* 19 February 1996, p. 16. The linking of corporate sponsors and sports teams/groups (even nations) should not be too surprising: witness the college bowl links with corporate sponsors, the blatant hawking of product by golf and bowling sponsors, the Gatorade Ironman Triathlon, etc. What is somewhat remarkable is that the myth was betrayed—that nationalism has now evolved into multinationalism—and that *Sports Illustrated*'s mild rebuff of chairman Phil Knight drew very little response from the readership: in the 11 March 1996 issue, two letters were printed. In one, the writer suggested that Phil Knight "stick that swoosh in his big mouth" (Pat Sweeney, letter to the editor, *Sports Illustrated,* 11 March 1996, p. 10); in the other letter, Nike chairman Phil Knight responded that Nike "has now signed the U.S. men's and women's soccer teams" and several other United States teams (Phil Knight, letter to the editor, *Sports Illustrated,* 11 March 1996, pp. 10, 12).

25. Jochen Schulte-Sasse, "Foreword: Theory of Modernism versus Theory of the Avant-Garde," in *Theory of the Avant-Garde,* ed. Peter Bürger (Minneapolis: University of Minnesota Press, 1984), pp. xxxv–xxxvi.

26. Ibid., p. xxxvi.

27. See Michael A. Messner, *Power at Play: Sports and the Problem of Masculinity* (Boston: Beacon, 1992), pp. 9–10.

28. See Robert Dunn, "Postmodernism: Populism, Mass Culture, and Avant-Garde," *Theory, Culture, and Society* 8 (1991): 111–135.

29. See Gablik, *Has Modernism Failed?*

30. Dunn, "Postmodernism," p. 112 (his emphasis).

31. Renato Poggioli, *The Theory of the Avant-Garde* (Cambridge, Mass.: Belknap Press, 1968), p. 8.

32. *The Random House Dictionary of the English Language* (New York: Random House, 1969), p. 102.

33. Andreas Huyssen, "The Hidden Dialectic: The Avant-Garde—Technology—Mass Culture," in *The Myths of Information: Technology and Postindustrial Culture,* ed. Kathleen Woodward (Madison, Wisc.: Coda Press, 1980), p. 153.

34. Henri de Saint Simon, *Opinions littéraires, philosophiques et industrielles* (1825), cited in Huyssen, "The Hidden Dialectic," p. 152.

35. Mann, *The Theory-Death of the Avant Garde,* p. 13.

36. This concept is similar to Williams's emergent culture: "What matters . . . in understanding emergent culture . . . is that it is never only a matter of immediate practice; indeed it depends crucially on finding new forms or adaptations of form." In Raymond Williams, *Marxism and Literature* (Oxford: Oxford University Press, 1977), p. 126. For examples of subtle acts of resistance (which certainly might be described as avant-garde, in many senses), see James C. Scott, *Weapons of the Weak: Everyday Forms of Peasant Resistance* (New Haven: Yale University Press, 1985), esp. chap. 8; and Forrest D. Colburn, ed., *Everyday Forms of Peasant Resistance* (Armonk, N.Y.: M. E. Sharpe, 1989).

37. In fact, the disparity between contemporary "poetry" and "sport" is lessening. Witness, for example, the (self-claimed) Chicago innovation of "poetry slams," cited in the *Chicago Tribune* (3 February 1992, sec. 2, p. 3): "Reputedly inspired by wrestling matches, Chicago's slams have given unprecedented visibility to the city's poets. . . . [Paul] Hoover [who has been "identified with the avant-garde"] has become a chief voice of dissent . . . [saying] the slams encourage people to 'consume' poetry exclusively as theater."

38. See James Clifford, "On Ethnographic Authority," *Representations* 1, no. 2 (1983): 118–146.

39. Margaret P. Battin, John Fisher, Ronald Moore, and Anita Silvers, *Puzzles about Art* (New York: St. Martin's Press, 1989), pp. 21–22.

40. Henry M. Sayre, *The Object of Performance: The American Avant-Garde since 1970* (Chicago: University of Chicago Press, 1989), p. 230.

41. Ibid.

42. Ibid.

43. See Gablik, *Has Modernism Failed?*

44. Susan L. Greendorfer, "Sport and the Mass Media," in *Handbook of Social Science of Sport,* ed. Günther R. F. Lueschen and George H. Sage (Champaign, Ill: Stipes Publishing Co., 1981), pp. 160–180.

45. And, it might be added, a part of the contemporary sport tourist discourse. See chapter 8.

46. Bob Cannon, "How They Do That Halftime Show: Greatest Show on Turf," *Entertainment Weekly,* 11 February 1994, p. 53.

47. "WWF," Fox Channel KTVU (Ch. 2), Oakland/San Francisco, 20 July 1991.

48. Ben Brown, "Hawaiian Achieves Sumo Breakthrough," *USA Today,* 26 January 1993, p. C1.

49. Of course, the avant-garde of modernism opposed the death of creativity as exemplified within structures of commoditization and mythically had no interest in its "effectiveness" with the masses. See, for example, Rosalind E. Krauss, "The Originality of the Avant-Garde," in *The Originality of the Avant-Garde and Other Modernist Myths* (Cambridge, Mass.: MIT Press, 1986), pp. 51–170.

50. Singular entertainment "types" such as Marilyn Monroe and Madonna, who successfully re-created themselves, have served as models for the likes of Dennis Rodman. The impulse, of course, is multidirectional: workers in the entertainment industry borrow from one another to perfect their trade. See, for example, Kathryn N. Benzel, "The Body as Art: Still Photographs of Marilyn Monroe," *Journal of Popular Culture* 25, no. 2 (1991): 1–29; Richard Hoffer, "The Importance of Being Barry: The Giants' Barry Bonds Is the Best Player in the Game Today—Just Ask Him," *Sports Illustrated,* 24 May 1993, pp. 12–21; Michael Silver, "Rodman Unchained," *Sports Illustrated,* 29 May 1995, pp. 20–29.

51. Silver, "Rodman Unchained," p. 22. Interestingly, one of the components that may distinguish the postmodern sport star from the modern sport star is a heightened self-awareness, which plays out of a deeper "practical consciousness." Dennis Rodman is certainly aware of his place on the commodity chain—and he voices his opinion vociferously and articulately.

52. As reported on CNN News (4 October 1991), NFL players' careers average 3.7 years.

53. Johannes Birringer, "Imprints and Re-Visions: Carolee Schneemann's Visual Archeology," *Performing Arts Journal* 44 (1993): 31.

54. Decidedly "politically incorrect," this gesture, eschewed for a time by Jane Fonda and her husband, Turner Broadcasting head Ted Turner (but then heartily adopted), was carried over into the 1992 season—and adopted by fans of such teams as the Kansas City Chiefs—and continues in 1997 (in the 1997 National League Championship Series, Florida Marlins fans skewered the so-called Tomahawk Chop with their version, called the Mock Chop).

55. CBS Sports, National League Playoff Series, 5 October 1991. The instrumental nature of the offensive gesture was thus justified.

56. William Oscar Johnson, "Wrestling with Success," *Sports Illustrated,* 25 March 1991, p. 44.

57. Ken Tucker, "Party Out of Bounds," *Entertainment Weekly,* 11 February 1994, pp. 52–53.

58. "Get Ready for Onslaught of 'Super Ads,'" *Idaho State Journal,* 26 January 1996, p. C3.

59. Ibid.

60. From "The Official WWF™ Merchandise Catalog," in World Wrestling Federation Program, vol. 190, Spring/Summer 1991; "The Official WWF™ Merchandise Catalog," in *WWF Magazine,* September 1991; and from the live show merchandise display.

61. Michael A. Lipton and Irvin Muchnick, "Incredible Hulk? He Denies It, but Colleagues Say Hogan's Bulk Was Built on a Steroid Foundation," *People,* 23 March 1992, p. 91.

62. Gerald W. Morton and George M. O'Brien, *Wrestling to Rasslin': Ancient Sport to American Spectacle* (Bowling Green, Ohio: Bowling Green State University Popular Press, 1985), p. 51.

63. For the term "trash sport," see George Sage, *Power and Ideology in American Sport: A Critical Perspective* (Champaign, Ill: Human Kinetics Books, 1990).

64. An interesting example of this type of behavior is the New York Giants–San

Diego Chargers football game on 23 December 1995, at which fans threw ice balls onto the field. See Mike Freeman, "Amid Hail of Snowballs, Giants Suffer Meltdown," *New York Times,* 24 December 1995, sec. 8, pp. 1–2; Dave Anderson, "Throwing Snowballs in Hell," *New York Times,* 24 December 1995, sec. 8, p. 1.

65. Johnson, "Wrestling," p. 51.

66. See, for example, Sharon Mazer, "The Doggie Doggie World of Professional Wrestling," *Drama Review* 34 (1990): 96–121; or Morton and O'Brien, *Wrestling to Rasslin',* esp. chap. 2, "Sinew and Sequins: Wrestling in the Age of Electronics."

67. First aired on 26 August 1991, pay-per-view.

68. NBC Sports, 5 October 1991.

69. Much as Greek theatre performers make broad, almost caricatural gestures for their audiences—and the subtle nuances of film acting (the facial tic, the furrowed brow) would be lost upon their "coarser" audiences. But Greek theatre is considered "high" theatre.

70. As cited in *USA Today,* 8 October 1991, p. 7C.

71. See Johnson, "Wrestling."

72. See, for example, Manthia Diawara, "Black British Cinema: Spectatorship and Identity Formation in *Territories,*" *Public Culture* 3, no. 1 (1990): 33–47.

73. Linda Hutcheon, *A Theory of Parody: The Teachings of Twentieth-Century Art Forms* (New York: Methuen, 1985), p. 96. The cultural competence of the "reader" of such texts is, of course, critical: the cultural competence of sports aficionados is legend.

74. Overheard at the World Wrestling Federation™ live show, 30 May 1991, Assembly Hall, Champaign, Ill.

75. See Dunn, "Postmodernism."

76. Popular culture is an archeological dig for future culturists; thus value judgments that privilege so-called "high" over "low" forms of culture (be they art, sport, or electronic storytelling) remain inappropriate because they establish canons that may limit study. See chapters 1 and 2. See Anna Quindlen, "If You Turn Off the Television, You Tune Out Popular Culture," *Champaign-Urbana News-Gazette,* 4 December 1991, p. A–4. Thus, the choice to utilize *USA Today* for many of the newspaper texts studied is a conscious one, one that limits regional influences and biases to an extent, and one that assumes a cultural homogenization which further needs to be studied.

5. SPORT AS EPIPHANIC MARKER

1. Moreover, the question of how to convey these experiences—and how they would be received—becomes an interesting problematic. If, as many ethnographers have chosen to do, I decided to pretend to convey an "objective" view of the Super Bowl, I would lose much of the emotional feel of my object. If, on the other hand, I wrote strictly of the sensory experience, many problems would crop up: I would rouse the rancor of colleagues who avoid affect, because it (like many other concepts) ultimately is not "quantifiable"; I would move outside academic discourse, at least the majority of that discourse which is current within sport studies; I would open up the question of the seductive nature of writing itself (not necessarily a bad thing); I would be taking on an impossible task, since experience is

modified when we speak (or write) about it; I would be avoiding cognition, itself a human experience.

2. Norman K. Denzin, "Representing Lived Experiences in Ethnographic Texts," *Studies in Symbolic Interaction* 12 (1991): 63.

3. Norman K. Denzin, *Images of Postmodern Society: Social Theory and Contemporary Cinema* (London: Sage Publications, 1991), p. 139.

4. Ibid., p. 11.

5. In fact, football players often check the large-screen video monitor atop the stadium to *see what they have just done*. Similarly, spectators' images are often projected onto the same screen, perhaps to remind everyone in attendance just how much fun this really is (and as we have seen in the example given in chapter 2 about Pamela Anderson Lee, this "fifteen minutes of fame" carries with it unbridled hope of instant success). Denzin (*Images of Postmodern Society,* p. 11), citing Steve Connor, *Postmodernist Culture* (Oxford: Basil Blackwood, 1989), speaks of the rock concert aficionado performing this very gesture. This reinforces an important similarity between art (music) and sport: their performative natures.

6. Denzin, *Images of Postmodern Society,* 11.

7. The "how-to-write" literature is certainly worthy of examination in this regard: How does one make writing "artful," "truthful," "provocative"? In my opinion, some of the better books discussing these options central to writing include John Gardner, *The Art of Fiction: Notes on Craft for Young Writers* (New York: Vintage Books, 1983); Natalie Goldberg, *Writing Down the Bones: Freeing the Writer Within* (Boston: Shambhala, 1986); Brenda Ueland, *If You Want to Write: A Book about Art, Independence and Spirit,* 2nd ed. (Saint Paul, Minn.: Graywolf Press, 1987 [1938]); and Monica Wood, *Description* (Cincinnati, Ohio: Writer's Digest Books, 1995).

Of course, more specifically, there exists a whole body of literature about qualitative research, and the process (and product) of ethnography. For a start: Norman K. Denzin and Yvonna S. Lincoln, eds., *Handbook of Qualitative Research* (Thousand Oaks, Calif.: Sage Publications, 1994); John Van Maanen, ed., *Representation in Ethnography* (Thousand Oaks, Calif.: Sage Publications, 1995).

8. By calling it a "story," I have already shifted the focus from raw experience to mediated experience, and will continue to follow that convention. However, I am not utilizing the dramatic framework for this story: thus, the "structure" might more appropriately be seen as non-narrative.

9. See Victor Turner, *Dramas, Fields, and Metaphors: Symbolic Action in Human Society* (Symbol, Myth, and Ritual Series) (Ithaca, N.Y.: Cornell University Press, 1974), pp. 166–230. Interestingly, another site of pilgrimage for the professional football fan—generic, not team-affiliated—is Canton, Ohio, where the NFL Football Hall of Fame is located—and there is no intrusion of the secular. There is only one NFL game played there annually—no distraction to the pilgrims' interests, since it is symbolic, the first pre-season contest.

10. *Regis and Kathie Lee Live!* WCIA (CBS), Champaign, Ill., January 1992.

11. For example, see Charles Fruehling Springwood, *Cooperstown to Dyersville: A Geography of Baseball Nostalgia* (Boulder, Colo.: Westview Press, 1996); John D. Dorst, *The Written Suburb: An American Site, An Ethnographic Dilemma* (Philadelphia: University of Pennsylvania Press, 1989).

12. See Jean Baudrillard, *Simulations* (New York: Semiotext(e), 1983).

13. Erik Cohen, "Tourism as Play," *Religion* 15 (1985): 296

14. Anthony F. C. Wallace, *Religion: An Anthropological View* (New York: Random House, 1966).

15. Ibid.

16. Gerald Redmond, "Ghosts Linger in Memories," *Windsor Star,* 9 March 1996, p. A11.

17. See Jeff Pelline, "Silicon Valley's Power Growing: Bid to Rename Candlestick to 3Com a Coup," *San Francisco Chronicle,* 7 September 1995, pp. D1–D2; Stefan Fatsis, "Stadium Names Get Businesslike in the Minors," *Wall Street Journal,* 10 April 1996, pp. B1, B10.

18. David Shoalts, "Hockey Fan Comes First in New Arena," *Globe and Mail,* 15 March 1996, p. D1.

19. Rachel Shuster, "NFL Honor Has Sterling History," *USA Today,* 26 January 1993, p. 5C.

20. Ibid.

21. C. Wright Mills, *The Sociological Imagination* (London: Oxford University Press, 1959), p. 169.

22. Ibid., p. 170.

23. I have searched for the exact source of this pithy term, and the closest I can come is note 4 in Edward M. Bruner, "The Story of Abraham Lincoln: A Postmodern Perspective," paper first presented at the University of Wisconsin, Department of Anthropology Lecture, Madison, Wisc., 4 May 1990, wherein Bruner writes, "'Soft struggle' was suggested . . . by Daphne Berdahl" based upon Bourdieu's work. It seems to me that Bruner has used the term "velvet noose" in this context as well, but I may have imagined it.

24. Michel Foucault, *Discipline and Punish: The Birth of the Prison* (New York: Pantheon Books, 1977).

25. "Being Seen," *USA Today,* 17 January 1992, p. 4C.

26. See Mary Schmitt, "Wolves Worth Watching, Too," *Saint Paul Pioneer Press,* 24 January 1992, pp. 1D, 4D.

27. See Randy Furst, "The Weekend Belongs to a Wave of High Rollers," Minneapolis *Star Tribune,* 26 January 1992, pp. 1A, 15A.

28. As quoted from the 1-800 Directory of *USA Today* advertisers (13 January 1992, p. 5D).

29. "The Point After," Minneapolis *Star Tribune,* 26 January 1992, p. 1A.

30. The descriptive question of ascribed or achieved status for attendees at the Super Bowl is mildly tempting, but beyond the scope and concerns of this chapter.

31. Wallace, *Religion,* p. 65.

32. See, for example, ESPN's broadcast "Autumn Ritual"; Jay Coakley, "Sport and Religion," in *Sport in Society: Issues and Controversies,* 3rd ed. (St. Louis: Times Mirror/Mosby College Publishing, 1986), pp. 317–330.

33. Wallace, *Religion,* p. xii.

34. Ibid., p. 64.

35. Thorstein Veblen, *The Theory of the Leisure Class* (New York: Penguin Books, 1979 [1899]), p. 34.

36. Wallace, *Religion,* p. 64.

37. Though David Sansone (*Greek Athletics and the Genesis of Sport* [Berkeley:

University of California Press, 1988], p. 37) defers: "It is important to recognize that sacrifice is not necessarily, or originally, an offering of a gift to a deity." In popular culture, which often ignores too-fine distinctions, the provision of sacrifice, I think, follows my rough outline.

38. Ibid., p. 37.

39. Chris Rojek, *Capitalism and Leisure Theory* (London: Tavistock Publications, 1985), p. 71.

40. Sansone, *Greek Athletics*, p. 36.

41. The previously mentioned Pro Football Hall of Fame in Canton, Ohio, and the St. Olaf Catholic Church's sign provide examples of this blurring. The pious seriousness with which advertisers juxtapose the use of their product with relaxation after watching a game for three to five hours ("It's Miller time!" one shouts. "Know when to say when," another insists) provides a further indication of intentionality in the blurring of "importance" and "frivolity."

42. This might be sport touristic discourse—a return to the nostalgic, remembered traditions (which may never have existed in reality) in which a fan could, unhindered, enjoy the simplicity of (usually men) playing sports. See Redmond, "Ghosts Linger in Memories," for a good example of such discourse.

43. Lawrence A. Wenner, "The Super Bowl Pregame Show: Cultural Fantasies and Political Subtext," in *Media, Sports, and Society*, ed. Wenner (Newbury Park, Calif.: Sage Publications, 1989), p. 159.

44. See Michel Picard, "Cultural Heritage and Tourist Capital: Cultural Tourism in Bali," in *International Tourism: Identity and Change*, ed. Marie-Françoise Lanfant, John B. Allcock, and Edward M. Bruner (London: Sage Publications, 1995), pp. 44–66.

45. See Richard Gruneau, "Making Spectacle: A Case Study in Television Sports Production," in *Media, Sports, and Society*, ed. Lawrence A. Wenner (Newbury Park, Calif.: Sage Publications, 1989), pp. 134–154.

46. That is, primarily the media, sponsors, spectators; but owners, the television viewing audience—the whole infrastructure may be implicated as players of and with sport.

47. Ron Roizen, "Understanding Conflict between Coaches and Officials," Sociological Aspects of Sports Discussion, 3 March 1996.

48. Thus the specific methodology utilized in chapter 8, in which I take on the participative mode of an international sport tourist.

49. See Norman K. Denzin, *Interpretive Interactionism* (Newbury Park, Calif.: Sage Publications, 1989), p. 131 (from Samuel Taylor Coleridge, "Biographia Literaria").

50. A term borrowed from Synthia S. Slowikowski, "How We Remember," paper presented at the annual American Alliance for Health, Physical Education, Recreation, and Dance Conference, Indianapolis, 9 April 1992. Professor Slowikowski derives this term from Paul Connerton, *How Societies Remember* (Cambridge: Cambridge University Press, 1989).

51. Denzin, *Interpretive Interactionism*, pp. 129–131.

52. Henry M. Sayre, "Pursuing Authenticity: The Vernacular Moment in Contemporary American Art," *South Atlantic Quarterly* 91 (1992): 148.

53. Donald Hall, "O Fenway Park," in Donald Hall, *Fathers Playing Catch with*

Sons: Essays on Sport [Mostly Baseball] (San Francisco: North Point Press, 1985), p. 53.

54. Dean MacCannell, *The Tourist: A New Theory of the Leisure Class* (New York: Schocken Books, 1989), p. 110.

55. Ibid.

56. John J. MacAloon, "Olympic Games and the Theory of Spectacle in Modern Societies," in *Rite, Drama, Festival, Spectacle: Rehearsals toward a Theory of Cultural Performance,* ed. John J. MacAloon (Philadelphia: Institute for the Study of Human Issues, 1984), p. 276 (fn. 21).

57. I recently was given the opportunity to look at a scrapbook of sports keepsakes collected by a friend's grandfather, Julian Hayward, who graduated from Wesleyan in 1911. Among the items was a passport-sized folder containing a mint-condition Olympic Stadium pass to the Tenth Olympiad, held in 1932 in Los Angeles. The cost? $22.00. The green engraving is reminiscent of the intricate designs on U.S. currency. Along with the Olympic Stadium pass, there were golf scorecards from the Middletown Golf Club Inc. in Cromwell, Connecticut; the Brooklawn Country Club in Bridgeport, Connecticut; and the Rhode Island Country Club in Nayatt, Rhode Island. Thanks to Steve Hayward.

58. Wenner, "The Super Bowl Pregame Show," pp. 162–163.

59. See, e.g., Clifford Geertz, *The Interpretation of Cultures* (New York: Basic Books, 1973); Clifford Geertz, *Works and Lives: The Anthropologist as Author* (Stanford, Calif.: Stanford University Press, 1988); James Clifford and George Marcus, eds., *Writing Culture* (Berkeley: University of California Press, 1986).

60. Patricia Ticineto Clough, *The End(s) of Ethnography: From Social Realism to Social Criticism* (Newbury Park, Calif.: Sage Publications, 1992), p. 131.

61. Tzvetan Todorov, *Mikhail Bakhtin: The Dialogical Principle,* trans. Wlad Godzich (Minneapolis: University of Minnesota Press, 1984), p. 106.

62. Mikhail Bakhtin, *Problems of Dostoevesky's Poetics,* appendix II, ed. and trans. Caryl Emerson (Minneapolis: University of Minnesota Press, 1984), cited in Todorov, *Mikhail Bakhtin,* p. 107.

63. The co-writing project is taking on many adherents whose writings inscribe a postmodern, multi-subject, dialogic project that mirrors a cultural intertextuality. Some of the scholars who are encouraging this new project include Karen McCarthy Brown, *Mama Lola: A Voodou Priestess in Brooklyn* (Berkeley: University of California Press, 1991); Clough, *The End(s) of Ethnography;* and Ariel Dorfman, profiled in Debra E. Blum, "Giving Voice to the Tragedy of Oppression," *Chronicle of Higher Education,* 8 April 1992, p. A5.

6. SPORT AS POSTMODERN CONSTRUCTION

1. See, e.g., Johan Huizinga, *Homo Ludens: A Study of the Play Element in Culture* (Boston: Beacon Press, 1955); George A. Sheehan, "Playing," in *Sport and Religion,* ed. Shirley J. Hoffman (Champaign, Ill: Human Kinetics Books, 1992), pp. 83–87. I am grateful to Ann Sebren for the concept of "cosmological significance" regarding the games children play. The thesis for this type of game is not undiscovered, yet appears to be largely unexplored.

2. See Allen Guttmann, *From Ritual to Record: The Nature of Modern Sports*

(New York: Columbia University Press, 1978); B. C. Postow, "Women and Masculine Sports," in *Philosophic Inquiry in Sport* 2nd ed., ed. William J. Morgan and Klaus V. Meier (Champaign, Ill: Human Kinetics, 1995), pp. 323–328.

3. See Chris Rojek, *Decentring Leisure: Rethinking Leisure Theory* (London: Sage Publications, 1995), p. 6.

4. See Victor Turner, *Dramas, Fields, and Metaphors: Symbolic Action in Human Society* (Symbol, Myth, and Ritual Series) (Ithaca, N.Y.: Cornell University Press, 1974), p. 237. Turner might use the term "liminal," meaning "the midpoint of transition in a status-sequence between two positions" specifically, but a series of midpoints of transition generally. The emphasis I wish to make here is the processual nature of the change and the fruitfulness of studying processes when they have not become reified—Turner calls it "a self-certifying myth, sealed off from empirical disproof" (p. 29), particularly "in the periods during which they first appeared in their full social and cultural settings and in their subsequent expansion and modification in changing fields of social relations" (p. 28).

5. See American Paintball League, 20 June 1993. Though, as I have argued elsewhere (Robert Rinehart, "Symbolic Dimensions of Contemporary Sport Forms," in F. van der Merwe, ed., *Sport as Symbol, Symbols in Sport: Proceedings of the 3rd ISHPES Congress* [Berlin: Academia Verlag, 1996], pp. 259–269), the fact that paintball is an emergent form has already changed the quality of production: ESPN broadcast the "Paintball World Cup" in a series of shows (less than two years later, but of course with a great deal more of monetary investment, from February to September 1995) which demonstrated consistently higher production standards.

6. Ernesto Laclau and Chantal Mouffe, *Hegemony and Socialist Strategy: Towards a Radical Democratic Politics* (London: Verso, 1985), p. 163.

7. Ibid.

8. Jean Baudrillard, *Simulacra and Simulation*, trans. Sheila Faria Glaser (Ann Arbor: University of Michigan Press, 1994), p. 75.

9. Using the term "postmodern" (which of course they are) may divert attention from discussion of the forms themselves and onto heated debate regarding modernism, postmodernism, postfordism, poststructuralism, and such. These discussions are certainly critical arguments, and the stance one takes toward such terms—and practices—indicates a deeply felt politicism. However, for the purposes of this chapter, I do not wish to engage that particular debate. Suffice it to say that there exists a postmodernism, that through its reach it has insinuated itself into sport, and that the sport forms I am talking about, particularly in this and the following chapter, are exemplars of the postmodern element in sport. Thus I use the terms "postmodern" and "contemporary" interchangeably in describing sport.

10. As well as of residual forms of sport, forms that are neither emergent or dominant, forms such as mountain climbing, skydiving, surfing. (Of course, much of this discussion of dominant, residual, and emergent forms owes to Raymond Williams, *Marxism and Literature* [Oxford: Oxford University Press, 1977]). In Pocatello, Idaho, for example, there is a grassroots group that has formed which calls itself the Silent Sports (SS) alliance. In the SS alliance, mountain and road bike cycling, running, water sports, Nordic skiing, rock climbing, camping, and hiking are the "focus groups" included.

11. Susan Birrell and John W. Loy, Jr., "Media Sport: Hot and Cool," in *Sport, Culture, and Society: A Reader on the Sociology of Sport,* 2nd ed., ed. John W. Loy, Gerald S. Kenyon, and Barry D. McPherson (Philadelphia: Lea and Febiger, 1981), pp. 296–307.

12. See Ellen Neuborne, "Road to Final Four Paved in Green for Colleges," *USA Today,* 28 March 1996, p. 1B. Neuborne cites three major "payoffs" for the colleges whose basketball teams achieved Final Four status in 1996: increases in merchandise sales, enrollment applications, and alumni donations. See also a six-part series documenting the disparities between NCAA administrators' and college athletes' "perks": "Inside the NCAA: Revenues Dominate College Sports World," *Kansas City Star,* beginning 5 October 1997.

13. Jean Baudrillard, *Simulations* (New York: Semiotext(e), 1983), p. 12. As he also writes (p. 4), "Never again will the real have to be produced."

14. And if so, do these new sport forms lose their creative uniqueness as soon as they are appropriated and commoditized by the media?

15. See, for example, Mikhail Bakhtin, *Rabelais and His World,* trans. Hélène Iswolsky) (Bloomington: Indiana University Press, 1984 [1936]); Tzvetan Todorov, *Mikhail Bakhtin: The Dialogical Principle,* trans. Wlad Godzich (Minneapolis: University of Minnesota Press, 1984); Williams, *Marxism and Literature.*

16. Todorov, *Mikhail Bakhtin,* p. 11.

17. For example, see Melvin L. Adelman, *A Sporting Time: New York City and the Rise of Modern Athletics, 1820–70* (Urbana: University of Illinois Press, 1986); Richard E. Lapchick, *Fractured Focus: Sport as a Reflection of Society* (Lexington, Mass.: D. C. Heath and Co., 1986); Phil Patton, *Razzle-Dazzle: The Curious Marriage of Television and Professional Football* (Garden City, N.Y.: Dial Press, 1984); Benjamin G. Rader, *American Sports: From the Age of Folk Games to the Age of Televised Sports* (Englewood Cliffs, N.J.: Prentice-Hall, 1990); Stephen A. Reiss, *City Games: The Evolution of American Urban Society and the Rise of Sports* (Urbana: University of Illinois Press, 1989); and Randy Roberts and James S. Olsen, *Winning Is the Only Thing: Sports in America since 1945* (Baltimore: Johns Hopkins University Press, 1989).

18. George Sage, *Power and Ideology in American Sport: A Critical Perspective* (Champaign, Ill.: Human Kinetics Books, 1990), p. 126.

19. "Amateur Sports across the USA," *USA Today,* 30 December 1994, p. 8C. Admittedly the AAU is more welcoming than other sanctioning organizations, recognizing many new variants of sports. But the power of the AAU's "recognition" is almost nil: see chapter 7 for discussion of the liminality of grassroots to mass-appeal sports (and sport figures).

20. By "demise," I do not mean that the sport will not continue to exist, just that its diffusion and mass recognition will never come to fruition. However, see my "Symbolic Dimensions of Contemporary Sport Forms," in which I discuss the penetration of contemporary sport into visually literate markets.

21. Broadcast on NBC-TV, 3 September 1994, though this is certainly not a "participant" type of sport in the same sense that the others might be. It is NFL stars who "play," and their status as NFL players is the primary reason for their selection as participants. Thus the audience rarely, if ever, participates in a home-grown "Run to Daylight," but rather may practice its component parts. The "Run to

Daylight" is more in keeping with Sage's term of "trash sport," sport forms created by television promoters primarily for the sake of monetary reward.

22. Harry F. Waters, "'Rough, Tough and Rotten': Two New 'Sports' Shows, So Outrageous They Hurt," *Newsweek,* 14 August 1989, p. 64.

23. Desiree R. Schild, "Brothers (and Sisters) in Arms: The Area's Best Arm Wrestlers Show Up at the State Fair," *Idaho State Journal,* 5 September 1993, p. A1.

24. Mike Snider, "Faux Sumo Wrestling Is Bellying Up to Bars," *USA Today,* 4 October, 1993, p. 1D.

25. Peter Brewington, "3-on-3 Game Grows from Teen Dream," *USA Today,* 6 July 1993, pp. 1C, 2C.

26. Thom Marshall, "Disc Golf: It's a Far Cry from the Days of Lid Tossing," *Champaign-Urbana News Gazette,* 3 July 1993), p. B–3.

27. Interestingly, the World Championships of Cutter and Chariot Racing gain little recognition, yet in 1992 the Utah state finals had 4,000 spectators. They are not as yet televised. For example, see Greg Boeck, "When in Pocatello, Do As the Romans Do," *USA Today,* 30 March 1992, p. 2C.

28. Margaret Carlisle Duncan and Cynthia A. Hasbrook, "Denial of Power in Televised Women's Sports," *Sociology of Sport Journal* 5 (1988): 16.

29. By placing the term "sport" in quotes, I draw attention to the contested nature of "what is sport."

30. And yet fans more and more are asked to be generalists: consumers, knowledgeable fans, eager spectators, interested and involved observers.

31. Susan L. Greendorfer, "Sport and the Mass Media," in *Handbook of Social Science of Sport,* ed. Günther R. F. Lueschen and George H. Sage (Champaign, Ill.: Stipes Publishing Co., 1981), pp. 160–180.

32. Indeed, to the uninitiated, paintball resembles the war games of military organizations—but at the beginner, recreational level, players form into teams nearly arbitrarily, and there is little real strategy, only a great deal of the posturing, and the pretense, of strategy. The emphasis at this level, it seems, may be more on Caillois's "mimicry" (ilinx) than on "agon." R. Callois, *Man, Play and Games* (New York: Free Press, 1961), p. 36.

33. Deobold B. Van Dalen and Bruce L. Bennett, *A History of Physical Education: Cultural, Philosophical, Comparative,* 2nd ed. (Englewood Cliffs, N.J.: Prentice Hall, 1971), p. 102.

34. Ibid, p. 103.

35. Editor, CO_2 mail, *Action Pursuit Games* 8, no. 10 (October 1994): 8.

36. Steve Mitchell, letter to the editor (CO_2 mail), *Action Pursuit Games* 8, no. 10 (October 1994): 7.

37. Darwin Britton, "Paintball Pride," in "Firing Line" (letters to the editor), *Paintball Sports International* 7 (November 1995): 23.

38. Laurel Richardson, "Postmodern Social Theory," *Sociological Theory* 9 (1991): 173.

39. Joy B. Reeves, "The Survival Game: Who Plays and Why," *Sociology of Sport Journal* 3 (1986): 60. In this study, paintball—or a very close description of the form this sport takes—is named "the National Survival Game."

40. B. J. Given, "Zen Handgun: Sports Ritual and Experience," *Journal of Ritual Studies* 7, no. 1 (1993): 145.

41. Len Canter, "The Editor Speaks Out," *Paintcheck International* 5, no. 9 (1993): 24.

42. In fact, the business risk for paintball shops remains high: an indoor paintball site opened up in Pocatello in early 1995; one year later, it was gone.

43. These categories are illustrative only of varying motivations; certainly they are not exhaustive as categories, nor have I looked descriptively at the "data" on "reasons to play," though in an earlier study, Reeves ("The Survival Game") attempted to ferret out reasons for playing the National Survival Game.

44. This turns the exemplar of paintball into an important cultural creation: Could paintball be utilized by "hate groups," for example, instrumentally? Might the seemingly benign "game" culture, inspired by war-like strategies, turn back upon itself and become a training ground for war games? James A. Aho, who wrote *This Thing of Darkness: A Sociology of the Enemy,* finds this premise ironic; he says, "If they [white supremacist groups] played it at all, it might be for real" (personal communication, 1995).

45. Van Dalen and Bennett, *A History of Physical Education.*

46. Paintball Sam's "American War Games," North Highlands, Calif., October 1994.

47. Usually small groups of friends joined with other small groups just prior to contact with the other team; the specific game rules were given immediately prior to the whistle starting play: few, if any, team "strategies" were ever conveyed—and outsiders to each group were made even less privy to any "game plan."

48. *Paintball Sports* 6, no. 64 (November 1994): 3.

49. Ibid., p. 12.

50. Ibid., p. 45.

51. Hollywood, "Fun with Scenario Games: Attack on Peenemunde," *Action Pursuit Games* 8, no. 10 (October 1994): 44–47; Hollywood, "Attack on Peenemunde!" *Paintball Sports* 6, no. 64 (November 1994): 42–44. Scenario games are specifically designed to nostalgically re-create past battles in paintball scenarios.

52. Mark L. Berry and Laurie Balsamo, "Flying into Action, *Again!* A Tradition among Friends," *Paintball Sports International* 6, no. 69 (April 1995): 40–44.

53. American Paintball League program, 20 June 1993, The Sports Channel, Urbana, Ill.

54. One advertisement capitalizes upon this attitudinal disparity: entitled "Play for fun," the ad queries, "Remember the sport of paintball? Remember hearing 'great shot,' 'flag capture,' 'didn't hear you,' and 'wait 'til next time'? The object of the sport was capturing the flag, not simply hosing down your opponent with paint." "Play for Fun," *Paintcheck International* 5, no. 9 (November 1993): 1.

55. Virginia Allen, personal communication, October 1994.

56. Which leads to an interesting thought: What if a paintball-type activity became a symbolic substitution for war? Or if by playing such a sport/game, little boys (and girls) learned how much it hurt to get hit—even by a small paint pellet? Or if players were not in actuality being entirely "duped" by the purveyors of paintball, but in fact were active (re)producers of their own simulacra?

57. The magazines, wherever I found them, are placed in racks alongside the hunting magazines.

58. See B. C. Postow, "Women and Masculine Sports," in *Philosophic Inquiry in*

Sport, ed. William J. Morgan and Klaus V. Meier, 2nd ed. (Champaign, Ill.: Human Kinetics Books, 1995), pp. 323–328.

59. Alicia Winder, personal communication, October 1994.

60. *Paintcheck International* 5, no. 9 (November 1993): 31. In April 1995 (*Paintball Sports International,* p. 23), professional paintball player Dave Youngblood wrote a letter to the editor telling his "fans" that he is now a police officer in San Diego. This is an interesting twist on the classic rags-to-riches story embedded in professional sport: in this case, the upward mobility climb goes from professional athlete to professional police officer!

61. This "rogue model" might include outlaw games (consisting of groups who are unaffiliated, who rent fields for their own use, and who control their own structures) and games of affiliated groups whose instrumental intent is primary over the secondary enjoyment of the game itself. Groups of the latter category might include, for example, skinhead and other so-called "hate" groups.

62. Richardson, "Postmodern Social Theory," p. 173.

63. Edward M. Bruner, "The Story of Abraham Lincoln: A Postmodern Perspective," paper first presented at the University of Wisconsin, Department of Anthropology Lecture, Madison, Wisc., 4 May 1990.

64. Laclau and Mouffe, *Hegemony and Socialist Strategy,* p. 164.

65. Jack Schaefer, *Shane* (New York: Bantam Pathfinder Editions, 1949), p. 105.

66. Ibid., p. 113.

67. Michael Polanyi, *Personal Knowledge: Towards a Post-Critical Philosophy* (Chicago: University of Chicago Press, 1958).

68. Anthony Giddens, *The Constitution of Society* (Berkeley: University of California Press, 1984).

69. See Clifford Geertz, "Deep Play: Notes on the Balinese Cockfight," *Daedalus* 101 (1972): 1–37.

7. SPORT AS CONSTRUCTED AUDIENCE

1. There are notable exceptions, of course. One of the most outstanding examinations of sport logic formation is Richard Gruneau, "Making Spectacle: A Case Study in Television Sports Production," in *Media, Sports, and Society* , ed. Lawrence A. Wenner (Newbury Park, Calif.: Sage Publications, 1989), pp. 134–154.

2. Alain Coulon, *Ethnomethodology* (Thousand Oaks, Calif.: Sage Publications, 1995), p. 2.

3. This chapter is a study of the ESPN coverage of *The eXtreme Games,* which was broadcast from 24 June to 3 July 1995. Both ESPN and ESPN-2 aired the event. Though I did not study ESPN-2's coverage, I did examine twenty-seven hours of ESPN's coverage.

4. The discussion of Alistair McIntyre's concepts of practices and institutions, cited in William J. Morgan, *Leftist Theories of Sport: A Critique and Reconstruction* (Urbana: University of Illinois Press, 1994), is germane to this question. See also Alasdair MacIntyre, *After Virtue: A Study in Moral Theory,* 2nd ed. (Notre Dame, Ind.: University of Notre Dame Press, 1984).

5. This common language is but one of the indications of shared practices (in this case, of television sports viewers); see Morgan, *Leftist Theories of Sport,* chap. 3.

6. See Norman K. Denzin, *Images of Postmodern Society: Social Theory and Contemporary Cinema* (London: Sage Publications, 1991), p. 55: "Treating each postmodern subject as an universal singular (Sartre, 1981: ix–x), universalized by this historical moment, but unique in the reproduction of it as an individuality, postmodern theory must uncover how, in epiphanal moments, each person lives this time of history into existence."

7. Mountain Dew commercial, ESPN, 24, 25, 26, 27, 28, 29, 30 June and 1, 2, 3 July 1995.

8. Indeed, Lyotard "defines 'postmodern as incredulity toward metanarratives'" (cited in Chris Rojek, *Decentring Leisure: Rethinking Leisure Theory* [London: Sage Publications, 1995], p. 6). Rojek explains that "it is still a matter of debate whether we live in the age of postmodernity or in an age of transition" (ibid.).

9. *The eXtreme Games* Preview Show, ESPN, 24 June 1995.

10. Chris Fowler, *The eXtreme Games,* ESPN, 25 June 1995.

11. Charles Fruehling Springwood, *Cooperstown to Dyersville: A Geography of Baseball Nostalgia* (Boulder, Colo.: Westview Press, 1996), p. 22.

12. When in-line skater Chris Edwards, a favorite, was eliminated on the first day of verts, viewers were told that the officials and fellow in-line competitors got together to reestablish a corrected order. Chris Edwards became a qualifier. One competitor, who went from 7th place (qualifying) to 12th place (non-qualifying), is claimed to have said that Chris Edwards deserved it: after all, Edwards has been skating eight years, the other young man only two years.

13. Stuart Scott, *The eXtreme Games,* ESPN, 26 June 1995.

14. In fact, during *The eXtreme Games* in 1995, television viewers were encouraged to "become interactive" with the sky surfing event on the World Wide Web.

15. *The eXtreme Games,* ESPN, 25 June 1995.

16. Ibid.

17. Chris Fowler, ibid.

18. Stuart Scott, *The eXtreme Games,* ESPN, 26 June 1995.

19. *The eXtreme Games* Preview Show, ESPN, 24 June 1995.

20. Chris Fowler, *The eXtreme Games,* ESPN, 25 June 1995.

21. NBC-TV, "Gatorade Ironman Triathlon Championship," 20 June 1993.

22. Gaye Tuchman, "Historical Social Science: Methodologies, Methods, and Meanings," in *Handbook of Qualitative Research,* ed. Norman K. Denzin and Yvonna S. Lincoln (Thousand Oaks, Calif.: Sage Publications, 1994), pp. 315–316.

23. Rojek, *Decentring Leisure,* p. 6.

24. I feel that postmodernism, in fact, subsumes modernism—co-opting modernist strategies to its own ends.

25. See Coulon, *Ethnomethodology,* p. 17. Indexicality, in Coulon's view (drawn from Garfinkel), "is a technical word adapted from linguistics. It means that although a word has a transsituational signification, it also has a distinct significance in each particular situation in which it is used." Thus interactions are symbolic, working for individuals on various levels, including (often) what we *assume* is meant for most receivers, and what we *think* is meant in a given, specific case.

26. See Synthia S. Slowikowski, "Burning Desire: Nostalgia, Ritual, and the Sport-Festival Flame Ceremony," *Sociology of Sport Journal* 8 (1991): 239–257, and

Synthia S. Slowikowski and John W. Loy, "Ancient Athletic Motifs and the Modern Olympic Games: An Analysis of Rituals and Representations," in *Sport in Social Development: Traditions, Transitions, and Transformations,* ed. Alan G. Ingham and John W. Loy (Champaign, Ill: Human Kinetics Publishers, 1993), pp. 21–49.

27. See Eric Hobsbawm and Terence Ranger, eds., *The Invention of Tradition* (Cambridge: Cambridge University Press, 1983).

28. Suzy Kolber, *The eXtreme Games,* ESPN, 1 July 1995.

29. The term "extreme" is as omnipresent as is "NFL" in the Super Bowl, "American Gladiators" in *The American Gladiators,* or "WWF" in the World Wrestling Federation presentations. Yet in *The eXtreme Games* (perhaps since its use has not yet become naturalized), the self-promotion is mildly irritating; in the others, it is something audiences have come to expect.

30. *The eXtreme Games,* ESPN, 25 June 1995.

31. Scott Smith, *The eXtreme Games,* ESPN, 26 June 1995.

32. *The eXtreme Games,* ESPN, 25 June 1995.

33. Suzy Kolber, ibid.

34. Ibid.

35. This strategy echoes—or is echoed by—the Nike campaign for NBA stars, in which different mediated images solidify different segments of the market for Nike products.

36. See Gruneau, "Making Spectacle."

37. Jim Forkan, "Crazy—Like a Fox," *Cablevision,* 3 July 1995, p. 11.

38. Ibid.

39. See, for example, chapters 2 and 4; see also Suzi Gablik *Has Modernism Failed?* (New York: Thames and Hudson, 1984). One well-known example of such a co-opting by commercial interests is the artwork of the self, self-made, of and by Andy Warhol.

40. This is an interesting dilemma for many "outlaw" sport practitioners; see, for an examination of the various subgroups of skateboarding, Becky Beal, "Disqualifying the Official: An Exploration of Social Resistance through the Subculture of Skateboarding," *Sociology of Sport Journal* 12, no. 3 (1995): 252–267. The "variety of subgroups [which] resisted . . . [included] those involved in corporate bureaucratic skating as 'rats,' individuals who bought the commercially produced paraphernalia and plastered all their belongings with corporate logos" (p. 255).

41. Shura McComb, quoted in Lisa Feinberg Densmore, "Taking Extreme Mainstream," *InLine: The Skate Magazine* 4, no. 8 (November 1995): 37.

42. "For Love or Money? Extreme Showcase Predictably Network," *Thrasher,* October 1995, pp. 50–53.

43. See, for example, B. F. Skinner, *About Behaviorism* (New York: Knopf, 1974); B. F. Skinner, *Walden Two* (New York: Macmillan, 1948); B. F. Skinner, *Beyond Freedom and Dignity* (New York: Knopf, 1971).

8. SPORT AS POSTMODERN TOURISM

1. This introduction echoes work by Edward M. Bruner, "Abraham Lincoln as Authentic Reproduction," paper presented at Le Tourisme International entre Tradition et Modernité, Nice, France, 19–21 November 1992.

2. Oftentimes the individual parts do not add up to the sum of the whole. The experience of reading and enjoying poetry versus analyzing component characteristics of a poem may be a good example. While educated analysis may inform and increase the positive aspects of the experience, it is not necessary. Similarly, though safety, prediction, and fulfillment of expectation often define the experienced tourists' goals, some experience celebrates the uncertainty of total immersion (if only for a short time) within a given (in this case, sport) culture. This is not to say that there is no difference between natives and tourists; rather, it is to say that a kind of temporal privileging occurs within scholarly travel and ethnographic discourse which assumes that a longer period of immersion in an unfamiliar culture leads to greater insight into that culture. While this may often be the case, it does not necessarily follow: what may appear as verisimilitude may, in fact, be only a better disguised and more practiced rendering of professional ethnography. In other words, the experience of the individual who only occasionally travels to "foreign," "exotic" realms, may be qualitatively (as well as quantitatively) different from that of the professional tourist/ethnographer. How, then, to capture this experience?

A second problem occurs in the privileging of length of stay. If we study only phenomena that occur over time (rather than, as Baudrillard seems to say in *America*, in an instant), we may miss significant-impact, more ephemeral events. In one sense, of course, the process of being human allows us leave to study such ephemera, but it opens us up to criticism from an academy spawned of the Age of Reason (see, e.g., Stuart Hampshire, ed., *The Age of Reason: The 17th Century Philosophers* [New York: New American Library, 1956]), which little values that which is not replicable.

3. Edward M. Bruner, "Of Cannibals, Tourists, and Ethnographers," *Cultural Anthropology* 4 (1989): 440.

4. See Ludwig Giesz, "Kitsch-Man as Tourist," in *Kitsch: A World of Bad Taste,* ed. Gillo Dorfles (New York: Bell Publishing Co., 1968), pp. 156–174.

5. Barbara Kirshenblatt-Gimblett, "Objects of Ethnography," in *Exhibiting Cultures: The Poetics and Politics of Museum Display,* ed. Ivan Karp and Steven D. Lavine (Washington, D.C.: Smithsonian Institute Press, 1991), p. 413.

6. This distinction has been alluded to by Dean MacCannell, *The Tourist: A New Theory of the Leisure Class* (New York: Schocken Books, 1976; reprint, 1989), p. xvii: "But it would be theoretically and morally wrong to equate the forced nomadism and homelessness of the refugee and the impoverished with the supercilious voluntaristic Abercrombie and Fitch tourist or other soldiers of fortune."

7. bell hooks, *Yearning: Race, Gender, and Cultural Politics* (Boston, Mass.: South End Press, 1990), pp. 150–151.

8. Cited in Malcolm Crick, "Representations of International Tourism in the Social Sciences: Sun, Sex, Sights, Savings, and Servility," *Annual Reviews of Anthropology* 18 (1989): 322, from MacCannell, *The Tourist,* p. 165.

9. Alexander Wolff, "The Games: Showing Their Stripes," *Sports Illustrated,* 22 July 1992, p. 22.

10. Steve Woodward, "Little Things Define Memory of Games," *USA Today,* 7 December 1992, p. 14C.

11. See Allan Hanson, "The Making of the Maori: Culture Invention and Its Logic," *American Anthropologist* 91 (1989): 890–902.

12. Bruner, "Of Cannibals," p. 440.

13. Ibid.

14. Aligned with Olson-Travelworld™, Ltd., out of Manhattan Beach, California, whose initial communications for the potential "Olympic Games Enthusiast" included a set of two winter and two summer Olympic brochures. The glossy, full-color brochures provided an overview of the *XVI Olympic Winter Games* (Olson-Travelworld, Ltd., 1990) and the *Games of the XXV Olympiad* (Olson-Travelworld, Ltd., 1990), as well as *Olympic Ticket Information* (Olson-Travelworld, Ltd., 1991) for each of the games. Follow-up mailings included ticket confirmations (for various venues), and an "Exclusive Olympic Games Travel Kit" which "includes the 1992 AT&T Olympic Summer Games Traveler's Companion, the USA Olympic Team baseball cap and the Spectator credential" (Olson-Travelworld, Ltd., July 1992).

15. Although, interestingly enough, according to a letter written by Jan Katzoff (President, Olympic Division) to "Dear Olympic Enthusiast," "The year 1992 promises to be an incredible one in Europe and the Olympic Games will provide a front row seat to watch history unfold. In addition to the Olympic Games, Spain will host the '92 World Expo in Seville and celebrate the 500th year anniversary of Christopher Columbus' discovery of America. Combine all of this with the Olympic Cultural Festival, the long history and tradition of Barcelona and the stage is set for a memorable Olympic experience" (Letter accompanying *Games of the XXV Olympiad*, Manhattan Beach, Calif.: Olson-Travelworld, 1990, p. 3). I met quite a few other sport tourists who were combining vacations with attendance at the Olympics; in fact, my length of stay in Europe, not to say Spain, may have been well under the norm for Olympic attendees from the United States. But the Olympic spectators' primary interest was sport, as demonstrated in a paper describing a survey conducted in Barcelona during the Olympics: see Lisa Delpy, "The Spectator in Barcelona: Creation of Narratives," paper presented at the annual meeting of the North American Society for Sport Sociology, Toledo, Ohio, 7 November 1992. Her results showed that an "Important" factor that "particularly attracted" people to the Games was "Excellent Athletic Competition" (59.3 percent). The "Most Important" attraction for respondents cited was "Excellent Athletic Competition" (37.3 percent), followed by "A Cultural Experience," with 22.9 percent.

16. Crick, "Sun, Sex, Sights, Savings," p. 313.

17. Barbara A. Babcock, "By Way of Introduction," *Inventing the Southwest*, Special Issue, *Journal of the Southwest* 32, no. 4 (1990): 385 (my emphasis).

18. An example: the coining of Olympic money by the Spanish government. I have an España 25 ptas. coin (1991) with Juan Carlos I's visage on one side and a figure of a high jumper "Fosbury-flopping" over a bar, with the words "Barcelona '92" and the Barcelona Olympics symbol, on the other side. Of course, this may also be considered a souvenir, a "collector's item," and in fact it is utilized by many for just such a purpose.

19. See, as an example, Edward M. Bruner, "The Ethnographer/Tourist in Indo-

nesia," in *International Tourism: Identity and Change,* ed. Marie-Françoise Lanfant, John B. Allcock, and Edward M. Bruner (London: Sage Publications, 1995), pp. 224–241. However, mediated sport has managed to retain an aura of self-conscious-lessness: see chapter 5.

20. See Suzy Kruhse-MountBurton, "Sex Tourism and Traditional Australian Male Identity," in *International Tourism: Identity and Change,* ed. Marie-Françoise Lanfant, John B. Allcock, and Edward M. Bruner (London:. Sage Publications, 1995), pp. 192–204.

21. See Brian Currid, "'We Are Family': House Music and Queer Performativity," in *Cruising the Performative: Interventions into the Representation of Ethnicity, Nationality, and Sexuality,* ed. Sue-Ellen Case, Philip Brett, and Susan Leigh Foster (Bloomington: Indiana University Press, 1995), pp. 165–196.

22. Eric Hobsbawm and Terence Ranger, ed., *The Invention of Tradition* (Cambridge: Cambridge University Press, 1983).

23. "Go for the Gold: Use Your Visa Card to Receive Exclusive Discounts from Prestigious Olympic Sponsors," VISA Sales Brochure, 1992.

24. Tom Kacich, "Urbana Man Pines for Olympics Pins," *Champaign-Urbana News-Gazette,* 16 February 1992, p. E–3.

25. C. W. Nevius, "Olympics: A Small World," San Francisco *Chronicle,* 23 July 1992, pp. B1, B5.

26. Ben Wattenberg, "Olympics Highlight Good Things," *Champaign-Urbana News-Gazette,* 2 August 1992, p. B–2.

27. Coca-Cola commercial, "Opening Ceremonies," NBC-TV, 25 July 1992.

28. See, e.g., Richard D. Mandell, *The Nazi Olympics* (Urbana: University of Illinois Press, 1987); Benjamin Rader, *American Sports: From the Age of Folk Games to the Age of Televised Sports* (Englewood Cliffs, N.J.: Prentice-Hall, 1990); or Allen Guttmann, *The Olympics: A History of the Modern Games* (Urbana: University of Illinois Press, 1992), for discussions of Hitler's 1936 Berlin Olympics, the Black Power movement at the Mexico City Olympics, the 1972 Munich tragedy, and various boycotts and exclusions. During the opening ceremonies broadcast on NBC TV (25 July 1992), commentators Bob Costas and Dick Enberg waxed nostalgic about the legacy of these Games as the flag symbolizing each incarnation of the Olympics was run out to take its proper place in Olympic history.

29. "In Catalonia, Of Course," *Time,* 27 July 1992, pp. 5, 7.

30. Sally B. Donnelly, "Decathlon: Dave on His Own," *Time,* 27 July 1992, p. 62. The emphasis on the dramatic metaphor is intensified when the author of the article begins, "This was not the way the script was supposed to turn out." See chapter 1 of this volume.

31. Nelson H. H. Graburn, "The Evolution of Tourist Arts," *Annals of Tourism Research* 11 (1984): 413.

32. Some might go so far as to call it cynicism: in fact, though we got along quite well at the women's basketball venue in Badalona, two older women physical educators from a college in the Midwest seemed puzzled that I would study the Olympics as a participant-observer spectator. Their wonder at the merit of such a study is not uncommon in physical education (and kinesiology) circles. Like marketers of happy-face buttons, many physical educators tend to form a non-

critical exclusive circle around any problems, since they perceive in the general populace a common discrediting of their work. Such defensiveness is, however, compounded in kinesiology for sociologists studying sport. The marginality of sociologists in general and sport sociologists in particular has been well documented.

33. Edward Bruner, "Transformation of Self in Tourism," *Annals of Tourism Research* 18 (1991): 240.

34. I allude to Kirshenblatt-Gimblett, "Objects of Ethnography," p. 407, for her use of the term "quotidian," as well as Virginia R. Dominguez, "The Marketing of Heritage," *American Ethnologist* 13, no. 3 (1986): 549, for her discussion of Hobsbawm and Ranger's *The Invention of Tradition:* "It concerns practices of the 'civilized' and not the 'exotic' or 'primitive.'" Sports have traditionally (if they have been studied at all) been relegated to the realm of insignificance and the taken-for-granted. Interest in the constructed nature of sports has been limited to a few sport scholars, rarely to the media (for whose self-interest perpetuation of the myth of non-construction serves), and not at all in the popular mind.

35. For an interesting discussion of time perception as it pertains to athletics, see Conrad Phillip Kottak, "Swimming in Cross-Cultural Currents," in *Applying Anthropology: An Introductory Reader,* ed. Aaron Podolefsky and Peter J. Brown (Mountain View, Calif.: Mayfield Publishing Co., 1989), pp. 126–131. Expensive travel puts a premium on time and scheduling, which smacks of economic/class distinctions, primarily because the travel infrastructure has promoted leisure, service, and having one's needs met as requirements for "the good life." Such dependency, structure, and coddling, however, by definition give the packagers of touristic experience, not necessarily the recipients of the experience, more control over the experience. On this last point, see Edward M. Bruner, "Between Tourism and Ethnography: A Postmodern Tour Guide in Bali," TMs, Anthro. 450 course packet, University of Illinois, Urbana-Champaign, Fall 1992.

36. See Victor Turner, *Dramas, Fields, and Metaphors: Symbolic Action in Human Society* (Symbol, Myth, and Ritual Series) (Ithaca, N.Y.: Cornell University Press, 1974), chap. 6, passim.

37. Among them, Australian Olympic committee officials who gave me a "Sydney 2000" pin in support of their bid for the upcoming Olympics.

38. A few of the U.S. team members carried cameras, to solidify the moment; David Robinson even held a video camera up to the NBC camera and laughed at the absurdity (irony) of filming himself being filmed.

39. For a discussion that touches on this point in regard to the seemingly encyclopedic collections housed in the Christian C. Sanderson Museum at Chadd's Ford, see John D. Dorst, *The Written Suburb: An American Site, An Ethnographic Dilemma* (Philadelphia: University of Pennsylvania Press, 1989), pp. 192–203.

40. For example, New Year's Day parades, halftime entertainment, cheerleaders, etc. Another, more commonplace example: the University of Illinois' "1993 Fighting Illini Football: Student Ticket Lottery" flyer reads "ENJOY FOOD . . . FUN . . . MARCHING ILLINI . . . STUDENT BLOCKS . . . CHEERLEADERS . . . HARD-HITTING BIG TEN ACTION." The total entertainment package, as written by someone in Sports Information at the Division of Intercollegiate Athletics at the

University of Illinois, sells "football" sixth out of six attractions.

41. See Hobsbawm and Ranger, *Invention of Tradition.*

42. Interestingly, I have had to watch the taped version of NBC's televised broadcast (25 July 1992) to confirm and help illustrate (in terms of names, etc.) my initial impressions. Such is the nature of a "seamless" televisual production. (Such is the nature of "seamless" authorship that I conflate the NBC version of the Olympics with the Spanish Channel 3 version within the text.)

43. My week-long special "Bitllet Olimpic"—Olympic Ticket—purchased for "2.000 ptas.," does not include this RENFE train ride. It costs me an extra 4.50 ptas. per trip.

44. Built for the 1919 World's Fair, refurbished for this Olympiad, but not completed in time, so it appears that the "rabble" is excluded for the duration. But this is not true. We wander inside the next day, see architectural drawings and models of how it was proposed to look. Apparently, tonight is some privileged bash for Olympic officials and government VIPs.

45. Or maybe I am becoming overwhelmed by it all, and need a break from intensive study of the sport milieu. It doesn't feel that way, but re-reading my notes, I get the feeling that the intensity of the events ("This is the Olympics!" etc.), combined with unfamiliar surroundings and a certain loneliness, may conspire to undermine enthusiasm. But, of course, this is all a part of the process for the (single) tourist as well. I talk with people, and pretty much know I will never see them again. It lends a certain giddiness to conversations, yet in the end is a rather empty feeling. This may be the tack MacCannell was taking in *The Tourist*, when he insisted that tourists are authenticity-seekers.

46. Deborah Tannen, *You Just Don't Understand: Women and Men in Conversation* (New York: Ballantine Books, 1990), p. 246.

47. Crick, "Sun, Sex, Sights, Savings," p. 307.

48. Jules Brown, *The Real Guide: Barcelona* (New York: Prentice Hall Travel, 1992), p. 282.

49. Or "host." See Valene L. Smith, ed., *Hosts and Guests: The Anthropology of Tourism,* 2nd ed. (Philadelphia: University of Pennsylvania Press, 1989).

50. Mikhail Bakhtin, *Rabelais and His World,* trans. Hélène Iswolsky (Cambridge, Mass.: MIT Press, 1968; Bloomington: Indiana University Press, 1984), p. 71.

51. Bruner, "Transformation," p. 240.

52. Edward M. Bruner, "Tourism, Creativity, and Authenticity," *Studies in Symbolic Interaction* 10 (1989): 110.

53. See Milton J. Esman, "Commentary," in *Everyday Forms of Peasant Resistance,* ed. Forrest D. Colburn (Armonk, N.Y.: M. E. Sharpe, 1989), p. 223 and his n. 5.

54. Robert Rinehart, "'Fists Flew and Blood Flowed': Symbolic Resistance and International Response in Hungarian Water Polo at the Melbourne Olympics, 1956," *Journal of Sport History* (in press).

55. Graburn, "The Evolution of Tourist Arts," p. 406, writes analogously that "some ethnic groups have gone from florescence through change and nihilism, to a reintegrated but new florescence."

56. Dorst, *Suburb,* p. 196.

57. The U.S. team later lost two games, and did not medal.

58. See Susan Stewart, *On Longing: Narratives of the Miniature, the Gigantic, the*

Souvenir, the Collection (Baltimore: Johns Hopkins University Press, 1984); Dorst, *Suburb.*

59. Jean Baudrillard, *America,* trans. Chris Turner (Paris: Bernard Grasset, 1986; London: Verso, 1988), pp. 6, 9.

60. Certainly "high" in terms of other sport forms, but also "high" in aesthetics, and "high" in cultural terms as well. The (Barcelona) Olympics is so expansive, its alignment with art includes poster and stamp contests and a "celebration" that implicitly ties traditional Catalonian painting, sculpture, literature, architecture, and music in with the Olympic movement.

61. These distinctions, I feel, are exercises in degree: writing, reading, and constructing and viewing are, of course, experience as well.

62. Rob Gloster, "Cobi the Pooch Not Your Average Olympic Mascot," Anchorage *Daily News,* 5 July 1992, p. E–7.

63. John Updike, "The Heart and Soul of the Olympic Games," *Official Souvenir Program: Games of the XXV Olympiad, Barcelona '92* (Barcelona: Cayfosa, 1992), pp. 26–31 passim.

INDEX

Index

Index

Index

Index

8–9, 18
Postow, B. C., 96
Privileging of sport forms, 10–13, 143n52

Quinn, Bob, ix

Rader, Benjamin G., 31
Rashad, Ahmad, 82
Realism, 6
Redmond, Gerald, 73
Reebok, 14; "Dave and Dan" ad campaign, 5, 117
Religion, 72–73, 76–77, 165n41
Richardson, Laurel, 92
Robinson, David, 8, 26, 177n38
Rock 'n' Wrestling, 43
Rodman, Dennis, ix, 26, 58; avant-garde characteristics of, 63–64, 161n50, 161n51
Roizen, Ron, 79
Rojek, Chris, 55, 76–77, 172n8
Roller derby, 43, 89
Ross, Dorothy, 12
Rowan, Chad, 63
Roy, Tom, 30–31
Rozelle, Pete, 26
Rust, Bill, 71

Sage, George, 11, 33, 44, 88, 150n55
San Francisco 49ers, 22, 91
Sansone, David, 36–37, 76, 77, 164n37
Savage, Randy "Macho Man," 5, 64, 67
Sayre, Henry M., 4, 13, 150n42
Schneemann, Carolee, 4
Schroeder, Terry, 132
Schulte-Sasse, Jochen, 59
Shaw, Gary, 2
Sheppard, Anne, 155n29
Silent Sports (SS) alliance, 167n10
Singer, Linda, 64
Sky surfing, 27, 102, 106, 149n37
Slo-motion replays, 30, 150n48
Slowikowski, Synthia S., 165n50
Smith, Tommy, 59
Socialization, 41, 153n1
Spectacle sport, 12, 42, 90
Spectators: as audience to performance art, 4–5, 8; bond to favorite teams, 29; collective nostalgic past of, 82; creation of in emerging sports, 88; epiphanic markers of, 79–82; experience of live vs. televised sporting events, 7, 16–18, 28, 41–42, 145n77; fan-

tasy chaining by, 78; identification with sport, 64; interactions with players in new sport forms, 27–28, 79, 149n38; lived experience in sport, 28–31; participation by, 42, 66–68, 161n64; as performers before television cameras, 28, 163n5; "play" of, 16; as privileged few at live events, 11, 75–76, 82; and the sport-as-drama metaphor, x, 8, 21–22; as sport tourists, 16, 77–79; Super Bowl pilgrimages of, 71–73, 76; television audience as participants in sport, 42; total "sporting experience" sought by, 7, 16–17

Sponsors. *See* Corporate sponsors
Sport: Americanization of, 6, 141n23; as art, 23; broad inclusive definition of, 36; commoditization of, 2, 12, 73–75; emerging sports, 87–88; as entertainment, 62, 65; expressive vs. spectacle sports, 12; high vs. low continuum in, 45; idealization of, 27, 149n39; institutions of, x–xiii; kitsch in, 43, 45, 47–52, 154n13; marginal sports, 43–46; as mirror of society, 23, 24, 146n7; on the modern/postmodern cusp, 38, 104; modernization of forms of, 89; naturalization of sport discourse, 23; new sport forms, 27–28; Oedipal logic of, 28–29, 150n44; as performance, 4–8, 78–79, 142n28; "play" as secondary to, 16; politicization of, 12; predetermined outcomes in, 33, 36; privileging of certain sports, 10–13, 143n52; as religious experience, 72–73, 76–77, 165n41; rhythmicity in, 3; society as permeated by, 14–15; spectacle sports, 12, 42, 90; "sporting experience" distinguished from, 7; "traditional" sports, 43, 154n14, 154n15; "trash" sports, 33, 44, 45–46, 88–89; as war, 23, 146n7
—avant-garde metaphor for, 21, 23–25, 34, 39–40; "high" vs. "low" culture dichotomy collapsed by, 56–57; icons of, 58, 62–64; individual/group interaction in, 25–27; as invigorating for sport, 59; kitsch compared to, 43, 47, 49, 55, 154n13; narrativity question in, 24; and new sport forms, 27–28; and spectators' lived experience in sport, 28–31; in sport studies, 35–37; in Super Bowl merchandising, 74–75; and technology, 56; in the World Wrestling Federation, 62–68
—drama metaphor for, x, 21–23, 139n3; high

Index

vs. low drama in, 24, 33, 34; and narrativity, 24–25; in paintball, 87–88; predetermined results in, 33, 151n64, 151n65; in sport studies, 31–34, 150n55
—postmodern sport forms: emergence of, 87–88, 167n9; in *The eXtreme Games,* 99; paintball as, 19–20, 87–88, 91–97, 167n9, 169n32; problems of sanctioning of, 88–91, 168n20
—studies of, 2–3, 8–9; avant-garde metaphor for, 19, 35–37, 39; canonization of sports in, 9–13, 18, 37, 142n37; dramatic metaphors in, 31–34, 150n55; modernist definition of sport in, 36; and postmodernism, 8–9, 18; and reflexivity in, 13, 19, 143n56
Sports Direct, xi
Sportscasters, 25–26
St. Paul Winter Carnival, 71
Starrett, Robert McPherson, 97
Statistics, sport, 2–3
Steeg, Jim, 62
Subjectivity, 14
Sumo wrestling, 50, 63, 89, 156n44, 156n46
Sun-Tzu, 84
Super Bowl XXVI (1992), 19, 69, 162n1, commoditization of, 73–75; epiphanic markers for, 81–82; nostalgia of, 81–82; pilgrimages to, 71–73, 76; religious aspects of, 72–73, 76 77, 165n41; as seasonal ritual, 70 71; site as football shrine, 72; tickets reserved for the select few, xii, 75–76, 82, 164n30; touristic discourse on, 77–79
Super Bowls: advertising campaigns for, 65; certainty of outcome in, 36; commoditized as drama, 24; corporate sponsors of, xi; as entertainment, 62, 65; parties, 7, 71, 82; pastiche in, 5; player introduction rituals in, 7; Vince Lombardi Trophy, 74. *See also* Super Bowl XXVI
Super Sports, 43
Sutton, Mike, 132
Swimming: rhythms of breathing in, 3

Tannen, Deborah, 127
Taylor, Lawrence, 75
Televised sports, 29–31, 41–42, 150n48; avant-garde, 56; dramatic tension in, 58–59; economics of, 29–31; as entertainment, 62–68; football coverage, 26, 41, 148n24; and kitsch, 47–48, 53, 56; marginal sports programs, 43–44; mass consumption of, 41;

metanarratives in, 100–105; paintball telecasts, 86–87, 95; pay-per-view, 66; as preferable to attending live events, 16, 41; as sanctioning mechanism for sport forms, 89–91; slo-motion replays, 30, 150n48; and socialization of children, 41, 153n1; sportscasters' role in, 25–26; women's sports coverage, 90. *See also The American Gladiators;* ESPN's *The eXtreme Games*
Texts: readers' creation of, 28–29
Thomas, Jim, 13
Thompson, Jenny, 122
Tick, Steven, xii
Tinley, Scott, 67
Todorov, Tzvetan, 83
Tourists, sport, x, 12, 20; at the Barcelona Olympics, 112, 117, 118–35, 175n15; as critical thinkers, 117; experiences collected by, 1–2, 16–17, 139n1(2); irony and self-referentiality of, 131–32; natives compared to, 113; package tourists, 114–15; resistance by, 131; spectators as, 16, 77–79
Trash sports, 33, 44, 45–46, 88–89
Triplett, Norman, 79
Turner, Victor, 22, 70, 120, 151n71, 167n4, on root metaphor, 32–33

Ueberroth, Peter, ix
Uecker, Bob, 26
Ultimate Warrior, 64, 67
Universal singulars, 4, 29
Updike, John, 138

Van Dalen, Deobold B., 91–92
Verducci, Tom, ix
Visser, Leslie, 75
Volleyball, college, 7, 142n28
Voyeurism, 50, 156n50

Wallace, Anthony F. C., 72, 76
War: avant-garde in, 23, 147n12; sport as, 23, 146n7
Warhol, Andy, 58, 68, 173n39
Waters, Harry, 37
Watten, Barrett, 12, 24
Weber, Max, 76–77
Weiss, Don, 74
Wenner, Lawrence A., 77–78, 82
Wertz, Spencer K., 34
Williams, Raymond, 160n36
Wilson, Joan, 108

Index

ROBERT E. RINEHART is an independent scholar. His work has been published in *Sociology of Sport Journal, Aethlon,* the *Journal of Sport History,* the *Journal of Sport and Social Issues,* and *Cultural Studies: A Research Annual.*